CLASSIC

CW01371711

CLASSIC RACERS

NEW ZEALAND'S GRAND PRIX GREATS

EOIN YOUNG

Harper*Sports*
An imprint of HarperCollins*Publishers*

To my grandson, Alfred

National Library of New Zealand Cataloguing-in-Publication Data

Young, Eoin S.
Classic racers : New Zealand's Grand Prix greats / Eoin Young.
ISBN 1-86950-460-7
1. Automobile racing drivers—New Zealand—History.
2. Grand Prix racing—History. 3. Automobiles, Racing. I. Title.
796.72092293—dc 21

Harper*Sports*
An imprint of HarperCollins*Publishers*

First published 2003
HarperCollins*Publishers (New Zealand) Limited*
P.O. Box 1, Auckland

Copyright © Eoin Young 2003

Eoin Young asserts the moral right to be identified as the author of this work.

The photo of Norman Smith (C-25903-1/2-; New Zealand Free Lance Collection) appears with the permission of the Alexander Turnbull Library.

All rights reserved. No part of this publication may be reproduced, stored in a retrieval system or transmitted in any form or by any means, electronic, mechanical, photocopying, recording or otherwise, without the prior written permission of the publishers.

ISBN 1 86950 460 7

Designed by Murray Dewhurst
Typeset by Graeme Leather
Printed by Griffin Press, Australia

FOREWORD

I said to Eoin recently, 'You can't ask a man that!'
'Why not?' he said. 'At worst he'll say no, but he might say yes.'

My first impression of ESY was not great, to say the least. It was around 1963, at Teretonga, that this bumptious young bank clerk from Timaru asked Len Gilbert if he could have a drive of his 250F Maserati, as he wanted to write about it. Len Gilbert said yes. When the car shot backwards off the track in the first hundred yards I bet he wished he had said no, or at least told the lad it had a central accelerator.

After such an embarrassing start to a journalistic career, one would have thought banking was looking pretty sweet. But our man is made of sterner stuff. Thank goodness, or we would have missed out on years of wonderful, entertaining insights into the human side of motor sport worldwide.

To say Eoin had limited mechanical knowledge would be an understatement. Changing a tap washer was a challenge well beyond him, but I did once watch him change a wheel. He was driving, and we were on our way to a party. He thought the car was handling strangely, and when we arrived at the function, a rear tyre was just on flat. He suggested I might help him change the wheel but I pointed out that it was his car, his puncture. I did come out and make several helpful comments, which he apparently didn't take kindly to, perhaps because I had a glass of red in my hand and he didn't. 'Furious' is a word that comes to mind. But he got a column out of it, and it was hilarious.

People, not power curves, are his thing, and he knows them all. Up to the present-day overpaid prima donnas, that is. If they matter.

Not only did Eoin wine and dine with all the top people in racing in the Good Old Days, but they were also good friends. Take Denis Jenkinson, for instance; or DSJ, as he appeared at the foot of his writings in *Motor Sport*. 'Jenks' — the prickly little bearded gem of a journalist who rode with Stirling Moss when he won the Mille Miglia, a 1000-mile race round Italy, in a Mercedes back in 1955. Not only was Eoin welcome at his house, he knew where it was. Now we can cash in on all that inside knowledge of the people who made racing tick, in this wonderful collection of memories of the drivers and the races in New Zealand, of the people and the history they made. To relive it all, read on.

Euan Sarginson

CONTENTS

Conversion table   9

A blast from the past   11

1. Bruce McLaren   15
2. Denis Hulme   23
3. Chris Amon   42
4. Howden Ganley   53
5. Ron Roycroft   76
6. Ross Jensen   88
7. Tom Clark   111
8. Johnny Mansel   119
9. The blue Ferrari   133
10. Ernie Sprague   139
11. The Lycoming Special   145
12. The Stanton Crop-duster   152
13. Bill Hamilton   159
14. The Indy Stutz   168
15. Norman 'Wizard' Smith   176
16. Reviving lost Ferraris   186
17. Nuvolari's P3 Alfa Romeo   195
18. The Bramwell Blower   203

19.	Black Hawk blazing	209
20.	The Mille Miglia Ferrari and Le Mans C-Type Jaguar	213
21.	Those New Zealand races	220
22.	Young and free in a Triumph TR2	233
23.	CanAm testing with Bruce McLaren	239
24.	Goodbye Denny	244

Conversion table

1 inch	25.40 millimetres
1 foot (12 inches)	30.48 centimetres
1 yard (3 feet)	91.44 centimetres
1 mile (1760 yards)	1.61 kilometres
1 pound	453.60 grams
1 stone (14 pounds)	6.35 kilograms
1 ton (2240 pounds, 160 stone)	1.02 tonnes
1 brake horsepower (bhp)	0.746 kilowatts (kW)
1 gallon	4.55 litres
1 US gallon	3.79 litres
1 acre	0.40 hectare

A BLAST FROM THE PAST

I started writing about motor racing in New Zealand on a manual typewriter at the Timaru sub-branch of the ANZ Bank in the late 1950s and, half a century on, I'd like to think I've moved on from my first report for the *Timaru Herald* — words that I virtually adzed out of stone. I couldn't believe that writing could be so difficult. I had met up with David Young, who had an XK120 Jaguar drophead, and we had been to a few races when he decided that he would like have a go himself. He won easily first time out on a Christchurch beach, comfortably heading our local Timaru hero, Ernie Sprague, in his tuned-up Ford Zephyr — which wouldn't have been all that difficult, now that I think back. The course was straight up and straight back, with a couple of hairpins. Horsepower beat skill. Not that David didn't have the latter, he just had more of the former than Ernie did that day.

Ernie was our hometown hero. We would go down to his garage on North Street and just sort of hang around and talk what we thought might be racing talk when Ernie had got rid of his road-car customers and started work on his racing car at the end of the day.

So my mate David actually winning the race and beating Ernie needed a better headline than 'Timaru Driver Placed Third in Car Race'. I was Mr Angry on Monday, striding up the stairs to the newspaper editorial office and demanding to speak to the Sports Editor. The Sports Editor was probably well used to Mr Angrys coming up his stairs and he suggested that if I knew more about the race than the NZPA perhaps I should write the report to put right whatever I felt had been wrong.

I spent *hours* at the bank's typewriter, pecking out a version that I hoped would give David his dues. The headline the next morning was 'Timaru Driver Won Saloon Race at Christchurch'. Journalism didn't seem to be as easy as I had always imagined when I only had to read it rather than write it.

I must have been irritatingly persistent, because the newspaper eventually gave me a weekly motor sporting column to indulge myself, albeit on 'The Teenager's Page', and when I discovered that Bruce McLaren's sister, Pat, lived in Timaru, I had an inside line to the top. I devoured every handwritten letter that Bruce sent to Pat from Europe. For a young, pre-OE Kiwi this was just about as good as being there. Two years later, I was. The summer of 1961 was spent with Denny Hulme on the Formula Junior circuit around Europe and the next year I was travelling the world as Bruce's secretary, the first McLaren employee. Bruce won the Monaco Grand Prix at the start of the summer that season and it sort of kept on going from there. I started with a weekly motor racing column in the *Timaru Herald* and in 1967 graduated to a weekly motor racing *page* in the prestigious *Autocar* magazine that lasted for 32 years.

In this new century I'm using a state-of-the-art electronic laptop, tapping out the intro for a collection of my favourite pieces on New Zealand racing and the personalities in it over the years. I have included a number of features on different aspects of Denny Hulme, mainly because they cover his career, his reasons for retirement — and the fact that there has never been a book on the only New Zealander ever to be a World Champion. This spectacular achievement was disgracefully ignored when a Sporting Hall of Fame was set up in New Zealand and Denny was not included!

Of course, there are other people I should have included, but I've been based in Britain for much of the time. Though I was able to enjoy the Tasman summers with the McLaren team during the sixties, I've spent less time with local racing since those days.

I've put together a collection of features and profiles written over the years and there will always be personalities who deserve to be in it, but have not been included simply because our paths never crossed and paused for a glass of something at the right time.

Roly Levis is one of the people I would like to have profiled, if only because he was inadvertently the driver who set me free of the bank and out into the world of motor racing. I walked out of the bank in

Timaru one afternoon when it was still called the Bank of Australasia, and saw this quite superb little cycle-guarded RAL Special sports car with luggage strapped on its tail and a guy who looked every inch a racing driver with his glamorous wife. That was the moment in time when I realised that there really was another way to live life other than the pursuit of a guaranteed income and pension if I could survive the bank.

I suppose I should dedicate this book to Roly and apologise for the fact that he isn't in it.

I'm told that I now write the way I speak, which, if true, is a huge compliment. Writing should be like that. A projection in print of what you want to say. There have been so many dinners over a Grand Prix weekend somewhere in the world with Denis Jenkinson, Alan Henry, Nigel Roebuck and Maurice Hamilton where someone would launch into a tale. When the laughter had died away, someone else would eventually say, 'Why can't you write the way you talk?' That was always the ultimate dinner table put-down.

Denis Jenkinson ('Jenks' to his mates) was the doyen of motor racing writers and with a reputation of being severe and stand-offish. My problem was that nobody told me how difficult he could be, and I just bowled up to him in the pit-lane at Rouen in 1961 and started chatting. We were friends from then on and my friends became his, which is how we snapped the photograph of Jenks and Euan Sarginson at the famous Barley Mow pub in Horsley.

If I'm able to write the way I talk, as opposed to those hauntingly original few inches I achieved in the *Timaru Herald* that Monday afternoon, then I guess my forty-odd years in the pursuit of motor racing writing hasn't entirely been misplaced.

Every motoring enthusiast has owned a car that he wished he had never sold. Mine was the 1928 5.3-litre supercharged straight-8 Stutz Black Hawk that was rescued and immaculately restored for Allan Bramwell by the late Murray Jones and Auto Restorations. It was gloriously unoriginal, but it was a wonderful motoring experience and I had some memorable rallies and drives in the South Island with that rather special historic car. But at the end of the day there are always two ideal days in car ownership: the day you buy it and the day you sell it. I was equally delighted to buy and to sell the Stutz, but now I wish I could afford to still own it instead of having to remember it in print . . .

The international series in New Zealand in the sixties was always covered for *Autosport* by Peter Greenslade, with Euan Sarginson as his photographer. They also produced the excellent Shell-sponsored annuals at the end of each season, in the days when we enjoyed what amounted to an international Grand Prix with all the top drivers and cars from overseas here during January. 'Sarge' and I have been friends ever since and many of the best photographs in this book are his. He also wrote the foreword, most of which I thank him for.

My thanks also for the original appearances of these various features and profiles in *F1 Magazine*, *Classic Car*, *Autosport*, *Motor Sport* and *Autocar* in the UK, and especially *New Zealand Classic Car*. Thanks to editor Allan Walton for permission to use the features I had written for him on the top New Zealand drivers over the years, some of whom were the subject of major profiles for the first time in their career. Thanks also to Milan Fistonic, who lives near Auckland but could be at my elbow in Surrey for the way he has been able to answer any question — and I've had many — by electronic reply after a quick whizz through his amazing motor racing reference library.

It's been better than working in the bank . . .

CHAPTER 1

BRUCE MCLAREN

Bruce McLaren was killed on 2 June 1970, and since then I have written a book on his racing career and his team and I have written numerous features on the New Zealander who gave his name to the team that is still in the top ranks of international Formula One. This article was written for New Zealand Classic Car *as part of a series in 2001.*

Bruce McLaren put me wherever I am today. In hindsight, he gave me the most valuable of all gifts — the opportunity to be introduced to the rarefied world of Grand Prix racing in 1962 as his friend and secretary. The fact that I was a journalist as well didn't seem to bother anyone. If I was a mate of Bruce's, I was a mate of theirs. It would simply never have happened if I had been a Pom, but I arrived in Europe as a Kiwi when New Zealand was the racing flavour of the decade. It sure as hell wouldn't — couldn't — happen today.

I remember my first meeting with Bruce, at Teretonga in 1958. I took photographs of him with my Kodak 127 and proudly pasted them in my motor racing album — and spelled his name 'MacLaren' in my spidery handwritten caption. I knew he had entered our local loose-metal hill climb at Clelands, and asked if he would like to go to the local Saturday-night dance at Caroline Bay. He was on his own, so he went, and it was there that he met Pat Broad, the local beauty he would woo by mail and eventually marry. The rest, as they say, is history.

Bruce led the Cooper Grand Prix team, won Le Mans for Ford, dominated CanAm sports-car racing in North America, and won a Grand Prix in his own McLaren car. All this having spent two years of his boyhood strapped to a wheeled frame, specialists fearing he would never walk again. The determination to prove his doctors wrong was an early manifestation of his quiet fighting spirit, which underlay his subsequent will to win on the track.

Everyone remembers his cheerful, almost shy, schoolboy smile and his infectious enthusiasm for just about anything. He led from the ranks, worked shoulder to shoulder with his mechanics and taught by experience. He was one of them. Young guys, in their twenties, they all worked together as a team. Not that it seemed like work. At the very least they reckoned they were working *with* Bruce rather than for him. It was a fine line but an important one for a hand-picked team that operated almost as a family. It was Bruce's team, but he seldom made a point of it. If they won, it was a joint effort. Denny Hulme came from the same Kiwi mould, and they teamed well together. When Bruce was killed, testing a CanAm car at Goodwood on 2 June 1970, it was Denny who talked the team through its darkest day and held them together.

Bruce was among the first of the engineer drivers, along with Jack Brabham and Richie Ginther — drivers who could think as well as race. He won the last Grand Prix of the 1950s — the US at Sebring — and the first of the 1960s — the Argentine — for Cooper, and a McLaren car, driven by Denny Hulme, won the final Grand Prix of the 1960s, in Mexico. The McLaren decade saw the progression from driver to team-owner and car-builder.

Brabham left Cooper to build his own cars in 1962, and Bruce was promoted to team leader, stepping out to win the Monaco Grand Prix and the non-title Grand Prix at Reims. But the spark had gone from Cooper. John Cooper's father, Charles, believed Jack Brabham had betrayed their trust by leaving, and he wasn't about to let Bruce promote his own Formula One technical ideas; so Bruce had no option but to establish a team of his own to build bespoke cars for the Tasman Series in New Zealand and Australia that incorporated all his improvements but were called Coopers to ease tension in Surbiton, Cooper's southwest London home. It was the genesis of the modern McLaren team.

Bruce McLaren Motor Racing Ltd had a shield-shaped badge featuring a racing car and a Kiwi, designed by artist Michael Turner, and loosely based on the British Racing Drivers' Club badge. The first garage facility was shared with a road grader in nearby New Malden, where the Climax 4-cylinder engine in the Cooper-based Zerex Special, pensioned off by team owner Roger Penske, was swapped for an F85 aluminium-block 3.5-litre Oldsmobile V8. The conversion was done in haste, and the engine sported aggressive stack-pipe exhausts.

It seemed like luxury to move to a 4000 sq ft factory block in a run-down estate behind Feltham, in Middlesex. Robin Herd and then Gordon Coppuck were hired from the aerospace industry as designers. I was Bruce's secretary and a founder director of the company, with a sign on my office door that read DON'T KNOCK — WE DON'T HAVE THAT SORT OF TIME. Well, it seemed very American and trendy at the time. Bruce had a sign on his desk that read WINNING ISN'T EVERYTHING BUT IT BEATS THE HELL OUT OF BEING SECOND.

The McLaren credo for success was enthusiasm. 'Not just mild, but burning enthusiasm,' Bruce wrote in one of his early magazine columns.

> To succeed in motor racing it must be the most important thing in your life, because if it isn't the most important thing to you, there are a dozen others for whom it is. Those are the people you have to beat. You must eat, live and think motor racing. The more you think about it and plan, the better you will do. On second thoughts, 'scheme' is probably a better word than 'think'.

New Zealand racing-car builder George Begg spent a year as a sort of senior-citizen mechanic with McLaren in 1968 and was able to observe Bruce from a detached point of view.

> Y'know there are all sorts of modern terms for these things. There are lateral thinkers and upward thinkers and there's all this modern claptrap but at the end of the day, Bruce just used to sit down and nut it out. He wouldn't have known what a lateral thinker was. Bruce built cars for the sake of creating something. He certainly didn't do it for the money because there was practically no money in it then. He wanted to create something better that would go out and *win*. That was his driving force. Fame and fortune didn't feature very highly in his list of human priorities.

Wally Willmott, who became Bruce's personal racing mechanic and one of the original team members, reflects on the change from seat-of-the-pants intuitive engineering to computer-generated input: 'In the early 1960s when I first came over, Bruce was the principle source of information and everything that happened in the team came from the cockpit of the car. Forty years on, the driver has some input but most of it comes from the computer screen.'

When the formula doubled from 1.5 to 3 litres in 1966, Bruce was already building sports cars for CanAm racing and felt ready for Formula One. He won and lost with Ford in 1966. He co-drove the winning Ford at Le Mans with fellow countryman Chris Amon, but his ambitious project to convert a Ford Indianapolis engine to Formula One was a dismal failure. He was forced to compromise with various different engines, and it was not until the Ford-Cosworth DFV became available to teams other than Lotus in 1968 that McLarens became Grand Prix winners. It was ironic that when Bruce won the 1968 Belgian Grand Prix at Spa in a car with his own name on the nose, he didn't realise he had. He thought he had finished second.

The team was now based in a 20,000 sq ft factory at Colnbrook beneath the Heathrow Airport flight path, and Bruce was spending more time over the factory than in it, commuting to and from Grands Prix and CanAm races and doing corporate work with sponsors Gulf Oil and Reynolds Aluminum.

The steamroller success of the orange McLarens in North America made the Formula One struggles in the mid-1960s so much more difficult to accept. In fact the rich CanAm wins were paying for the Grand Prix shortfalls. After his team's first season in North America, Bruce said, 'I reckon we've collected more prize money in this series than we could have won in three years in England.'

It was part of racing folklore that if you were a New Zealand mechanic and turned up at the McLaren factory, you were guaranteed a job. Team manager Alastair Caldwell, himself a Kiwi (of course), said he reckoned every countryman mechanic who applied had already passed a 10,000-mile initiative test just getting there. One of those Kiwis who passed the mileage test was Bruce Harré.

> I remember when we were building the cars and racing them the next day and it'd get to midnight and we'd say, 'Look, McLaren, you'd better go home and get some sleep.' And he wouldn't go and we'd say, 'Go, or we'll *take* you home.' He wouldn't leave working on the cars. And when he was testing or practising, we'd think he was daydreaming and we'd say, 'McLaren *race* the effing thing. Don't sit there on the track redesigning it. *Race* it!'

Bruce's personal drive and determination to succeed probably stemmed from his long months as a boy in a hospital bed in Auckland recovering from Perthe's disease, which all but destroyed his hip joint. 'I spent my tenth and eleventh birthdays in a home for crippled children, then came the big day when I was allowed to get up,' he recalled in his autobiography, *From the Cockpit*.

> The doctor told me to stand, not to try and walk, but just try and stand normally. My legs had been hanging in the air for a couple of years and I suppose I must have forgotten how to stand on my own. At the end of 1949 the doctors told me I could go home, where I graduated from crutches to a couple of sticks but I had to spend a year at home before I could lead a normal boy's life.

Bruce's father, Les, owned a garage and service station in the wealthy Auckland suburb of Remuera and had always been interested in motor sports, starting out with motorcycles before graduating to a Singer Le Mans and then an SS Jaguar. He bought an Ulster Austin 7 in bits and passed it on to young Bruce to maintain, modify and race. This was where it all began. Bruce would later recall his early Austin 7 experience as an essential part of growing up in race engineering. Colin Chapman had done the same, he would say.

Jack Brabham was influential in Bruce's early career, first of all selling a bobtail sports car to Les for his son, then bringing single-seaters out to New Zealand each season as 'spares' for sale at the right price. In fact, Brabham had met the McLarens in 1954 when he had entered a Cooper-Bristol in the New Zealand Grand Prix. It was his first international event, and he stayed at Les McLaren's home over the race weekend, an introduction having been arranged by RedEx, Brabham's first sponsor.

In 1958 Bruce won the inaugural Driver to Europe scholarship funded by the New Zealand International Grand Prix Association, an achievement that was to launch him into a career that he could scarcely have imagined at the time. Brabham was his mentor, introducing him to the Cooper team and coaching him in Formula Two.

Bruce made his name in the 1958 German Grand Prix — his first — on the old mountain 14.2-mile Nürburgring, where skill certainly told. He was in his own 1500 cc Formula Two Cooper, a car he had built himself under a tarpaulin in the Cooper yard, in a separate section of the event for 2.5-litre Formula One cars. He finished fifth overall, having left the German Formula Two works Porsches and Phil Hill (also in his first Grand Prix) in the works Formula Two Ferrari in his wake and carved through the Formula One field.

Tony Brooks won for Vanwall from the Coopers of Maurice Trintignant and Roy Salvadori. Wolfgang von Trips was fourth for Ferrari. Exalted company. When asked later how he had managed to score on the most difficult circuit in the world, Bruce said, 'I suppose it was because I thought nothing of putting a wheel up a bank if necessary.' John Cooper was not the only team manager who was impressed.

Cooper signed Bruce for his Formula One team in 1959, a season that would end with Bruce scoring his first Grand Prix victory when Brabham ran out of fuel in the closing laps while Bruce was following dutifully in second place.

At 22, Bruce was the youngest driver to win a Grand Prix. Six years later, with his own small team building and racing his own sports cars, he faced the pleasant if vaguely embarrassing problem of being asked to supply replicas of his totally dominant CanAm machines. The £6,000 price tag tended to put off some of his prospective customers, but that was OK with Bruce because he only had a staff of six and they simply couldn't cope with building and preparing the works cars *and* a production programme. The problem was solved when Peter Agg's Elva company took over a run of customer cars. I remember spending a whole afternoon in Agg's company boardroom arguing over whether the cars would be called McLaren-Elvas or Elva-McLarens. I won.

The CanAm series was known as 'The Bruce and Denny Show' because Bruce McLaren and Denny Hulme almost totally dominated it. It was difficult to understand how a small, energetic team using American Chevrolet horsepower could beat the American teams so devastatingly in their own back yard. They enjoyed themselves both on and off the track.

Bruce's dream of building a McLaren road car dated back to the time of his earliest involvement with cars, and the days when his father used to bring sales brochures and motor-racing books for him to read while he was cooped up in his hospital bed as a boy. With the Elva involvement in late 1964 came a proposal to build a run of GT cars based on the first M6 CanAm monocoque. The glass-fibre coupé body was striking, but the project foundered amid Fédération International de l'Automobile (FIA) red tape, so Bruce built a road car to his own personal recipe. It was a shapely road rocket, basic beyond belief but reasonably tamed for traffic. The driver froze in winter and fried in summer, but Bruce loved it. Had it ever been civilised, the M6GT would have been the precursor of the centre-seat McLaren Formula One road car that eventually came from Gordon Murray's drawing board, but the project died with Bruce in 1970.

When other drivers were killed, Bruce was fond of saying that life wasn't measured in time alone, but also in terms of achievement and the sheer enjoyment of talent. His words are an eloquent commentary on his own life and career. It is hard to credit he could have crammed so much into just 32 years.

Would Bruce have retired, given the chance? It was definitely in his mind, and earnest efforts were made to hire Jochen Rindt for the Formula One team in 1970. Ironically, Rindt's main reason for refusing was because there was no place for him in the CanAm team. Bruce would have stepped down from Formula One but planned to keep his CanAm seat, so he would still have been testing on that fateful day in June.

The Bruce McLaren Trust has been established in New Zealand in recent years by Bruce's sisters, Pat and Jan, and a group of enthusiasts to ensure that the McLaren name and achievements are remembered. Bruce was survived by his wife, Patty, and their daughter, Amanda, who was four when he was killed.

CHAPTER 2

DENIS HULME

In 1961 I travelled the European Formula Junior series with Denny Hulme, who, six years later, would become the only New Zealander to win the Formula One World Championship. This article was written in 1974, shortly before Denny announced his retirement.

Grand Prix racing is a selfish ego trip where the winners take the spoils and satisfy their ambitions. The also-rans satisfy their lesser egos merely by being involved, by being part of the elite international scene. Being a Grand Prix driver is as near as many will ever get to being a Grand Prix winner, and their greatest triumph will be to retire with their life. To retire wealthy is a bonus, but retiring alive is the goal for most. And knowing when to retire is probably the most important decision a Grand Prix driver ever takes.

Denny Hulme built himself a granite reputation as a tough individual, a craggy Kiwi who couldn't care less about the human side of racing; the cares and the worries at home, the elation of winning or the gloom of defeat — it was all the same to 'The Bear'. But Denny worked hard to build a wall round his private feelings, so very few people really knew him away from the race track, or knew that he and his wife, Greeta, discussed retirement shortly after the death of his great friend and team-mate, Bruce McLaren, and decided he would race for only two more seasons. Those two seasons stretched into a third, in 1974, but following a series of accidents Denny determined to hang up his hat at the end of it.

We started the interview for this piece the week after the 1974 Italian Grand Prix, in which Denny had run a dogged sixth with a performance that could scarcely have impressed the racer who had won the world championship in 1967 and come close to winning it again in 1968. We skirted the subject of impending retirement without actually mentioning it, but when we began talking about racing accidents and how they affected other drivers, all Denny's concerns about racing came flooding out, along with the reasons for his decision to retire.

Denny had been close behind Jochen Rindt when Rindt's Lotus had crashed at Monza in 1970. Did an accident like that have an effect on him? 'Jochen's crash was just a big shower of dust and rubbish and wheels flying everywhere. No, it didn't affect me because at the time I had the spirit to keep going and I wanted to keep going, but after Francois Cevert's accident at the Glen . . . That was a particularly terrible accident because a lot of the drivers stopped.'

He sighed, and then settled down to the real and human reasons why a racing driver doesn't want to race any more.

> Most of the drivers were kicking themselves that they hadn't stopped at Zandvoort to try and save Roger Williamson, so at the Glen they stopped to see if anything could be done. The whole thing was just a mess; the car hadn't caught fire so some of the drivers had gone right in. This affected Jody Scheckter very badly and he said straight afterwards that he was going to quit, no way was he going to continue, he was too young for this sort of nonsense. Then you began to wonder. It had all happened so damned quickly and there was another driver gone and it was all very sad, and I went over to Paris for the funeral and I thought, 'Oh Christ, can it all be worth it?', and I made up my mind that I'd do one more season and that would be it.

The 1974 season started well for Denny when he won the Argentine Grand Prix in the Texaco-Marlboro McLaren, but then in South Africa the spectre came back with the Peter Revson crash during prerace testing. Denny was one of the first on the scene. 'I saw all the shambles and I thought well, bugger it, that's it. I just can't wait for the end of the year to get it all over with.' And for the rest of the summer Denny was a turned-down racer, staying out of trouble on the racetrack, admitting that his career was over but going to the races to fulfil contractual obligations.

> That probably wasn't the right attitude from the team's point of view, but I don't really think the team suffered, because Emerson Fittipaldi was way up there in the championship and I was the block at the back. If I'd been up there with him, I'm sure things would have been really hectic and they would have had to divide their attentions. I think — I *hope* — they won't be disappointed after the Glen. Sure, I won Argentina. I was lucky because Carlos dropped out but I was happy to win. So I've had a win and a second place and finished sixth what seems like a dozen times.

At 38, Denny candidly admitted he was too old to be racing:

You have less worries or cares when you're young. But when you take time out to think, 'Am I doing the right thing?'. . . You've got a family, responsibilities, and here you are thundering around a racetrack like an idiot. I don't think that's the right attitude for a man in his mid-thirties. I still enjoy what I'm doing but I basically know that it's not right for me to be doing it. And for Graham Hill to be still racing — I think that's pretty foolish because for sure he doesn't *have* to do it. Jackie Stewart made the right decision to finish while he was on top.

Denny Hulme was almost a has-been before he even started seriously in Formula One racing. He began with an MG TF at club races in New Zealand, driving in shorts and bare feet. When he arrived in England in 1960 as one of two Drivers to Europe that season, he was still racing his Formula Two Cooper in bare feet because he maintained it gave him a better feel of the accelerator. With shoes and a veneer of civilisation, he raced Formula Two and Formula Junior Coopers throughout Europe that summer. *Autosport* referred to him first as David Hulme, then as George Hulme when he won the Grand Prix de Pescara in his Formula Junior car in August 1960. In September his New Zealand team-mate, George Lawton, was killed in a crash on Denmark's Roskildering, and later that month Denny drove in his first Formula One race at Snetterton in a Yeoman Credit Cooper-Climax, a drive originally arranged for Lawton.

In 1961 and 1962, Denny campaigned his own Formula Junior Cooper, but he had missed the main chance the Driver to Europe scholarship had given its first recipient, Bruce McLaren, by then established as a Cooper works Grand Prix driver. Team manger Ken Tyrrell didn't rate Denny highly as a driver then — he doesn't now, really — even though Denny drove his cars on occasion.

By 1963 Denny had sold his updated Cooper and was working in the nuts-and-bolts end of Jack Brabham's customer garage, racing other people's cars as a journeyman driver when asked to do so at weekends. Tasmanian Gavin Youl was the works driver-in-waiting in those fledgling days of the Brabham empire, but when he broke his collarbone, Denny stepped in to take his place at Crystal Palace and later in the year, on Boxing Day, at Brands Hatch. Phil Kerr, then

Brabham's manager, was a champion of the Hulme cause, and it was through his insistence that Brabham gave Denny a chance. Denny raced the works Formula Junior Brabham during 1963, was upgraded to partner Jack in the works Formula Two team in 1964 with the Brabham-Hondas, and, that season, was given a Formula One drive at Karlskoga. He drove the transporter up to Sweden.

When Brabham decided to try his hand at retirement in 1965, Denny took his place in the team, but come 1966, with Brabham back in harness with new Repco engines for the 3-litre formula, Denny was his regular number two. That was Brabham's year to take the title. In 1967 it was Denny's championship, and he won the Monaco and German Grands Prix, on the two toughest tracks of the season, having led in South Africa and Canada. Although presumably satisfied that one of his cars had won the world title, Brabham would have preferred to do the winning personally.

Denny felt Brabham might have tripped himself by experimenting during the season with new parts for the engine. 'If the experiments had worked they would have been an improvement, but they let him down. Maybe he would have finished higher but he was always trying something new while I had a nuts-and-bolts engine.'

There was tension in the Brabham team, and tension is something Denny has never really been equipped to cope with. Offered a CanAm McLaren at the end of the 1967 season, he thoroughly enjoyed the new atmosphere as 'The Bruce and Denny Show' began its domination of the CanAm series. McLaren won that year, while Denny won in 1968 and 1970. In 1968 Denny switched to the McLaren team in Formula One as well, and looked like retaining his world championship right up until the last round in Mexico City, but a suspension breakage put him into the wall and out of the chase.

'I realise now that it was bad of me to go away and leave Jack after winning the championship in 1967, but I think I did the right thing because Jochen Rindt drove for him in 1968 and they had a disastrous season, whereas the McLaren was running like a dream.'

Denny won two Grands Prix in 1968, in Italy and Canada.

That dreamy summer, driving the M8 winged McLaren-Chevrolet, was one of Denny's happiest racing seasons. 'We were so far ahead of the opposition in those days that we went water skiing one afternoon when we should have been practising.'

He won three of the six races and the championship.

That M8A McLaren was Denny's ideal motorcar, and he would like to buy one of the ex-works cars to restore it:

> People can't understand why I don't have a Boxer Ferrari or a Lamborghini or something like that. It's just that I've driven what I consider to be one of the best cars ever made, and I'm probably one of only a dozen guys who has ever driven one. Nothing else measures up. It's like going to the moon. There are only a few guys who have ever gone up there, and I'll bet they're pleased too.

Denny was very much the reluctant champion when he won the title in 1967, but he looks back on his lack of grace with no regrets:

> It put me on the map, right? I won the world championship, but I don't think 1967 was my happiest year. Sure, it was exhilarating building up to it, and the chances that you'd win the title, but you were also on tenterhooks wondering if you'd do it and you only needed a couple of things to go wrong and it wouldn't have happened. OK, we scraped through and got enough points to win, but I felt a lot happier the following year with Bruce.
>
> It was more enjoyable being CanAm champion those two years than it was being world champion in 1967. I knew when I won the world championship that I'd have to do this and do that, make speeches and give interviews; it's something that I still dread to this day. I'm not so bad when I actually get there, but it's the thought of having to do it, preparing myself to go to these places. As far as I'm concerned I'd rather stay at home, but I know you're obliged to go out and do these things. When I won the CanAm series, there was only the prize-giving at the end of the series and that was it. We'd won the series, had a good time, a lot of fun, met a lot of people, but there was no big deal afterwards, which suited me just fine. When I won the world championship I was forever making speeches and wondering what I'd let myself in for.

It's nice to win the world championship, sure, and I felt everything was justified once I'd done it. I'd justified my family's decision to let me go racing and justified my own ambition to try and press on and do it. Once I'd done all that I was quite happy within myself, but then I had what was, from my point of view, the aggravation of going and doing all the things that a world champion is supposed to do, and that's what I shunned. I really hated it. I suppose I was lucky to get away with it as well as I did without being ridiculed and people saying what a right bastard I was.

Bruce McLaren's death early in June 1970 caught Denny at a very low personal ebb, still recovering from severe burns to his hands from when the MI5 McLaren caught fire during practice at Indianapolis, and it was at this point that he started seriously to consider his future. Until then, accidents had been things that happened to other people. His 10 days in hospital in Indianapolis gave him time to dwell on the shortening odds.

There was always the chance element, the chance that it wouldn't happen again. But it did. In the opening laps of the Road Atlanta CanAm race in 1972, Denny was tucked into the slipstream of George Follmer's 917 turbo-Porsche, shaping up to pass, when his McLaren flipped over backwards and skated to a halt upside down. A flash flame was immediately extinguished, and the heavy car was man-handled back on to its wheels. The incident provided more food for thought. Denny could so easily have been killed in a crash he would have known nothing about, a crash he had escaped from with only a bump on the head.

> Then I realised how you could be wiped off the face of the earth without really knowing it. I was following Follmer and I don't remember anything to this day except coming to in hospital. It was an indication that you could be snuffed out painlessly without even knowing you'd been killed. The car could have caught fire or destroyed itself, but fortunately it stayed intact and there was no damage to me except a bump on the nut. Then you start to realise how easy it is for it all to go wrong . . . just too easy . . .

Denny said this experience of the vagaries of aerodynamics snatching control from him had an effect on his racing from then on:

> It stopped me from racing right close to people, trying to dice and frig about with them. If I couldn't run clean or get past them cleanly I wouldn't bother to get too close to them. I think that had an effect on me in Formula One as well. I do not like running close to anyone in Formula One cars — not right up their exhaust pipes. Ever since that Atlanta flip I've worried that something is going to lift and the car will skate out.
>
> Ronnie Peterson said in Austria this year that he tucked in behind me on the first lap and his car just washed completely out across the road and nearly hit the guardrail. I *know* that's what it's going to do — I don't need anyone to tell me that's what's likely to happen. So I don't run within cooee of anyone for that reason. Maybe I don't race as well as I used to, but I know how easy it is to get yourself sucked in and flung off the road. It's just one of those things. The older you get the more you begin to realise that it's more difficult than it looks. All right, it might never happen again, but I'm just not prepared to take that risk, tucking right in behind and hoping to dive out at the end of the straight and go by. I'd probably dive out but I know I'm only faking because I know I'm nowhere near enough to go past them under braking unless they make a mistake.

Just what does Denny Hulme plan to do with himself now he has retired? Frankly, he doesn't know. He says he has saved enough money to live comfortably for the rest of his life without having to work again. He will eventually take his family back to live in New Zealand, and he talks vaguely of a small farm, a comfortable home, enough land to keep neighbours at bay. A few cows, perhaps. Some sheep. A garden where he could grow enough vegetables to be self-sufficient, independent.

Denny's fierce disapproval of regimentation and officialdom in its many forms at racetracks met its match at Indianapolis. The Speedway adheres to rules and principles that could have been drafted at the time of the Civil War and is administered by men who look as though they may have taken part in it. When Denny arrived at Indianapolis he was a very small cog in a large machine and was constantly reminded of the fact. Instead of rebelling, he actually came to appreciate, even like, the weird rites of the place.

But it was a type of racing that outpaced him. In 1967 he was fourth in the '500' driving for Smokey Yunick; in 1968 he was fourth again, this time in one of Dan Gurney's Eagles. In 1969 he was lying second when the clutch of his Eagle failed. In 1970 he missed the race while recovering from burns, and in 1971, with the new MI6 McLaren, he qualified fourth but dropped out with engine failure. Peter Revson started in pole that year in a car identical to his, and that was enough for him. Denny never raced at Indy again.

> I stopped racing at Indy because it was very, very difficult for me to qualify. I could race all right, but I couldn't qualify like those guys who could tweak themselves up and get a good quick time just for four laps. When the race starts they're all right, they're in the race, the pressure's off and they go round and round to try and pick up the money. I enjoyed the race but I didn't enjoy the first three weeks at Indy, trying to get up to speed and qualify. It just became a big problem and I figured I was better off without all the aggravation, so I thought, 'To hell with it.' I didn't want to go back and the team wanted a better driver, so it was a good arrangement. I didn't go back and they picked up Gordon Johncock. If 38 is too old to go racing, what is the right age?
>
> If you could plonk your bum in the seat of a Formula One car by the time you're 20, that's the time when you get the best feel for a car. I don't say you'll win then, but you'll get the feel and in a few years you'll have the feel, the technique and the whole works put together that will enable you to win races. You might win a couple when you're 21, but you'll only do it on sheer guts, no brains sort of thing. After a while you get the technique and it works for everything — brains, feel, guts and the whole thing. You understand it much better.
>
> It's important to get the breaks, of course. If you're an unknown, with no persuasion, and have to buy your own car and go through the whole rigmarole, you're going to be 30 before you're in Formula One,

but if you're lucky and can find a good talker and a good sponsor, you'll get in younger with a much better opportunity.

It comes as no surprise to hear Denny talking about Jody Scheckter as the driver with most potential, because it was Denny who acted as coach and mentor to the impressionable young South African when he began his Formula One career with the McLaren team. He was a young colonial, as Denny had been when he first arrived on the European scene, and Denny was giving him a break, the benefits of his experience. Another driver might have been content to let the young charger find out for himself — some drivers made a point of doing just that — but Denny took Scheckter under his wing:

> I think without a doubt Jody is the driver with the most potential, although I think on the day Ronnie [Peterson] is the guy who can screw himself up the most, who can pull out that extra little bit. I know that Emerson is very quick but he drives very much within himself; he's racing at nine-tenths with just a fraction in hand. I know Ronnie steps over the limit and goes ten-tenths or more, and Jody does on occasion, but not that often. I think Jody backs off a wee bit as well. Most of the others drive right on their limit, but it's generally a limit that's lower than the guys I've mentioned.

Boredom is one of the factors that could prompt a racing driver to put off retirement, but Denny has never been a jet-set socialite, flitting between the bright lights as a member of an international celebrity group. He almost gives the impression that race weekends intruded on his lawn-mowing, or pottering around the gardens of his modern new home in St George's Hill, the wealthy private park near Weybridge, in Surrey, where the address can double the price of a dwelling:

> I don't think I'll be bored. I know I'll miss a certain kind of life that I've semi-enjoyed, but I've never been overawed by grandiose things. Staying at posh hotels and having flunkies open the door bothers me more than it makes me happy. I'd sooner hump my own bags into the

hotel, get my own lift, and do things for myself. I guess I grew up different to other people. I just can't accept that these guys aren't spongers. Most people think that that's a flunky's job, but to me they're spongers.

Denny drives a 4.2-litre XJ6; the economics of a 5.3-litre V12 confuse him, and he's happy with the 4.2. He may get a Range Rover for New Zealand. Something to tow a boat. He's tracked down and bought back the MG he first raced and is planning its leisurely restoration; he's trying to buy the first of the M23 Formula One McLarens as well as an M8 CanAm car to form the basis of a small private collection, and he talks of equipping a small machine shop to help with his hobby.

Steam shows in England have taken his fancy recently, and stationary engines, steam or petrol, from the early 1900s look like being a hobby soon. He already has a 1912 Amoco engine, bought on a summer trip home two years ago.

This further look back at Denny Hulme, the man and his career, was written for New Zealand Classic Car *in 2000.*

The records show that Denny Hulme raced in 112 Grands Prix in 10 years of Formula One competition. He won eight of these and set seven fastest laps, yet started only one Grand Prix in pole position — the South African in 1973. He was Rookie of the Year at Indianapolis in 1967. He won two CanAm crowns and notched up a total of 22 wins in the McLaren CanAm sports cars.

For his bravery in Crete in the Second World War, his father, Clive Hulme, was awarded the Victoria Cross. Courage obviously runs in the family, because it certainly takes courage to make the decision to retire from Grand Prix racing.

Denny Hulme was dubbed 'The Bear', but his gruff exterior was a façade he was happy to relax behind. How you felt about him really depended on what type of bear you saw him as. Some in the motorsports press saw him as a grizzly, but there was a lot of Paddington and Pooh about the happy-go-lucky Hulme, who grew up in the tiny Bay of Plenty settlement of Pongakawa and learned to drive in the lorries of his father's transport business.

Denis Clive Hulme won the 1967 world championship for Brabham and the CanAm sports-car title in North America in 1968 for McLaren. Denny — he was only Denis when he was in trouble — won the CanAm crown again in 1970, but that summer it was off the track that he revealed the true depth of his inner strength, proving there was a real hero behind the ragged grin and tittering laugh.

He was testing the first Indianapolis McLaren in May when a fuel breather cap popped open and methanol fuel was blown back to the Offenhauser's red-hot turbocharger. The shimmering 'whoomph' of heat gave him only seconds to escape. His visor became welded to his helmet, and his flameproof overalls started to char. The leather of his gloves shrank his hands into painful claws as he battled with the buckle of his seat harness. He thought he had slowed the car to a crawl, but when he went over the side he guessed it was probably still doing 70 mph. The rescue truck sped past him, chasing the burning car; the crew didn't realise the driver on the track was also on fire.

Bruce McLaren and other team members visited Denny in the Indianapolis hospital every day. His burns were extremely serious, and there was an unspoken recognition that he could lose some fingers on his left hand. In the end the fingers were saved, but when Denny had recovered enough to race again, he continued to wear dressings on his hands under his gauntlets. The skin on his fingers remained so tender he sometimes sliced it opening a newspaper. Bruce was terribly concerned at his team-mate's condition in hospital, the two men's closeness in this time of trouble as clear as when they had travelled together between races like a couple of kids.

When Bruce was killed at Goodwood three weeks later, Denny, who had withstood the pain of his burns without a tear, broke down in grief. But it was he who rallied the team in those dark days, urging them to stay together and win again for Bruce. He was their strength. Their new leader. This was the other side of the Hulme coin.

Clive Hulme's Victoria Cross was recognition of his valour in Crete during the Second World War, where he fought what amounted to a private battle as an anti-sniper sniper in the hills, picking off the enemy one at a time. He was a tough old guy in later years, with extraordinary powers as a diviner for water and oil. In retirement, after quitting Formula One at the end of the 1974 season, Denny came to mirror his dad, with his greying, curling, thinning hair.

Clive Hulme used to tell the story of how he once noticed a strange smell when young Denny was welding in the family-business workshop, and he realised his son was standing barefoot on a glowing welding spark that was burning into his sole, and he hadn't noticed. All Kiwi country kids went barefoot, and when, in 1960, Denny arrived in Britain to race, the establishment was mildly amazed to learn that he drove his Cooper in bare feet because he claimed it gave him a better feel of the pedals.

You pronounced Hulme as 'Hume' at your peril. Clive Hulme had told his family, 'Never let them knock the "l" out of Hulme.' It was always 'Hullm'.

Denny was born in 1936 and went from school to the family haulage business. His first sporting car was an MG TF that he drove in a few hill climbs, and then in 1958 he graduated to an MGA. The racing bug had bitten, and two years later Denny was winning in a 2-litre Cooper and earning the Driver to Europe award that he shared with George Lawton. This was the same scholarship that had launched Bruce McLaren two years earlier. The newcomers' overseas season started tragically when Lawton was killed in a race on Denmark's Roskildering.

Bruce and Denny had met at the 1960 scholarship awards ceremony in New Zealand, and when Denny arrived in Britain, Bruce lent him his Morris Minor for transport while he built his own Formula Junior Cooper in the Cooper workshops — the traditional method for any young driver to ensure his car was delivered on time.

Denny won at Salerno and Pescara, but these wins were small beer in New Zealand, where the newspapers were full of Bruce's Grand Prix victories. Denny hired a 2.5-litre Cooper single-seater from Reg Parnell for the pre-Tasman races in New Zealand in early 1961 and won the National Gold Star title. There were those who felt he would follow Bruce into Formula One that season, but there were others who realised that the Hulme intransigence — the insistence that driving ability, not diplomacy, should get you to the top — would not sit well with the establishment. A diplomat Denny was not, and this certainly cost him dear during those fallow seasons in the early 1960s, when he worked as a mechanic in Jack Brabham's customer garage while he waited for the opportunity that eventually came in 1963 with a works Brabham drive in Formula Junior.

I toured the 1961 Formula Junior series with Denny, towing his Cooper-Ford on a trailer behind a Mark 1 Ford Zodiac around the crowded European circuit, from Karlskoga in Sweden to Messina in Sicily. The rear seats of the Zodiac had been removed and the space crammed with spare parts and petrol cans. Denny used to fuel the racing car after each event, and then fill six five-gallon cans to get to the next race, courtesy of his modest fuel contract.

Denny's race management was a fairly freehand arrangement. We unloaded at Monza only to find that Denny hadn't entered that race: he had entered the Formula Junior race at Reims, a support event for the Grand Prix the same weekend. We loaded up and set off on an overnight thrash up through France. Dawn found us waiting for a petrol station to open while Denny scratched through a shoebox full of every denomination of European coin to get together enough francs for fuel. I remember the only map we had was a huge foldout of Western Europe, since Denny reasoned it was more convenient to have a single map rather than one for each country.

We got what must have been the last fleapit hotel room in Reims, and on the Sunday morning, as we were leaving, a guy in blue Dunlop racing overalls was coming out of the room next door. I asked Denny who it was. 'Dunno,' he said. 'Never seen him before.' Not many people had. It was Giancarlo Baghetti, who would win the Grand Prix for Ferrari that afternoon before fading back into obscurity.

Jack Brabham won the world championship in 1966, and teammate and supposedly number two driver Denny Hulme won it in 1967 before leaving to join the man who had lent him his Morris Minor seven years before.

During his 1967 championship season, Denny won at Monaco and at the Nürburgring — coincidentally, the two Grands Prix Stirling Moss won when he was clearly outpowered by the Ferraris in 1961, the two races that demanded precise skill. His fame took time to gather. When Monaco Clerk of the Course Louis Chiron was shepherding Denny to the royal box after his win, he whispered, 'By the way, monsieur, what is your name?' Fame was not what Denny was doing it for.

Denny remembered his win on the Nürburgring in detail:

> What really surprised me on the first lap was that three of us — Jim Clark, Dan Gurney and myself — quickly lost the others, and that Jim hadn't set off like a rocket as I had expected it. I tucked in close behind the Lotus and got a fantastic tow. The rev counter soared up to 8900 rpm in Jim's slipstream, which was a few hundreds more than

I wanted, but I was prepared to keep my foot down and determined not to lose contact.

That tow lasted for three laps of the 14.5-mile track, and continued for a while longer when Dan slipped by in the Eagle. On lap four, Jim was in trouble. I knew he was having problems because he was looking over his shoulder to see if anything was wrong with his car. I was close on his tail and there was nothing obviously the matter, but both Dan and I overtook him shortly after going into the country after the pits, and then I did all I could to get away from the Eagle. At Adenau he was still right on my tail and I knew he was beginning to get serious about it all. Then we came up to the big jump on the far side of the circuit, and I landed all crossed up. I should have changed gear, because in recovering from that effort I had slowed down, and while I was gathering speed again, Dan came past. Then I *knew* he was serious, because in certain parts of the circuit he was really trying and going very quickly. I hung on to my tow for a lap, but after that Dan broke away and started to extend his lead. He really had that Eagle sorted out, and it didn't seem to be leaving the ground on the brows as often as my car. This was important, because I'm sure most people found more bumps at the 'Ring through travelling so much quicker. There is, for example, a very nasty bump coming up the home straight which I'm sure no one realised was a bump until this year.

Dan pulled away to a very useful lead of 45 seconds, but then had the misfortune to break down on the circuit, surrounded by a pool of oil. That gave me a 45-second lead with three laps to go, which was a very comforting situation. I kept going as quickly as I could, but without using all the revs. I changed up earlier and concentrated on saving the car all I could. The engine never missed a beat all the way to the finish and the brakes stood up to the job wonderfully. The car suffered no damage at all during the race, but when I stepped out of the cockpit, I broke the windscreen.

When Denny clinched the championship in Mexico at the end of the 1967 season, having finished third, he was photographed on the rostrum inside a huge laurel wreath with race winner Jimmy Clark, and he joked that he didn't mind being the champion if Jimmy would do the public appearances.

Denny knew his limitations, and compared himself with Bruce:

> Bruce used to like going out and meeting people. He managed to cope even when they asked the most ridiculous questions, whereas my natural reaction was to think, 'What a bunch of idiots we've got here,' and either tell them so or not talk to them at all. But that's just the way I am. Bruce could spend the whole night entertaining people, and this is how he made lots of friends. He was the same with the press. He always had the time to talk to them. I've never been able to do that. For certain people in the press, yes, but for most of them, no. There's probably only half a dozen I can sit and talk to, but the rest of them — I feel they should do more homework and find out what it's all about.

In the late 1960s and early 1970s, I was working with the McLaren team sponsors and travelling with Denny on the weekly Atlantic flights shuttling back and forth — a CanAm or Indy-car race one weekend and a Grand Prix in Europe the next. I watched a classic Hulme 'Bear' performance when Canadian TV was shooting an hour-long documentary on the Gulf-McLaren team. Opening interviews were scheduled before the first race at Mosport. Peter Revson was all smoothness and style. The crew was pleased, but not a little nervous. They knew the Hulme reputation, and the man himself was next.

Denny huffed down the steps of the Gulf motor-home and the interviewer took his position with the microphone. I stood beside the soundman. I never did find out what the first question was but I heard the reply. So did the soundman. He flinched inside his headphones, and Denny was staring straight at me and saying, 'Eoin, tell this **** to stop asking such stupid ****ing questions!' And with that he stomped back into the motor-home and slammed the door.

I thought the interviewer was going to burst into tears. It was even worse than they had imagined. It was certainly worse than *I* had imagined. I saw my new job coming to an early, grinding halt. I went into the motor-home to find Denny slumped in an armchair, giggling — that titter, with his tongue between his teeth, that was his trademark.

'Denis,' I said, because he was in trouble, 'what *are* you doing? You're *ruining* this ****ing documentary!'

He looked almost surprised. 'Aw, c'mon,' he said, 'I was just getting their attention.' And with that he ambled out, threw a big arm round the interviewer's shoulders and settled down to a long friendly chat that made great footage when it aired later in the season.

The McLaren duo made the CanAm series their own — 'The Bruce and Denny Show'. Another race, another win, more megabuck prize money and another good time. They thoroughly enjoyed everything about CanAm. I remember one night when we were staying at a big old tourist hotel at Elkhart Lake and I got back late to the big three-bedded room we were sharing. It was pitch dark, and I was tiptoeing in so as not to wake the drivers on the night before the race. I was startled when someone hissed to be quiet, and then I realised Bruce and Denny were peeking out of the window, shaking with silent glee as they watched a lothario pleasuring his lady on the veranda outside, unaware of his silent audience.

One famous weekend Bruce and Denny comfortably qualified fastest with times they figured wouldn't be beaten — and then went water skiing the next day. Denny didn't regard fitness as a necessity. 'It's difficult to say how fit you've got to be. You don't have to front up and run a four-minute mile — it's more important to be able to pace yourself, to know your own capacity and make it last the race. If you're strong from the waist up, especially in the shoulders, arms and neck muscles, you're able to concentrate better.'

Denny was interesting when he analysed the difference in driving style between Bruce and himself and the way this translated into different results in different areas:

> Bruce was quicker than me in CanAm, and I sort of *knew* he was going to be quicker. He would set his car up the way he wanted and he was very smooth. He liked CanAm racing. It was his one big thing

and that made the world of difference. He was the hardest guy to beat in a CanAm car, yet he could put the same amount of effort into a Grand Prix car and get nothing like the same results. I think one of the reasons for this was because he was so smooth. If you throw a CanAm car around you lose time, whereas the only way to get a Grand Prix car to go quickly is to hurl it round and really set it up for fast corners. I don't think Bruce liked doing this.

Racing wasn't the same for Denny after Bruce died. He could still win, and did so in the South African Grand Prix in 1972, in Sweden in 1973 and in Argentina in 1974, but the shine was going. He was one of the first drivers to the scene of Peter Revson's fatal crash, testing at Kyalami before the 1974 Grand Prix, an incident that contributed to his decision to hang up his helmet at the end of the season. He moved back to New Zealand with his wife and family to enjoy retirement in the sun, but soon became restless and dabbled in truck racing and touring cars. His son, Martin, drowned while bathing in a lake and Denny was devastated. Father and son had been more like brothers, off-roading on motorcycles and travelling together.

In 1992 Denny was racing a BMW M3 in the 1000-kilometre race at Bathurst, a classic enduro on the mountain circuit, beamed live on TV all over Australia and New Zealand. The cameras were on him as he veered to the side of the track and angled down alongside the guardrail to park as though he had recognised a mechanical problem, or perhaps run out of fuel. But Denny was dead. At the age of 56 he had suffered a heart attack at the wheel. 'The Bear' was gone. I always felt that if you had asked him if that was the way he would have wanted to make his final exit, he would have said yes. But that didn't make it any easier for his family and his world of fans to cope with.

CHAPTER 3

CHRIS AMON

Chris Amon is always regarded as the third New Zealand driver on the international scene, after Bruce McLaren and Denny Hulme, but this is strictly historical, in that he was the youngest and last on the overseas racing stage. He was the most talented driver of the trio, but for whatever reasons, the unluckiest. However, as he points out today, some of the 'lucky' ones are no longer with us. This article was written for New Zealand Classic Car *in 2000.*

Baby-faced New Zealand driver Chris Amon goes down in the Formula One history book as the best driver never to win a world-championship Grand Prix. He had a huge natural talent. Jochen Rindt considered him and Jackie Stewart his only true rivals.

Chris learned to drive in a 1937 Ford V8 pick-up truck on his father's farm when he was as young as six, he had his pilot's licence by the time he turned 16, and he was racing a 1954 250F Grand Prix Maserati at the age of 17. Motor-racing history intrigued him, and he followed the careers of fellow Kiwis Bruce McLaren and Denny Hulme during their early racing years in Europe. He decided to try his own hand, buying an elderly Austin A40 Special — extra special because of its vintage Bugatti gearbox — and was soon at the wheel of the Maserati.

Chris raced against Stirling Moss and Jack Brabham as a teenager, and his prowess on New Zealand circuits in the early 1960s so impressed team-owner and former Grand Prix driver Reg Parnell that Parnell signed up the youngster to drive Formula One for him in 1963.

> I received a telegram at the farm saying PLEASE BE IN ENGLAND BY GOOD FRIDAY. That was just 10 days away, but fortunately I'd had the foresight to get a passport. I arrived in London on Good Friday evening — I'd never even seen a passenger jet plane before — had a seat-fitting and practised a 1.5-litre Formula One Lola-Climax at Goodwood at 10 o'clock the next morning, and raced it on Easter Monday. The first Formula One race I saw, I was in. I finished fifth.
>
> It had rained a bit before the start, and Reg had been telling someone about this bright young prospect from New Zealand. They had wattle screens at the Goodwood chicane, and Reg was just saying 'And here he comes now' when I demolished the screens right in front of him. There was no damage to the car and I kept on going, but his 'bright young prospect' had got it a bit wrong.

Reg Parnell was a top British Grand Prix racer and team manager who had valuable connections with engine-builders and the trade and ran what was, in effect, a Lotus number two team. He saw Chris as fresh new talent, and when he returned from the Tasman Series in February 1962, he said he hadn't seen a 250F driven with more style since the days of Fangio. Tragically, Reg died in January 1964 while Chris was still at home in New Zealand driving the Tasman Series, and Chris's life and career changed with the news he received when he walked into the office of the New Zealand Grand Prix organiser.

The Parnell team was taken over by Reg's son, Tim, who had learned management from his father but lacked his connections in the motor-racing industry. He fielded Lotus-BRMs for Chris, Mike Hailwood and Peter Revson, the three of them living in a rented house in Ditton Road, Surbiton, in Surrey, and becoming branded 'The Ditton Road Flyers'. Their parties were legendary.

Chris was generally reckoned to have a pure natural talent like that of Moss, Clark or Stewart, but his lack of luck was astounding. He proved he was one of the best, winning Le Mans with Bruce McLaren for Ford in 1966, being signed by Ferrari in 1967 and leading the team at the end of the decade, setting pole positions and leading Grands Prix — he holds the Formula One lap record for the old Spa-Francorchamps road circuit with an average 152 mph — but never scoring a win. It was typical of his fortune that when he did finally win a Grand Prix — in 1971 in Argentina, after switching to the French Matra team — it was a nonchampionship race. He was still a pacesetter with Matra, leading and losing races, but gradually his eagerness to compete was becoming dulled. The risk was starting to outweigh the rewards.

Jim Clark's death in 1968 stunned the racing world of the day in the way Ayrton Senna's fatal crash at Imola in 1994 affected the modern Formula One world. 'I don't think Jimmy's death slowed anybody down, but I think it probably cast some doubts in people's minds, because if it could happen to him it could happen to anyone. A lot of us had a sort of bulletproof attitude at the time, and it certainly put a dent in that.'

In his last race with Jim Clark's Lotus in the 1968 Tasman Series, at Sandown Park in Australia, Chris had crossed the finishing line in his Ferrari almost alongside Clark's cockpit.

A quirk of fate led Ferrari to fit seat belts for the German Grand Prix at the old Nürburgring, a mountainous 14.5-mile circuit through forests. The belts weren't for driver safety — they were simply a means of preventing the drivers being thrown out of the cockpit when negotiating the high-speed brows where the cars became airborne. They were left in for the next race, the Italian Grand Prix at Monza. Chris was lying second when a hydraulic pump activating the rear wing came adrift and pumped fluid on to a rear wheel. The Ferrari suddenly swapped ends at high speed, hit a guardrail backwards and was launched into a series of aerial somersaults through the top of some trackside trees and an advertising hoarding. Incredibly, the car landed on its wheels, and Chris emerged totally unharmed. The belts had kept him safe.

'I had no idea where I was. I was trying to figure out what had happened when John Surtees [who'd also come off the track] popped his head over the fence and said, "Jesus! Are you all right?" One of the spectators loaned us a motorbike and John drove to the pits with me on the pillion.'

Chris left Ferrari at the end of the 1969 season to drive for the new March team, simply to get hold of one of the new Ford-Cosworth DFV V8 engines and satisfy his fierce desire to compete on equal terms with Jackie Stewart, who was driving an identical March-Ford for Tyrrell. The two of them tied for pole position in the first race of the 1970 season in South Africa, but whereas Stewart stayed with Tyrrell for the rest of his career, winning three world championships before eventually retiring at the end of the 1973 season, Chris continued to switch from team to team, chasing a championship Formula One win that frustratingly never came his way.

Chris's time with the March team in 1970 was fraught with political infighting. He had understood that he would lead a one-car works team, but the situation deteriorated almost by the week as more drivers signed up for more cars with more sponsors. Then there were the fatal accidents that summer: Bruce McLaren at Goodwood in June, Piers Courage at Zandvoort 19 days later, and Jochen Rindt at Monza in September.

Jackie Stewart wrote of Chris's frustrations and outbursts during the summer of 1970 in his book *Faster — A Racer's Diary*:

> Chris is a very open and relaxed guy who's great fun to be with, although sometimes he gets terribly tied up, particularly during practice. Anger can boil up inside him which you never suspected was there, and by now his mechanics have a fairly thorough description of it. They call it Chris's 'wobblies'. There are three kinds, each corresponding to the intensity of his mood: the white, the rainbow and the purple wobblies. The white variety is when he gets out of his car, his face ashen, throws his gloves down and simply screams 'Fucking car,' and storms off. The rainbow type is when he explodes at everything, makes no discriminations and is close to outright hysteria. The purple wobblies, the peak of his outbursts, set in when he's completely without measure, his face beet red, his blood pressure up, eyes bulging and he's almost wrenching everybody apart.

During his two seasons with Matra in 1971–72, Chris flirted with success. He was one of the best-paid drivers, earning £1,000 a week, which pales to nothingness in comparison with Michael Schumacher's Ferrari income, but in those days it reflected his rating as the close equal of Stewart and Rindt. He really was that good.

In addition to his natural style, Chris was a top test driver in the days before computer generation. Most drivers preferred to race rather than test, but in 1965 Chris led the tyre-test team when Firestone signed with the fledgling McLaren outfit. A single-seater version of the CanAm McLaren sports-racer, a prototype for the new 3-litre Formula One, served as test vehicle.

'It was quite exhausting because we were probably doing 300 miles a day flat out. I used to drive pretty well right on my limit, because you had to really find out what you were doing. The car was heavy in the steering, so at the end of the day you really knew you'd done something.'

Chris had an inbuilt technical knack with tyre-testing that was proved, without his knowledge, one afternoon at Goodwood. The Firestone technicians thought they would reduce the boredom by taking a set of tyres and wheels off the McLaren when Chris stopped at the pits to report on the car's behaviour — and then refit the same set. As Chris rumbled down the pit lane, the technicians realised the implications of what they had done. If Chris did his scheduled laps and then delivered a report different from the one he'd given on his earlier run — with the same tyres — his diagnosis would be instantly suspect and they would have to confess what they had done. Chris stopped at the pits as scheduled and sat in the cockpit, puzzled. 'Y'know,' he said, after a pause. 'I don't understand this, but those tyres feel *exactly* the same as the ones you took off at the last stop.'

Looking back on those days, the racing world regards the Kiwis as a close-knit trio, but Chris says it wasn't quite like that:

> I knew Bruce and Denny in the early days, but not very well. People forget that I was three or four years behind them. Bruce and I had talked on a couple of occasions, but we had no real contact until I started driving for him. I certainly didn't know him very well. I probably hadn't met Denny at all by then. Denny didn't socialise a lot, and the same could be said for Bruce then, I suppose.

Bruce McLaren's game plan was that he and his young countryman, Chris Amon, would drive two new McLaren-Fords in Formula One when it doubled from 1500 cc to 3 litres for 1966. They won and lost with Ford that year. They paired up to win at Le Mans for Ford, but McLaren lost out hugely when, after trying unsuccessfully to persuade Ford in North America to bankroll an engine for Formula One, he tried to reduce a 4-cam 4.2-litre Ford Indianapolis V8 to 3 litres. 'It was an absolute disaster,' says Chris. 'They had so many engine problems that they never did build the second car for me.' He drove a works Cooper-Maserati in the French Grand Prix at Reims, but otherwise it was a lost season.

A year later Ford was in Formula One, not as a result of McLaren's freelance push, but thanks to Walter Hayes, Public Affairs Director at Ford of Britain, bankrolling a £100,000 project for Keith Duckworth and Mike Costin at Cosworth Engineering to build a Formula One engine — an engine that went on to dominate international motor racing for decades.

It was Chris's talent as a Firestone tester that brought him to the attention of Ferrari:

I was at Watkins Glen, spectating at the US Grand Prix, when Keith Ballisat, from Shell, approached me in the lobby of the Glen Motor Inn. He asked what I was doing the following weekend and I said I had a CanAm race, so he said, 'What about Sunday night, Monday and Tuesday?' I said, 'Probably not a lot,' and he said, 'Would you like to come over to Italy with me and meet Mr Ferrari?' Talk about a bolt from the blue. It took me about two whole seconds to say 'Yes!' Actually, I was in a difficult situation, because Bruce wanted me to stay at McLaren, but driving for Ferrari was also a boyhood ambition of mine.

Enzo Ferrari entertained the new young driver but refused to say more than 'maybe' about a Formula One drive:

There was no problem with an endurance sports-car drive, and he suggested that there would be no problem about Formula One, but he couldn't or wouldn't put it in writing. I never did find out why, but after a couple of endurance races he was as good as his word and I was entered for the first Grand Prix of the season, at Monaco.

I was absolutely in awe of him, as I think most people were. He was actually quite good at putting me at ease. We did the contractual negotiations then went over to the Cavallino restaurant, across the road from the factory at Maranello. We had a wonderful lunch and I sat there being very good, drinking mineral water with all this good food and wine on the table, and he said via his interpreter that it was always interesting having the first lunch with a new driver. He said Mike Hawthorn had had lunch and drunk a bottle of his best malt whisky, having signed the contract half an hour before. He always took a keen interest in his drivers' relations with the opposite sex. He had a superb intelligence set-up; in fact, I think he knew more about what we were doing than we did.

Enzo always did the best deal of the day, and when Jacky Ickx signed for the 1968 season, Chris soon found that the young Belgian was getting a far better deal than he was. 'I raised it with the old man, and he said, "No problem — we'll make yours the same."'

The Italian press has always baited foreign drivers:

> I had a sort of love-hate relationship with them which was probably more hate than love, I think. It was difficult for them because Ferrari was going through a fairly average period during most of my time there. If we won — not that I ever did in a single-seater — it was the car, and if we lost, it was down to the driver. It wasn't just the press. There were certain people within the team who had great difficulty in being convinced that the car wasn't up to scratch.
>
> If you're driving for Ferrari and living in Italy, you can live like royalty. The whole of Italy was behind motor racing, and I had three wonderful years there — three of the best years of my life, to be honest.

Back at McLaren, Chris thought Bruce felt somewhat betrayed. 'He felt that his Formula One team was on the brink of getting it right, and I guess he also felt he'd invested a couple of years in me, too. We always got on well, but I don't think it was ever quite as close as it used to be.'

Chris's Ferrari debut at Monaco in 1967 saw the death of his friend and team-mate, Lorenzo Bandini. 'I'd got to know him pretty well, and he was very supportive to me in the team. His death probably spurred me on because it was fairly obvious that I was quicker than the other two [Ludovico Scarfiotti and Mike Parkes] and so it really put more responsibility on me, which was probably good in the long run.'

Bandini crashed at the quayside chicane late in the race while in pursuit of Denny Hulme's Brabham, his Ferrari hitting hay bales, overturning and catching fire. Bandini died of burns.

> I think it was sheer fatigue. It was a long race, the thick end of three hours, and it was very hot that day. I know by about the 75th lap I was actually starting to get cold in the car, which meant that I was

totally dehydrated. I'm sure he went through the same thing and it was purely a lapse of concentration that caused him to run wide and hit the bales.'

In 1968 Chris flirted with great wins for Ferrari, but was always cheated by unreliability. Following Jim Clark's death, he and Ferrari were regarded as the pacesetters. He started from pole in the Spanish, Belgian, Dutch and Canadian Grands Prix, but suffered a string of delays or retirements. 'If I'd finished all the races I led from pole, I would have won the world championship.'

With Matra in 1971 and 1972, he again led a works team and had certain victory plucked from his grasp more than once. In the 1972 French Grand Prix, at Clermont Ferrand, he started from pole and led comfortably to half distance, when he picked up a puncture and the wheel jammed in the pits. 'They had a hell of a job getting it off and I think I lost a minute-and-a-half. I threw caution to the winds after that and just went for it. I ended up third, about 30 seconds behind Jackie Stewart, in what I reckon was one of my better drives.'

He started from pole with the Matra V12 in the Italian Grand Prix, and was leading, almost within sight of the flag, when he tried to peel one of the removable visors off his helmet and inadvertently peeled them *all* off. Full-face helmets in those days had a letter-box slot with several Perspex visors attached which could be removed one by one during the race if they became opaque with oil and track dirt. 'Suddenly I got a 200-mile-an-hour blast of wind in my eyes and finished a very gentle sixth.'

It could only have happened to Chris Amon. Mario Andretti was moved to observe that if Chris took up undertaking, people would stop dying.

By the end of 1975, Chris was virtually washed up after a run of one-off drives, substandard drives and even an unsuccessful attempt at building a Formula One car of his own. He accepted a drive in the underfunded but well-designed Ensign, but Morris Nunn's team was running elderly engines and although there were flashes of the old Amon brilliance, come 1976 his enthusiasm was flagging, and when Niki Lauda's flaming crash stopped the German Grand Prix on the old mountain Nürburgring, Chris announced he would not take the restart.

He arrived at the scene of Lauda's crash to find six or eight other cars had already stopped, so he climbed out of the Ensign and ran back down the road to warn drivers coming up behind. As the cars were forming up on the grid for the restart, he couldn't dispel how appalled he felt at the length of time it had taken for the ambulance to arrive, and at the fact that if other drivers hadn't stopped to rescue Lauda, it would have been all over for the German driver. The track facilities simply hadn't been equal to the accident.

Chris dwelt on a delayed start he had made in an earlier German Grand Prix, when he could have had a similar accident and there would have been no cars coming through for perhaps five minutes. It was also going through his mind that his mechanical record with the Ensign had not exactly been reassuring. He said to team owner Morris Nunn: 'Morris, I'm going home. I'm sorry, but it's just bloody ridiculous. It took five minutes for the ambulance to get there. It's not on.' And he walked back to the pit, out of the race and out of Formula One.

Jackie Stewart sat quietly on the pit rail with him, not so much trying to talk him into racing as offering alternatives. He could perhaps have started, taken it easy for a couple of laps and then parked, preserving his reputation. But in such a highly charged situation, it required more bravery to quit than to race against one's better judgement, and Chris was not to be swayed, showing what I considered that weekend to be amazing strength of character. I think Stewart admired his resolve, too. 'Chris had made his decision and stuck to it,' he said. 'I wouldn't condone it — but I certainly wouldn't condemn it either.' Two days later, Chris and Nunn agreed to terminate their contract.

There was a swansong Formula One entry on the edge of a CanAm deal with Austro-Canadian Walter Wolf, but following a crash in practice, Chris, in tragicomic style, didn't start in his last Grand Prix.

'I felt I'd had enough,' he says today.

I'd been racing for 13 years, and the travelling, the hotels, the aeroplanes, the airports — the whole thing starts to get to you after a while. It was probably more the way of life than the actual racing that prompted my final decision. It had inevitably reached the stage where it had become a job, and I'd got to the point where I didn't actually look forward to the next race. I must say, when I stopped I really felt I'd had enough and was quite happy to stop.

CHAPTER 4

HOWDEN GANLEY

Howden Ganley is today still regarded as something of a mystery man, even amongst enthusiasts in his home country. When this profile ran in New Zealand Classic Car *in 2001, the fact that there was actually a fourth Kiwi who had raced in Formula One was received with some surprise. This was the first major feature to be written on the New Zealander who started on the workshop floor and made it to the top.*

Howden Ganley was the 'Quiet Kiwi' of Formula One, a steady glow beside the dazzling brilliance of Bruce McLaren, Denny Hulme and Chris Amon. These days Howden is comfortable with his place in the world of motor racing as a director of the British Racing Drivers' Club (BRDC), a former British Racing Motors (BRM) and Williams driver in Formula One, and 1972 runner-up at Le Mans for Matra — to name the highlights of a frontline career in international motor sport that seemed to go largely unnoticed in Howden's native New Zealand.

Howden grew up beside the lake in Hamilton, a yachting enthusiast who raced a P-class every weekend and also crewed for his father in a Frostbite. Paradoxically, his younger brother, Denis, was a motor-racing enthusiast but would become a top yacht designer before his death in a motor accident in May 1997.

In 1955 Howden's father and Denis were going to the Grand Prix at Ardmore and asked Howden if he wanted to join them. He said he didn't: cars did nothing for him. But it so happened he changed his mind, and while their father, who knew one of the drivers, was in the pits, young Howden and Denis were parked out at the Cloverleaf corners. 'The Grand Prix was in two heats and a final, and I was amazed when Prince Bira come storming out on the parade lap for the first heat with the 250F Maserati in blue and gold Siamese colours. He blasted through our corners and I was hooked. Right there! Talk about finding religion. Wow!'

Howden's eyes still light up as he remembers his first sight of a Grand Prix car at speed. 'Peter Whitehead was there with his Ferrari, so was Tony Gaze, and Reg Hunt had his A6 GCS Maserati. By the end of the day, when Bira had won, I was saying to Denis, "Forget sailing. I'm going to be a Grand Prix driver."' He had just turned 14. 'I didn't really forget sailing because I enjoyed it. But let's say I'm not as keen on sailing as my brother-in-law, Grant Dalton.'

School in New Zealand was something you did as quickly as possible so you could get on with life. When your father drove an MG TF and your burning ambition was to get into motor sport, it was always going to be a bore. 'I took Latin and French for a time but I discovered that it wasn't going to do me any good if I drove for Ferrari because the Italians didn't speak Latin, although I thought French would be OK if I drove for Gordini.'

Howden left school, went to work on the *Waikato Times* and became a motoring correspondent. He began writing for all the North Island newspapers and magazines that would take his columns on cars and motor sport. At the same time, I was writing for South Island newspapers under the by-line Eoin S. Young, in imitation of my hero on *Road & Track*, Henry N. Manney III, who would become a good friend when I found my way to Europe. Howden wrote as James H. Ganley.

> I knew that BRM were using a 250F Maserati at the start of the 2.5-litre formula, so I wrote to Sir Alfred Owen [of the Owen Organization] and said I'd like to know all about his 250F. I got a letter back from Raymond Mays saying that my letter to Sir Alfred had been referred to him and that Mr [Tony] Rudd [chief engineer and team manager at BRM] was preparing a report for me. Imagine the cheek of it? A kid from New Zealand and Tony is taking time off preparing the BRMs so that he can write a two-page report for me!

Howden would race for BRM in 1971 and 1972 but he never broached the subject of Rudd's special report to a teenage Kiwi. I asked Tony Rudd about it on Howden's behalf but it turned out he had already moved on to Lotus. 'I never met Howden. That was Big Lou's era at BRM. If it was late in 1955 when he wrote to Sir Alfred, I might have written the report for him because I thought he wanted to buy the car.'

Howden wrote to other motor-racing luminaries.

> I wrote to Stirling Moss when I was at school and got his autographed photograph. I wrote to him about every month after that. When I was supposed to be doing prep in the common room in the evening and the other boys were getting letters from their mothers and reading them, I had a letter from Stirling Moss — even if it did only say that he was enclosing a signed fan-mail photograph. I was already on the inside and I hadn't left school yet!

Howden prevailed on his mother to lend him her Morris Minor for a hill climb and a sprint in the same way I persuaded my mother to have twin SUs fitted to her Austin A30 because it would improve fuel economy and then to lend it to me for the hill climb at Clelands Hill.

Len Gilbert showed me some proper speed when he took me round Levin in his Cooper Bristol (ex-Horace Gould, ex-Jim Palmer), which he had widened out to qualify as a sports car. He had kept the single-seater frame but hung a passenger seat off one side and made the bodywork symmetrical. I rode in that little passenger's seat for a couple of laps and then wrote a story for the *Waikato Times*. In hindsight I realise how dangerous it all was, but at the time it was just wonderful. When I later worked for Len, washing dishes (and preparing the sweets!) in his restaurant, his race cars were always parked just behind the food prep area, but I guess hygiene was not such an issue then. He eventually had the Owen Organisation 250F in there, and I probably knew more about its history than he did, thanks to my correspondence with Raymond Mays and Tony Rudd.

I thought I went quite well against the other Morrie Minors so I was ready for a proper racing car. The Lotus 11 that had been raced by Jim Palmer was now owned by Johnny Windleburn, and he had it for sale at £1,300. I had to have it. It had the full works, and I knew the car well from when Jim had had it because he lived in Hamilton and we all knew each other. Somehow I managed to scratch up the money by getting my grandmother to give me my 21st birthday money and all my birthday presents up to that. I sold *everything* I owned. I sold my bike, which was serious stuff then. I fitted my brothers up with all sorts of old rubbish and I raised £650, which was halfway there. The bloke who was going to come in with the other half reneged, so I managed to get my mother to loan me the other £650 and we bought the car.

It was beautiful. It had a Climax 1100 cc engine and was simply the business. The problem was that now I was skint. I didn't have a trailer, I didn't have a tow car and I had no money left. I did one race at Ardmore in December 1960 and my first full race on the 1961 Grand Prix weekend. I won my class in the sports car race (and £15), and I went in for the Ultimate Ecco race for New Zealand drivers that paid the phenomenal amount of £150 to win — and I *won* it!

Suddenly I could afford to go racing for the rest of the season. I talked Denis into buying an old 1936 Chevvy, and I borrowed the trailer that my father used to haul his Ford 10 Special sports car. We took the back seats out of the Chev, loaded the spares in and away we went, with Denis as my mechanic, to Levin and Wigram.

Howden lost at Levin, going into a spin while lying second on the last lap, but at Wigram he took class seconds in two races. When Denis went back to work, Alistair Caldwell, who would go on to make his name as chief mechanic with the McLaren Formula One team, used his holiday pay from the Post Office garages to help fund the Ganley race programme. A fuel line came adrift at Dunedin in the sports-car race, and Howden clouted a kerb in the main event. After Teretonga, the Ganley équipe headed for Queenstown with a like-minded crowd for some R and R before the race round the streets of Waimate. I travelled with Howden from Queenstown to Waimate, and it must have been my fault that we headed over the Crown Range — the highest motor road in New Zealand. I probably suggested it because it looked like the shortest route on the map. 'I remember the old Chevvy was coughing and wheezing trying to get over the loose-metal pass with the Lotus and trailer on the back.'

The 1962 season was a disaster for the Ganley Lotus équipe, with a best placing of fourth in the sports-car race at Wigram. Howden finished fifth in the Ken Wharton Memorial Trophy race at Ardmore but no prize monies were paid out because there were not enough starters.

The final race at Dunedin was run in pouring rain on the street circuit. Johnny Mansel was killed when his Cooper-Maserati skidded on the diesel-slicked bus-route road, and Howden also lost control in the same area, smashing the shapely front of the Lotus 11 against a telegraph pole. The car had been sold, and Howden's sights were set on a trip to Britain, but the Dunedin crash put those plans in jeopardy.

'The Lotus was brought home to Hamilton, and my father and

Pete Kerr rebuilt it, but my buyer, I suppose understandably, had second thoughts. The market had shrunk, and we got enough out of the car to pay for the repairs and repay the £650 loan from my mother, and by the time I got to England I had £25 in my pocket.'

Howden took a leaf out of Graham Hill's book and spent evenings in The Steering Wheel Club in London, nursing a pint of beer through the night so that he would be around if a drive became available.

New Zealand journalist Bill Gavin introduced me to Mike Mosley, who made Falcon sports cars, and told him that I was *much* faster than his regular driver. He entered us both in a race with Falcons, and I was quicker than the other guy, so Mosley said, 'Right. Now you're my driver, and you can be my development engineer as well.'

At that stage my mechanical knowledge was minimal so I had to learn pretty damn quick. Part of the deal was that when I got the new GT into production I could build a lightweight one for myself to race and I could have someone to help me, so I got Johnny Muller to come over from New Zealand. We did about five races and we were mixing it with the Marcoses in the GT category, but then, unfortunately, we got a new major shareholder who was also a major shareholder in Marcos, and he said he didn't want Falcon racing against Marcos because Marcos was his racing company and Falcon was to be for road cars. John and I said, 'No racing? Goodbye.'

The two Kiwis went to work as mechanics for George Henrotte, who was running the Gemini Formula Junior team, and at Brands Hatch Howden was given a drive in the second car and went fast enough to impress Henrotte into giving him a few races until the formula ended when 1000 cc Formula Three and Formula Two started in 1964 and Gemini withdrew.

Unemployed again, Howden was sitting in his flat when the phone rang. By historic coincidence it was me, calling from Bruce McLaren's home. 'You said Bruce wanted to talk to me. He came on the line and said he was building up a team and did I want to come and work for him? Did I? Of course I did.'

Howden joined McLaren when Tyler Alexander and Wally Willmott were working on the Zerex Special in the grubby earth-floored grader garage in New Malden, southwest London — a far cry from the gleaming McLaren workshops of today.

> The Zerex was balanced on a big wooden crate that had just arrived back from the Tasman Series, and as the new 'gopher' I was sent to the Cooper Car Company to get some tube to make axle stands. Bruce sorted it with John Cooper and I drove over in our Mini van. I bent the tubes, and when I got back the others had gone, so I set about welding up a set of axle stands. When they came in the next morning they asked who had made the axle stands, and when I confessed that I had, they said, 'You didn't tell us you could weld. Right — now you're the fabricator.' And they got another gopher.

One of Howden's projects was to build a new back end on the Tasman Cooper that Phil Hill was going to drive. McLaren had raced it the year before. 'I thought this was great because it meant I'd be going home for the Tasman Series, and I was devastated when Bruce told me I wouldn't be going.'

In fact, Bruce had promoted Howden to build the prototype of the new sports car for the following season. Those were the days when the new McLaren company worked as a true team, with McLaren, as the driver, working side by side with the mechanics. 'That was the thing with Bruce. When we came to run the modified Tasman car, and when he had the new car, he told me to bring my helmet, and I had a zing round in it. How many employers would do that for you?'

The McLaren team had now moved to a trading estate at Feltham, in Middlesex, and McLaren was doing development work on the Ford GT programme as well as leading the Cooper Formula One team.

> Bruce came in one day and announced that we were going to build a hush-hush lightweight version of the GT40 with an aluminium monocoque, and I had to go to John Wyer's J.W. Automotive factory and collect all the suspension units. Gary Knutson would be in charge

and I was to be his right-hand man. That was when Teddy Mayer built a shed within a shed at Feltham, a self-contained unit so that the project would be kept secret. Later on I had a better understanding of how these things worked. I thought we were doing a development project to help Ford, but now I suspect it was to help finance McLaren Racing at a difficult time.

We drew all the bits and pieces and we built the car with a nose that had been taken from the Ford raced by Phil Hill and Chris Amon at Le Mans. We had a Spyder-type central cockpit, standard GT40 suspension and a Hewland LG gearbox. The idea was to make it as light as possible.

I was given a development report from Ford's Kar Kraft division which explained the reasons we were doing this 'X-1' project car:

a. To provide further information on the potential of large engines in the sports categories of racing (sports prototype and modified sports).
b. To provide a basis for developing vehicle tailoring for the 'J' car now under development.
c. To provide an operative racing test unit for components such as engines, drivelines, brakes, tires, etc.

When we completed the car at Feltham, it weighed 1920 lbs (870 kg) with its heavy second-hand Le Mans nose. That made it almost 1000 lbs (450 kg) lighter than the Le Mans 7-litre Fords.

The first race for the big open X-1, nicknamed 'Big Ed' by the team, was the 1965 pre-CanAm sports-car race at Mosport, in Canada. Chris Amon drove but retired.

We were told by Ford to take the car down to Kar Kraft in Dearborn. They were making an open car similar to ours and they couldn't believe our Hewland transmission: 'That skinny little Limey transaxle ain't going to cope with these horses!' In fact, we were using a 7-litre with a single Holley and it didn't really make that much power, but they didn't believe the little lightweight gearbox would do it. We were told to put a Kar Kraft transmission on it — a massive thing designed by Pete Weismann. It could have had a 14-litre engine in it now!

The car was tested by Phil Hill before the race at Riverside, and Amon drove the car to fifth place behind proper CanAm cars. The next race for the big Ford was the Nassau Speed Weeks, but the engine failed. Gary Knutson was pulled from the X-1 project to work on the McLaren Formula One engine project with a 3-litre version of the Ford Indianapolis 4-cam V8. Howden was now in charge, but his first job was to install a full-size FIA-spec windscreen.

'I was working in a big old wooden hangar at Nassau with just my toolkit, no fabrication equipment, and I was supposed to graft this huge windscreen on to "Big Ed". I've no idea how I did it, but I somehow managed it and we went off to Daytona testing. That windscreen project was another indication of the sometimes unrealistic expectations of some of the Ford hierarchy.'

Howden was then seconded to Ford and worked in Dearborn on a variety of automatic transmissions.

They had a guy from General Motors who knew how the Chaparral transmission worked, and I suppose they couldn't believe how simple it was. It was a fluid flywheel with a great big crash box and you just yanked the lever through. We went down to test at Sebring for weeks with this 2-speed crash box transmission, and then T & C [Ford's Transmission and Chassis Division] built a full automatic transmission from a Galaxy and we were running that as well. They were having terrible cooling problems with the GT40 brakes but we had done ours differently. Instead of trying to defy the laws of physics and stuff cold air down the outside of the disc, we'd sussed that if you blew it into the centre, you cooled the disc. Ken Miles came and drove our car and he couldn't believe how good the brakes were. They didn't fade.

I think that's when things started to go pear shaped. I was told to take the car to Daytona for the 24-hour race, but it just sat there all weekend and didn't run. At the end of the weekend I was told the car wasn't my project any more and it went back to the Shelby race shop in Los Angeles. I think Ken Miles had been very impressed and had told the Ford hierarchy that it was pretty good, so Shelby took it and they won the Sebring 12-hour race with it and McLaren got *no* credit for it. That was the car that *we* built in the McLaren workshop at Feltham. After it won Sebring it was allegedly crushed so there was no trace of McLaren involvement.

Howden went on to work as a mechanic with the McLarens of Peter Revson and Skip Scott in the 1966 CanAm series, and the team came close to winning in Nassau.

By working with Ford on the X-1 project and then with Revvy and Scott on the CanAm series, I'd saved up enough money to buy a brand-new BT21 Formula Three Brabham. Ron Tauranac was very good to me. I'd told him before I went to the States that I would have enough to buy a new car when I came back, but at that moment I didn't even have enough money to pay the deposit. I asked him if he would keep a place for me in his production queue. Everyone said he wouldn't do it, but he did. McLaren got me a really good engine from Cosworth and passed on their discount to me.

I set off round the races in Europe in 1967, living from race to race. Bruce let me rebuild the car in their workshops over the winter, and for 1969 I bought a new Chevron. I was getting seconds and thirds and doing a lot of racing in Scandinavia because they paid proper starting money there. Ronnie Peterson and Reine Wisell were very helpful. They were good days in Formula Three. I did the first (and only) Formula Three 100 mph lap round Brands Hatch. I beat Emerson Fittipaldi at Crystal Palace and I nearly beat Tim Schenken at Cadwell Park, but he ran me on to the grass on the last lap and I was second.

Bruce had told me to keep him posted on what I was doing, so I used to get *Autosport* every week and highlight my name all through the Formula Three race reports. I would find out what hotel he was staying at in the States and then airmail the magazine to him. When he came back at the end of the 1969 season he called me up and said he was having a Formula One test at Goodwood. Wisell and I both drove the M7 Formula One McLaren, and at the end of the day Bruce took me aside and told me he was going to retire at the end of the 1970 season and he wanted me to be his protégé. He said he would run me in a couple of the early-season nonchampionship Formula One races in 1970 and he wanted me to do Formula 5000. He said he would find a sponsor. It all sounded pretty good to me.

The sponsor turned out to be financier Barry Newman, McLaren's next-door neighbour, and the deal was done over dinner.

Barry wrote out the cheque there and then. Bruce told Trojan to sell me a new McLaren M10B monocoque at cost and arranged a Goodyear tyre contract, John Nicholson built us a good Chev engine, Mike Hewland gave me a gearbox, and I put the car together. We finished second to Peter Gethin in the championship that year, but sadly Bruce didn't live to see it. I started 18 races, finished 16, never lower than fourth, but my chances of a Formula One McLaren drive had gone and Gethin got the slot.

McLaren was impressed by Howden's ability, perhaps seeing something of himself in the quiet approach, the engineering background and the ability to finish races. He had been discussing drivers with 'Big Lou' Stanley at BRM, and Howden was offered a fourth car for 1971 racing with Pedro Rodriguez, Jo Siffert and John Miles. Howden made such a good impression in the nonchampionship races that he was promoted to the third car, and he raced for BRM in 1971 and 1972.

Tim Parnell, BRM team manager, told me that he couldn't work out why Howden's practice times were so erratic when he first arrived at BRM.

He would do a few good laps and then lose a lot of time, then do some more good laps. I said, 'Howden, what the bloody hell are you doing? How are you losing time on those laps?' He said he'd been getting out of the way a bit for the faster drivers. I said, 'Bollocks to these faster drivers, Howden. If these drivers are any good, they'll get by you.

Bloody concentrate on your lap times and get cracking. Never mind your mirrors. Jack Brabham never looked in a bloody mirror in his life!'

Howden remembered his first visit to the BRM workshops in Bourne, in Lincolnshire, back in 1962, when he drove up with Timaru racer David Young, who was considering purchasing a P48 rear-engined BRM.

> It was a two-day camel ride in those days with no motorways. We went up in David's Jaguar for an appointment with Wilkie Wilkinson, who had been in charge of the Ecurie Ecosse Le Mans Jaguar team, and since David had raced his C-Type Jaguar in New Zealand, he was looking forward to the meeting. Like going to see God. We went into the Formula One workshops, and I was clicking away with my camera when suddenly a furious Wilkie was there, demanding to know how many shots I had taken. I said I'd only taken one, but I'd taken half a roll. He wanted to rip the film out of my camera. I never dared show anyone those photographs! Then he remembered that David might buy a car and he calmed down. In fact, David didn't buy a BRM, but Arnold Glass eventually did.

In 1971 Howden scored a fourth in the US Grand Prix, and he was fifth in that famous flying-blanket finish at Monza — five cars fighting nose to tail and side by side, slipstreaming and jinking all the way — when Peter Gethin, in his BRM, won from Ronnie Peterson by a mere one hundredth of a second. His best finish in 1972 was fourth in the German Grand Prix on the old Nürburgring.

Nigel Roebuck wrote a graphic look-back description of the 1971 Italian Grand Prix finish in *F1 Racing*. Chris Amon had the win in the palm of his driving glove — until he accidentally ripped all his visors away so that he was driving almost blind. He went on to finish a disappointed and distant sixth behind Howden's BRM. Howden wrote to Roebuck with his version of what it had been like in the middle of that battling bunch at Monza:

Bruce McLaren surveying the Lycoming Special he drove at Wigram in 1960 when his Cooper's engine failed.

Bruce McLaren in his Cooper at the Clelands Hillclimb near Timaru in 1958.

Patty McLaren, Bruce McLaren and Denny Hulme on the rostrum after the 1964 New Zealand Grand Prix, won by McLaren. Hulme was second.

Bruce McLaren relaxing beside his car at Edmonton on the 1969 CanAm series.

Bruce McLaren and Eoin Young snug in the cockpit of the McLaren CanAm car before some fast 'demo' laps at Goodwood.

London to Brighton veteran run in 1965. Bruce McLaren drives the 1904 Sunbeam, with Chris Amon beside him and Eoin Young in the back seat. NIGEL SNOWDON

Denny Hulme at Goodwood with the McLaren CanAm car.

Howden Ganley, in a McLaren M10B, leads the F5000 at Brands Hatch, 1970.

The short-lived Japanese Maki works Grand Prix team, Howden Ganley on right.

A young Howden Ganley in his Lotus Eleven.

Ron Roycroft in his P3 Alfa Romeo at Mairehau. EUAN SARGINSON

Ross Jensen (at the microphone) and Jack Brabham share the rostrum at the 1958 New Zealand Grand Prix. Brabham won, with Jensen second. BARRY MCKAY

Ross Jensen in the Maserati 250F Piccolo at Ardmore, 1959.

Ross Jensen (Maserati 250F) leads Ron Roycroft's Ferrari at the start of the 1958 Grand Prix at Ardmore.

I was surprised to learn that the lead had only changed 25 times, but of course that was based on who actually led across the line. In fact, whoever led over the line almost certainly did not lead by Curva Grande, and whoever led into Curva Grande probably did not lead by Lesmo 1. Again, whoever led out of Lesmo 2 was unlikely to be in front by Vialone, and then there would be one or more lead changes down the straight to Parabolica. Obviously all the intermediate positions changed as well. I would estimate that the lead actually changed between five and six times a *lap*.

Compare this with 30 years later, when we count ourselves fortunate to watch a Grand Prix with five changes of lead in a whole race. Of course, that Monza race was before the chicanes were put in to break up such slipstreaming battles; indeed, the chicanes were probably brought in *because* of the 1971 race.

Howden continues from the BRM cockpit:

It was impossible to make a break, as in those times one could pick up quite a good tow from 50 yards or more. Remembering that Clay had managed to make a break and win the previous year in the Ferrari, I worked hard on this, as my car was working extremely well at Lesmo 2. Several times I came out with what seemed like a good lead, and played all the usual tricks of flicking from one side of the road to the other in an attempt to break the tow, using as much of the old circuit as possible — and the grass! — at Vialone to keep the revs up, but by partway down the back straight someone else would be in the lead.

With about 10 or 12 laps to go we had all figured that it was down to the last corner. Some of us were struggling with mechanical problems, and we all went into cruise mode, which allowed Peter Gethin to catch up. I guess that because we were all convinced it was between the four of us — me, Peterson, Hailwood and Cevert — we were actually lapping quite slowly, after Chris had dropped back in the Matra. It was a case of driving around scheming: 'How am I going to trick these other guys on the last lap?'

I suppose I was the only one who got tricked. I started a terrific run out of Parabolica, on the power early while the others were all bouncing off each other, but I just got blown away on acceleration. I still find it hard to believe that my engine had deteriorated that much in the last few laps. Except for Mike Hailwood, we had all recently graduated from 1000 cc Formula Three, where you definitely had to learn to slipstream. I remember Mike saying he didn't understand it, but he certainly took to it pretty effectively.

Peter Gethin won the race for BRM at an all-time record average speed of 150.755 mph from Peterson's March, Cevert's Tyrrell, Hailwood's Surtees and Howden's BRM. Howden was just 0.61 of a second behind the winner.

At the 1971 Canadian Grand Prix, Jabby Crombac asked Howden if he would like to drive for Matra at Le Mans in 1972, and he teamed with Francois Cevert. They had a chance of winning, but had to settle for second place. Chris Amon was leading the Matra Grand Prix team, and Howden was able to test the Formula One car on occasion, but at the end of the season Matra announced it was withdrawing from Formula One and only running French drivers in endurance races.

Marlboro were interested in running a second Grand Prix team in addition to BRM, and I suggested they underwrite Matra and put Chris and me in as drivers. That idea got so far down the line and then died on the vine. The Marlboro money went to Williams and I went with it.

John Horsman asked me if I would do some tyre testing with the Gulf-Mirage endurance sports car at Goodwood, and I was invited to drive for them the following season. I also drove the BRM CanAm car in a few InterSerie races in Europe and in the Riverside CanAm race, where I finished third behind the two works McLarens. And I met a nice little American lady, who I subsequently married.

Howden and Judy now live in Marlow, in Buckinghamshire.

Late in 1972, Ganley started thinking about designing and building his own car for Formula One.

When you drive for teams and you are only one of a number of drivers and you can't get your way technically with the car, you get kind of frustrated. I had been building cars and working on them, and Bruce had taught me so much, as had Gary Knutson, and you just want to get the best piece of equipment you can.

I remember back in 1970 Bruce told me that one day I'd want to build my own car, and I told him that I had absolutely no ambition to do that. But I guess he was right because he'd suffered the same frustrations, knowing he could build a better car than the one he was racing at the time.

In late 1972 I was thinking about building a Formula Two car, but early in 1973 I decided it would be better to go all the way and build a car for Formula One. I hired Martin Read to help me with the design, and I had a little workshop where I'd based the Formula 5000 McLaren, so I went to auctions and bought a heliarc, rollers, a folder and all the metal-working kit that we would need. We set to and built the car, but of course I needed money to finish it off and run it. I eventually scratched up some money, bought a transporter, bought a couple of Cosworth engines and a gearbox — but I still needed running money.

I was racing for Frank Williams in his Marlboro-sponsored Formula One Iso cars. I had started with Yardley sponsorship with BRM and switched to Marlboro backing in 1972, and they helped my move to Williams for 1973. Marlboro offered to pick up my whole Formula One project and give it to Frank as the 1974 Williams. I really thought my car was further up the road than the Iso I was racing for him. My car had pull-rod rising-rate front suspension, minor ground effect and all that stuff at the end of 1973. It wasn't going to be all that far away, I didn't think. This was before Patrick Head had arrived at Williams, and Marlboro giving my car to Frank was going to be a master plan, but Frank wasn't enthusiastic. He thought I was trying to take over his team, but all I was doing was handing over the car and Marlboro were going to pay for it. I think Frank simply misunderstood the situation.

Howden later sold the engines and the gearbox, and the one and only

Ganley Grand Prix car has sat in a corner of his workshop ever since. No photographs of the car were ever taken because it was never put together as a runner, but Howden recently bought a mock-up Cosworth DFV V8 to put the car together as a full-size piece of personalised motor-racing memorabilia.

A season with Williams looks good on any driver's CV, but Howden's season in 1973 was ahead of the Williams glory days. He signed with March for 1974 but, as always with March, there were sponsorship problems.

> In fact, the March was developing into a good car, but Brambilla was there with his Beta Tools money, and Robin and Max were asking if I could find some of my own sponsorship. Times weren't good, but I had found myself in an odd situation. The phone calls started one evening when we were in Argentina for the first race of the season. There was this bloke with a Japanese singsong voice saying, 'Aah . . . Mr Ganrey, you rike to drive for us?' I figured it had to be Tim Schenken or Peter Gethin, so I played along, trying to suss out who it was. It could have been anyone. I said, 'Thanks very much, I'm driving for March, but call me again.' Then we went to Interlagos two weeks later. I hadn't told the guy where we were staying but I got this phone call: same guy, same voice. I thought, 'This is getting to be a rather prolonged joke here.'

Ganley laughs at the memory of the voice.

> I played along again but I still couldn't get a clue who it was. Then we went up to Brasilia for the nonchampionship race and I had *another* call. I said I was going back to England, why not call me there?
>
> Back in England there was another call, and I was starting to think there might be something to it. The guy said they had four cars and seven engines and two transporters — and they were going to offer me a lot of money to drive. I asked who would be my number two driver and he said, 'Aah . . . Mr Ganrey, no number two — all for you.' Bloody hell! It was a dream come true. In hindsight it was one of those things that if it sounds too good to be true, it usually is.

Faced with the uncertain financial situation at March and hearing a rumour that Honda was behind this new Japanese team, which called itself Maki, Howden decided to gamble.

> I did the deal with the Japanese and eventually this big shipping container turned up. They didn't have a workshop, but luckily I had one to rent them. Sure enough, they had four cars and spares for them and they went out and bought a transporter.
>
> There were two head guys. One said his name was Mr Yamamoto and the other said he was Mr Togo, and being a bit slack on my history I hadn't twigged that they were the two great architects of the raid on Pearl Harbor. For whatever reason, they were using assumed names while they set up the deal. Mr Yamamoto was Masao Ono: he would later design the Japanese Kojima and Dome cars. Mr Togo turned out to be Kenji Mimura, who also contributed to the design of the Maki.
>
> The unfortunate thing was that the seven engines had depleted to one engine, which wasn't looking so good, and then they were planning to service the engine themselves. They didn't think it necessary to have Cosworth involved. We did a lot of testing but the car was way off the pace and they simply would not modify it. We eventually got to midseason and we still hadn't been to a race, so we had a big shout-up. That seemed to make a difference. They worked nonstop for days and completely rebuilt the car with new bodywork and new radiators, in fact everything I'd been asking for.

Two days before the British Grand Prix at Brands Hatch in 1974, the car was loaded and ready for practice. Howden drove down for the first session, but there was no transporter and no car.

> I phoned back to talk to my mate at base and he said they were just sitting round drinking tea. He couldn't get anyone to come to the phone. Then he said they were leaving. Next practice session and still no car. By this time I'm getting really grumpy and I'm on the phone again. They arrived just after practice had finished, and I wasn't very happy about that, but at least we were ready for the second day.

When I eventually got out on the track it didn't seem all that bad considering I hadn't tested any of the mods. I did a time that wasn't quick enough to qualify. They had the wrong ratios in it and they didn't have any more, so I had to make do. If you compared the previous day's times, I would have been in the middle of the grid, but everyone improves over the day and we would have improved as well. It made me think that the thing wasn't that far adrift.

A fortnight later they were at the Nürburgring. Howden warmed up on the short pits loop, then stormed out on to the 14.2-mile circuit proper.

I set off on a flying lap, got about a mile out into the country, and was going down the straight pretty fast when all of a sudden the thing just turned sharp right, straight into the barrier — *BANG!* — ripping the front end off so my feet were sticking out in front. Then it had another go at the barrier, smashing my feet and legs, and finished up in the middle of the track with fuel spraying everywhere. One of the bottom suspension links had come off. It had had a fail-safe washer to stop it coming off, but unfortunately the washer was just slightly smaller than the diameter of the banjo, so it was completely useless.

Howden was rushed to hospital with serious fractures to his feet, ankles and lower legs.

I was wrapped in plaster, and the German doctor said I would be there for three months, which didn't sound good. Mike Hailwood arrived a couple of days later. He had crashed his Yardley-McLaren in the Grand Prix and he had leg injuries similar to mine.

On Monday morning Louis Stanley came to the hospital and asked if we'd like to go back to England. Of course we would. I must say he was tremendous. He said he'd get us on a helicopter up to Cologne and on a plane to London. The Germans said they couldn't land a helicopter in the little front garden of the hospital, so Big Lou said he'd get the RAF to do it — and then the Luftwaffe decided that they could do it after all.

British Airways at Cologne said they only took one stretcher per flight, but Big Lou told them that on this occasion they would be taking two. Sure enough, this big German military helicopter came clattering in and collected us. The pilot gave us a lap of the 'Ring because we were in plenty of time. Big Lou met us at Heathrow and rode with us in the ambulance to St Thomas's Hospital, and installed Mike and me in there. I was out in two-and-half weeks instead of the threatened three months, but poor old Mike was still in there. While I was in hospital I received a writ from the Maki team because I had failed to honour my contract and drive in the Austrian Grand Prix two weeks after the German.

He laughs now, but he was in no mood to laugh at the time.

My solicitor dealt with that pretty swiftly. That was the end of that. I got my money from the contract.
  I was determined to walk out of the hospital but that was about all I did. It was a long recuperation. I didn't race again until the 1000-kilometre race at the Nürburgring in May 1975, when Tim and I finished second in the Gulf-Mirage. Then there was a second and a third at the Nürburgring and Hockenheim with the Gulf-Mirage in the InterSerie races. In June 1976 I drove the Gulf-Mirage to fifth place in the Mid-Ohio CanAm race and won the 3-litre category — and then I hung up my helmet.

Howden and Tim Schenken shared a house as motor-racing bachelors until both were married. Late in 1975, Schenken came to see his old mate with a proposal from someone who wanted him to fund a Formula Ford project and start a small company.

He left it with me and I read through it, checked all the numbers to see how they stacked up, and called him back. I said, 'Hey, forget that other guy — you and I should do this if it's as good as it looks!' It had to be right. We decided that we needed to be in business for 1976. We didn't have time to do all the body moulds, but it so happened that my accountant owned Motor Racing Enterprises (MRE) and he wanted to get out of it, so we did a deal whereby we bought the company for no money down with some orders for a neat little Formula Ford, mainly to get the body moulds. Martin Read came back to help me — he had worked with me on my Ganley Formula One car — and he drew a complete new chassis that slotted inside the existing body because the time-consuming thing was getting the new body moulds made. We converted the MRE orders into Tiga orders.

'Tiga' was a combination of TIm and GAnley.

The first car was delivered to the Winfield Racing School. David Lang drove it in its first race, at Mallory Park, where he qualified on pole for the heat, won the heat, had pole for the final and won the final.

I thought, 'Boy this is easy' — but it got slightly harder from there. In 1976 we sold about 21 cars, all out of my little workshop in Windsor, and then we took over the old Amon/Fittipaldi workshop to build Sports 2000 cars.

John Webb wanted to start Sports 2000. I said I wasn't interested, but Tim was keen to do it. Eventually Tim said, 'If I can get three deposits, will you agree to design and build the car?' Then he came along with a guy who had designed a car; he had body moulds and all he wanted was to use our uprights and axles. He'd designed this fantastic chassis, but of course when he arrived with the drawings, it wasn't like that at all. It was a bit of a disaster but we cobbled the thing together, which I was somewhat embarrassed about. The following year I designed a completely new car, and at Silverstone, first time out, our two cars just ran away from the field. We sold 250 of them! We also built Group C cars, a couple of CanAm cars and quite a lot of Atlantic cars, and won lots of races and championships with our Tigas.

Mike Coughlan, now technical director at the Arrows Formula One team, started his design career with Tiga in 1982 on the sports-car project. 'Howden taught me a lot,' he recalls. 'Such as there's a right way to fabricate, a right way to design, and that you can make things look elegant. I owe him a great debt.'

Howden recalls:

When we started the company, I said to Tim that whatever happened, no matter how successful we were or weren't, I wasn't going to do this for one day more than 10 years. That was going to be *it*. When we got to 10 years we were on such a roll that we agreed to give it a bit longer, but at the end of 1987 I said I was quitting. I said I needed to get to know my wife now.

Ganley rented his factory to Vern Schuppan, who was building a Porsche-engined carbon-chassis road car. 'It was basically a carbon-chassis Porsche 962. Vern asked if I'd help, and I did a day a week, then it was two days a week, and pretty soon I was right up to my neck in it. And then the market collapsed and the Japanese didn't want any more supercars.'

Retirement seems elusive where Howden Ganley is concerned. He became a director of the BRDC and subsequently a director of Silverstone Circuits. 'I've spent a lot of time at Silverstone over the last seven years chasing various projects along where I could help, and I'm still doing it. I'm also trying to improve my golf handicap.'

Looking back over his long racing career since those first days in New Zealand with his mother's Morris Minor in Hamilton club events when he was a teenager, Howden sees the 1973 Canadian Grand Prix as one of his great what-ifs. He was driving the Iso-Marlboro Formula One car for the fledgling Williams team and had qualified twenty-second.

It was raining when the race started and we set off on wet tyres, but I decided to take a long shot and gamble on it drying out, so I left the car on dry settings. It was really seriously wet for the first part of the race, but then it stopped raining. I stayed out a bit longer than most people and so I took the lead. Tim Schenken was driving the other Williams, and as nobody had practised pit stops I waited until Schenken had made his before I made mine, because I wanted that little narrow pit road to be fairly empty of cars. I just wished they'd hurry up because I wanted to stop right then.

When I came in, the guys made a terrific stop because they didn't have to adjust the wings or anti-roll bars. When I went out again there was a shunt between Cevert and Scheckter, and they brought the pace car out. I steamed up to the pace car and went to overtake it but they waved me back. I thought I'd lost the lead during my stop but we subsequently looked at the lap chart and discovered that this probably wasn't the case.

After the pace car had pulled aside, we took off again and I thought I'd really have to go for it if I was to stay in the lead. At the end of the race, in theory, I'd been leading. The organisers' lap chart blew up, but my wife-to-be, Judy, was very good at lap-charting. [In fact, Judy Kondratief had been a racing driver who, among other achievements, had won her class at Sebring in 1970, sharing an Austin Healey Sprite with Janet Guthrie.] We went back over her chart and there was just one little blip in it. At worst I was third and at best I'd *won*, but they gave me sixth, probably because we hadn't been going all that well during the season.

I think really whoever got up and shouted loudest was the winner, and I was penalised very heavily. It was one of those things, very unfortunate, and I suppose Frank was not the strong entrant that he is today. Today he'd be up there battling, but back then I think he was a bit subdued. If they had given me the win, I would have been the first driver to win a Grand Prix for Williams, six years before Clay Regazzoni broke Frank's Grand Prix duck at Silverstone.

Like a number of other New Zealanders who made their name in various forms of international motor sport, Howden cites Bruce McLaren as a very significant influence in his career.

He bridged the gap for me between Formula Three and Formula One. No question about that. I wouldn't have gotten there without his help. He was a terrific leader. If Bruce had come into the workshop one morning and said, 'Well, chaps, we're not going to work on the cars today, we're going to march across the Sahara,' the boys would have said, 'Well, OK Bruce, if that's what you reckon.' He was such a leader, and everybody would go with him. If you had to do a couple of all-nighters in a row, everybody would pull together. He was so charismatic. He would help you in all sorts of ways. Even when I was a new mechanic — I think I was McLaren employee number three — he knew I wanted to be a driver and he would let me have laps while we were testing. He was the dominant influence in my career.

CHAPTER 5

RON ROYCROFT

Ron Roycroft was associated with some famous cars on New Zealand tracks in the 1950s. He raced the P3 Alfa Romeo that Tazio Nuvolari had driven to victory in the 1935 German Grand Prix at Nürburgring (this is our cover car) and later the 4.5-litre V12 Ferrari in which Frolian Gonzales had won Ferrari's first Grand Prix at Silverstone.

Ron Roycroft was a legend in New Zealand motor racing, with a works supercharged Austin 7, a Bugatti, a P3 Alfa Romeo — 'The Glen Murray Express' — and a 4.5-litre V12 Grand Prix Ferrari. He was a small man, prematurely old with thinning hair at the age of 40, when he led the 1957 New Zealand Grand Prix, with a determination to succeed and a quiet enthusiasm for old motoring in his retirement.

The supercharged Austin was one of four works cars built in 1931. The Bugatti was a 2-litre 1925 Type 35A, which Ron bought in 1951 and later fitted with a new 3.4-litre 6-cylinder XK120 Jaguar engine in place of the elderly French straight-8. In 1956 Ron imported a C-Type Jaguar cylinder head and D-Type pistons and carburettors. 'I remember it cost me £650 for the engine and gearbox new, £250 to have the motor installed and another £350 to buy the other racing parts later. And £1,000 was worth a lot more then than it is today.'

Ron owned the Bugatti himself but he raced the P3 Alfa Romeo for his father, A.J. (Albert James) Roycroft, always known as Roy. His father also bought the Ferrari, but Ron bought it off him after the first season.

The Alfa Romeo and the Ferrari were elderly Grand Prix cars of great pedigree, although this was not realised at the time. In the 1950s, when speedway champion Les Moore bought the P3 and a 2.3-litre supercharged four-seater sports car in England, they were regarded as well past their win-by dates and a sale to the colonies was a blessed relief. Historians would later discover that the *monoposto* Alfa Romeo was the actual car driven by Tazio Nuvolari when he humbled the mighty Mercedes-Benz and Auto Union teams in the German Grand Prix on the Nürburgring in 1935. The four-seater sports Alfa, meanwhile, was the car that Tim Birkin and Earl Howe had driven to win the Le Mans 24-hour race in 1931.

The big Tipo 375 Grand Prix Ferrari had an equally fine pedigree, having won the very first world-championship Grand Prix for the Ferrari team when the burly Argentinian Froilan Gonzales — nicknamed 'The Pampas Bull' — took the laurels in 1951 at Silverstone. It was a bitter irony that this Ferrari, with which Roycroft captivated the nation and focused the attention of overseas drivers by putting it in pole position for the 1957 Grand Prix at Ardmore, was a car that he battled with summer after summer and soon came to hate. It drove him to distraction.

The fact that the old Ferrari was eventually restored and sold back into Europe for a small fortune 20 years ago only serves to add poignancy to Roycroft's memories of the car he came to remember as a beast. His father had bought it from French champion Louis Rosier, who had bought it from the Ferrari factory in Grand Prix single-seater form, raced it until it had become uncompetitive, and then converted it to centre-seat sports-car form with a little seat stuck up on the side — which it was impossible to sit in, according to Ron, although it satisfied the regulations. The car arrived in New Zealand fitted with this shapely body.

I was down in the South Island racing the Bugatti-Jag when the Ferrari arrived too late for the 1956 New Zealand Grand Prix. My father collected the car from the wharf in Auckland, filled it with fuel and drove it round. It ran reasonably well, so he suggested that instead of racing the Bugatti in the Mairehau road race at Christchurch, I give the Ferrari a run. I flew back and drove the Ferrari straight down to Christchurch. It went pretty well, but I was disappointed that it didn't seem to go as well as I had been expecting. I never put a spanner on it, thinking that it had been sold to us in perfect order, but when it was being delivered from Rosier's home in mid-France to the docks in Marseilles, someone must have overrevved it and bent valves and done other internal damage that we didn't know about.

I didn't do very well in the race at Mairehau, breaking an axle. If we'd known what condition the car was in, we'd never have taken it out of Auckland. We sent it home and came back by train. When we did a motor check, we found it was running on about nine cylinders properly and the other three were limping. It was then that my father went to work and had a copy of the original single-seater body built on it. That was another mistake. We should have raced it exactly as it was.

They also discovered a major problem with the brakes. 'We couldn't figure why the linings specified by Ferrari were too small in the drums. The drums *looked* right, but you wouldn't believe how much they had ground those drums out. In practice, when it was too late to do anything, we found that the internal steel parts were buckling in the heat. When we started in the Grand Prix I didn't have much hope at all for the brakes.'

The Ferrari was recreated in single-seater form in time for the 1957 Grand Prix, and it was clear that the international opposition would come from Ken Wharton in his 250F Maserati and the Ferrari Super Squalos of Peter Whitehead and Reg Parnell. Perhaps national pride and misty memories tend to distort history, but Graham Vercoe writes in *The Golden Era of New Zealand Motor Racing*:

'It was to be the most exciting qualifying period for any race to date in this country for not only was Roycroft the fastest Kiwi, he was fastest overall! From the word go, Roycroft was consistently faster than Wharton, Whitehead and Parnell, while Clark was faster than the rest! By the end of practice, Roycroft had recorded 1min 29.2sec — 0.3sec faster than the experienced Wharton's best.'

In fact, Wharton had turned in a pole lap of 1 minute 28.5 seconds. This is not to nit-pick, rather to put Ron's amazing feat that weekend into more accurate perspective. To confuse the situation even more, the Roycroft Ferrari *did* start from pole position, but this was because Wharton had been killed in his Monza Ferrari in the sports-car race a few hours before and the grid had closed up.

Ron was short on charity when he talked to Penn McKay of *New Zealand Classic Car* in 1997:

Wharton was at the end of his prime. He was prone to make mistakes. He had a certain reputation in sports cars and he was determined to hold it up and the result was that he killed himself. He was leading and he never should have been doing what he was doing, but the New Zealander he was trying to pass should never have been where he was — only a Ford 10, which he would have got on the next lap anyhow.

The night before the race Ron had worked late, changing gear ratios for the first time. 'In the light of later knowledge I would never have changed the ratio because it was obviously good enough. It wasn't quite peaking at the end of the straight. My father didn't want me to change the ratios and he was trying to get me to go to bed. It was one thirty on race morning before we finished.'

Wharton's death was announced as the drivers took their places on the grid. Ron led the opening 10 laps of his home Grand Prix to the roaring delight of the crowd, but it didn't last.

> I started to drop back as the brakes went, but I knew I could keep going with them as they were. I still had the legs on the other cars but I didn't realise that it was also *me* that was going off. The air scoop in front of the windscreen that was fitted to the works Ferraris hadn't been copied on to my new body, and the heat from the engine dried me out. I wasn't properly fit either.

Ron was also 40 years old when he started that race on the old airfield circuit outside Auckland, a slight figure of a man with hearing problems after months of work on Bristol engines in aviation test sheds during the war — the same as Jack Brabham had done in Australia. Brabham would also lose his hearing, but he would blame this on his days of speedway racing on the cinder tracks without earplugs.

> When I made my first pit stop it was only for myself, not for the car. They poured a bottle of lemonade all over me and I went out again but I knew that I wouldn't make it. When I came in the next time, I was finished. Totally exhausted. I was quite ill for days after that and we gave Levin a miss. I never did like Levin much, and the Ferrari wasn't a good car to drive there anyway.
> At Wigram the same thing happened, only this time I had fumes as well as heat coming back. I made a pit stop to recover and drove the rest of the race poking my head outside the cockpit. I couldn't drive very well like that, but I did finish. Then we cut a great hole in the front of the body and we never had any more bothers like that. We should have done it in the first place.

For reasons that are now unclear, Ron bought the Ferrari from his father despite having an offer from Ron Frost and Arnold Stafford, who were teamed as Ecurie Pomme (a play on the French word for 'apple' and the term 'Pommie', since both Frost and Stafford were English) in Cooper 500s, together with motorcycle-racer Syd Jensen. They suggested that Ron buy a Mark 9 Cooper-Norton and join them.

> That's what I should have done. From there on the Coopers went from strength to strength, and I was stuck with the Ferrari. It was an expensive car to run. Rear tyres were £70 a pair then and you'd wear them out at every race, whereas the Coopers could race all season on the same rubber. I was tied in with BP and that helped with bonus money, but of course in those days I drove because I enjoyed driving. The thought of really making money out if it never entered my head.
>
> The last year I raced the Ferrari was 1960. I remember I had magneto trouble and it banged and cracked and by that time I was losing faith in it. I knew I couldn't do any good with it and was losing interest in motor racing as well. When you've raced from 1934 right through . . . I'd never had a decent holiday over the summer period and I was always working on the cars. The first couple of seasons after knocking off motor racing were wonderful.

The big blue Ferrari sat in Ron's garage at Glen Murray until there was a telephone call early one morning from Ernie Nunn in Australia. He wanted the 4.5-litre Ferrari engine for his powerboat and didn't seem bothered whether he bought just the engine or the car complete.

> The upshot was that I sold him the engine and spares and retained the car. He didn't even want the clutch. He used to start it with a piece of rope round the flywheel. I knew the motor was in poor shape because it kept hammering out the main bearings and I told him that I'd rather he inspected it, so he came over, checked it out and bought it. I sold the chassis to Ferris de Joux and he built up a GT from it with a Jaguar engine.

Gavin Bain eventually rescued the chassis and the engine and had the famous old Ferrari restored to perfection in the guise in which Gonzales drove it to win at Silverstone in 1951.

Ron Roycroft was born in 1915 into a motor-sporting family environment. His father was an early dealer in the Auckland motor trade and raced a Triumph TT motorcycle in the 1920s before switching to Bugattis for the local races on the beaches. In 1928 A.J. Roycroft floated the original company to run speedway races at Western Springs, importing riders from Australia and England.

Ron started competing on motorcycles with an Imperial purchased for '10 bob' before moving on to Rudges. His first car, in 1936, was a Wolseley Hornet, then in 1937 he bought a genuine 1928 Brooklands Riley.

> There used to be big crowds for the races on Muriwai Beach before the war, when there were events for touring cars, taxi drivers and full racing cars. I remember one meeting when I was a child when we had to wait until after dark before we could drive our car away from the beach because of the traffic jam. And it was a rough clay road for much of the way back to Auckland in those days. Most Muriwai meetings were held just north of the creek, but the first track ran 12.5 miles up the beach to make a 25-mile lap, and feature races were only four laps. They gradually reduced the circuit until the distance was a mile, but cars like the old Stutz and Sunbeam weren't made for short runs. It took a mile or so to reach their maximum.
>
> Gloucester Park was the first motor race I ever went into. It was a half-mile dirt track, pure and simple. Hennings was a mile-and-a-quarter dirt. In 1932 there was a Humber Snipe drophead that I took out, and I learned my first major lesson in that race. It was to make sure I always had plenty of fuel on board, because the big Snipe suffered from fuel starvation on the turns. I took along a cobber. We had no crash hats. We just jumped in the car, lined up and off we went. I threw that race away, because we had the fastest car.

When the speedway introduced midget cars, Ron was an immediate convert and won the championship one season, racing against seasoned campaigners such as Frank 'Satan' Brewer, who would go on to win in Australia and the USA.

During the war the Northern Sports Car Club was formed and Ron was the tenth member to join.

> Depending on the amount of gas coupons we had, we would go out and do hill climbs, choosing the hill on the day. We also raced along the beach at Orewa. It was a wilderness after the war, and lonely — there was hardly a soul on the beach. I remember marking out a measured quarter mile, one mark on the end of a shed, the other on a post, and we used to have time trials.
>
> At one stage my father had the ex-works off-set single-seater supercharged Austin 7 that had been imported by Austin agents Seabrook Fowlds in 1935 — one of four built by the factory for racing. I bought it in the late 1940s when events were starting at Wigram. The car was shared with Harry Chatteris and entered as CR Racing Team. It was always known as 'The Rubber Duck' from its racing days at Brooklands, and the name followed it to the colonies. It had the same wheelbase and track as an ordinary Austin 7 of the '20s. The engine, wheels and axles all looked very similar but they were very much stronger. The side-valve engine was only 750 cc, with a monstrous heavy crank and rods in it. There was a whole forest of cylinder-head studs, and the supercharger on the front was as big as the actual cylinder block on the engine. It was a Roots-type blower and it made it a very potent little car. It produced 60 bhp at 6000 rpm and was good for over 100 mph. It ran about 10–12 pounds of boost on alcohol, and I remember a major blow-up in the second Wigram in 1950. It would take on all sorts of odd angles when you drove it on a fast track like Wigram. It would sort of bend and twist, but you could hold it and do some wonderful things with it. The wheels used to buckle on it and they'd be at all angles. You see photographs of it racing then and it looks as though it was falling apart.

Ron nearly missed the first 100-mile New Zealand Championship Road Race at Wigram in 1949. The Austin had been sent by rail from Auckland and been delayed, not arriving at Wigram until the morning of the race. Without practice, Ron had to start from dead last on the grid of 22 cars, but he put his midget-racing experience to blinding effect. On just the first lap he was sixth down the long back straight, fourth into the esse bend and second, to Hec Green in his RA1 Wolseley Special, by the end. The 30,000 crowd was delighted. Ron and Green skirmished in the early part of the race, a local reporter noting: 'Particularly spectacular was the cornering of Green and Roycroft at the sweeping bend coming into the back straight. Several times Roycroft left the track momentarily and ran along the grass.'

Ron was running strongly, but his rear tyres were shot by three-quarter distance and during the pit stop to change them he oiled-up a spark plug, which necessitated a slow lap. A complete change of plugs and he was back in to win the handicap section. If he had fitted better tyres, he could probably have won overall.

There were a couple of seasons in XK120 Jaguars, including one of the rare aluminium-bodied prototype cars, and Ron also raced one of his speedway midgets in hill climbs. Ron had bought the Type 35 Bugatti, but his father had bought the P3 Alfa Romeo from Les Moore.

> I drove the P3 for my father in all the major races and used the Bugatti for hill climbs and sprints. The P3 was the most wonderful motorcar. It was a car that, if you were trying, it would try too. One of those *real* racing cars. I loved the P3 to drive. This was a 1935 model that I was racing in the 1950s, but it was *wonderful*. My first race with the P3 was at Mairehau in 1953, and I won the handicap and set fastest time. It was amazingly reliable. It was a pure Grand Prix car running on 90 per cent methanol and yet my father used to take it shopping. One pull on the handle and it started every time.

Ron remembers taking the Bugatti (now Jaguar-engined) to Dunedin to run it in the road-racing championship and having problems with cooling the modern engine. He tried various solutions and ended up with a Jaguar radiator lashed to the front. This was hardly an elegant solution, but it seemed to work.

The newspaper sports writers in Dunedin thought I might get about fifth. The car went well in practice on race morning and I was about to pack up and wait for the race when I found that a big aluminium casting that held the left front spring had broken and fallen right off, so a friend whipped it round to a workshop while another race was on. We heated a big iron bar and wrapped it round the aluminium casting and locked it together. In the race the Bugatti-Jag ran faultlessly and I led most of the way. John Horton in the HWM [Hersham and Walton Motors] overtook me at one point but he didn't last. I won that race, which pleased me very much. It was only afterwards that I realised how lucky I had been.

Driving back to the garage I could hear this *tick . . . tick . . . tick* noise coming from the back, and I found a large bridge spike sticking in the tyre — which had obviously been there for much of the race. I certainly had luck with me that day, and I've still got the spike as a souvenir.

The tyres on the Bugatti were amazing, because I was running on ordinary Firestone tyres that were never designed to go over 80 mph, yet at Ryal Bush I was timed at 155 mph! That felt pretty damned dangerous, I can tell you. In the race I was undergeared and I didn't have any spare ratios. I was pulling 7700 rpm in top gear but restricting it to 6000 rpm in the gears and feathering it in top. The hot air currents coming between the cuttings and hills at Ryal Bush, the fastest road course in New Zealand, really caused dramas in the Bugatti. The car would almost go off the road and I had to work to bring it back. In one dip the Bug was all over the place. Tom Clark was having the same problems with his cart-sprung Maserati 8CM. I had to have two wheels on the left-hand side in the gravel, and by the time I was down the dip and through the crossing my right wheels were on the other side of the road in the gravel.

The Grand Prix Ferrari was a huge disappointment to Ron — a car that should have brought him the success he so richly deserved in the autumn days of his racing career.

The Ferrari was a real old goat, you know. I couldn't handle it. I couldn't do *anything* with it. It was a pest of a car, that's the only way to say it. At speeds over 130 mph in the cockpit, your goggles wanted to float off and you were ripped about in the wind. And yet I'd been timed at the same speed in the old Bug and didn't get any wind thrashing, despite sitting up so high.

Ron said he had been invited to race the Ferrari in Australia.

I told them I'd never go anywhere with the car unless it was ready to race, and of course it was *never* completely ready to race. There was always troubleshooting with it. In all the years I had that car I never tuned it, simply because I never got round to it. It didn't run well enough long enough to tune it! The year that I was third in the Grand Prix at Ardmore I only had third and top gears for the whole race because in the selectors there was a little whisker of aluminium which jammed the bore and I couldn't select second at all. The selector wouldn't move. That was the sort of endless trouble I had to cope with. It was definitely *not* a car that I enjoyed.

When he stopped racing, Ron devoted his time to his family and to building up an impressive collection of old cars. He sought early Cadillacs hidden away in sheds and garages around New Zealand, and he also set about tracking down Bugatti parts.

'I realised that I was probably the only bloke in New Zealand who knew a Bug part when he saw it, so I got to work and spent a year-and-a-half systematically getting every Bugatti part I could lay my hands on. I wound up with the nucleus of five cars. I kept two but I swapped the other three away for other cars.'

One of the favourite Roycroft Bugatti stories concerned the Type 13 Brescia that Ron's father used as a road car from 1928 to 1932.

I discovered that the car had finally been cut up, just after the war. It was sliced up and made into two trailers. The engine and magnetos were driven off a shaft at the back, set on a platform, and the mags were set in the dashboard itself. They were saved, and the chap that had the engine was going to put it into a boat but it had a cracked block and he never got around to it. I was lucky and got the motor off him, but I was never able to trace the trailers. For years I went round looking at every trailer I saw. In fact, I knew the chap who had cut the Bug chassis in half and he told me what had happened to it. I did manage to trace the front axle. It was in a handcart at Helensville by the hot springs, and that's where it finished its days. I missed it by a matter of a couple of weeks. It was lying around not being used and it simply disappeared, dumped somewhere. The back axle had simply disappeared too.

Ron Roycroft died on 18 May 2000, after a life spanning several eras of New Zealand motor racing.

CHAPTER 6

ROSS JENSEN

Ross Jensen carried the torch for New Zealand in international racing between the end of the Roycroft era and the emergence of Bruce McLaren's star. This article was originally published over several issues of New Zealand Classic Car *in 2001. It stands as one of the first substantial records of the achievements of this Kiwi racing hero.*

Ross Jensen still has style. You know if he's in a room or at a racetrack: there's the booming voice, and the blazer with the British Racing Driver's Club lapel badge. But the style only hints at the substance: honour earned by dominating New Zealand racing in the late '50s; racing factory Lister-Jaguar sports-racers in Britain in 1958; turning down the offer of a BRM Grand Prix drive in 1959; winning back-to-back New Zealand Gold Stars when they were first awarded (1956/57 and 1957/58); clinching the saloon racing Gold Star title in 1960/61.

Ross did the hard yards, starting with an Austin 7 Special, building and racing Ford V8 coupés, graduating to an XK120 Jaguar, a brace of Austin Healeys, a Triumph TR2 and a Monza Ferrari, and then having the audacity to buy the beautiful 250F Maserati Stirling Moss had driven to win the 1956 New Zealand Grand Prix — and to better Stirling's lap time in it at Ardmore the following season.

Ross's achievements speak for themselves. He is the senior statesman of New Zealand motor racing, and although he will talk endlessly, seamlessly, about the sport in his country — its past and its future — it is almost impossible to get him to talk about his own career. I know this will raise eyebrows, because of the Jensen reputation for verbal grandstanding, but I have always found it to be true.

Ross's problem is that he has been around so long he has probably given up telling his stories of racing in the good old days, when he used to beat Bruce McLaren and spar his corner with the overseas drivers of the '50s. They're true, but in this new century there is every chance they would sound like skiting. They wouldn't be. Getting Ross to talk about his own career is like drawing teeth. His.

As a schoolboy, in the immediate prewar years, Ross grew up on his father's dairy farm at Mangere, outside Auckland. Henning's Speedway was just across the road, an unsealed speed-bowl created by George Henning. 'George was one of the very early pioneers of the motor industry in New Zealand, and he was enthused to the extent that he dammed off a salt basin off the Manukau Harbour and turned it into a racetrack.'

Ross drove farm vehicles from the age of 10, as farm kids do, and you can imagine him pretending he was racing at the track across the road. 'The public roads were not heavy with traffic the way they are today, and I confess to an amount of illegal road driving that culminated in my first traffic ticket at the age of 11. This shouldn't be taken as a boast. It was just something you did when you were helping on the farm.'

Now a respectable senior citizen, he doesn't tell me that the 'ticket' was for driving without a licence on the public highway — nor that he got away with it in the end by giving the cop the name of his elder brother, who had just got his licence. I found this out in a *Sports Car World* profile written by Alan Gibbons in 1958. It was entitled 'Ross Jensen — The Fastest Kiwi', and gave a detailed account of Ross's career at the time he was at his peak; but he was probably less than impressed with the 'continued' subhead later in the magazine: 'Ross Jenkins — The Fastest Kiwi'.

Ross's first races were on motorcycles against his brothers — impromptu scrambles with bolts sticking out of the tyres to improve traction. Then there were races at Hennings and at Gloucester Park, in Onehunga. 'A race at Gloucester Park in 1939 was my first ever meeting with the well-known Len Perry — now in his 80s and still riding!'

Ross won a few handicap races on two wheels, but it was all going to be different postwar. He spent two-and-a-half years in the Royal New Zealand Air Force, and in 1956 was discharged as a qualified fitter. He bought an Austin 7 and entered it in club events, but he soon got bored with the lack of performance and in 1948 set to work on a damaged 1937 Ford V8 coupé. This would run at around 90 mph, but Ross reasoned that an even better solution was to buy a 1934 Ford coupé and fit it with a modified Mercury V8.

> I rebuilt this to a useful standard, running it in hill climbs around Auckland, and in 1949 I took it down to a hill climb in Dunedin, where Sybil Lupp was the star turn. One of the Auckland hill climbs was up the roadways of Mount Eden.
>
> At this time, hill climbs were expedient, and racing yourself against the clock was a splendid way to hone your skills and extract

optimum performance. I developed the old Ford to the point where it was dispensing with most of its competitors, including the more exotic touring cars of the day.

Tom Clark's Jaguar was Jensen's most spirited opposition. The two men raced at Seagrove, Ohakea and on the sand of Muriwai Beach, and Jensen emerged at the end of the season with the Provincial Sedan Car Championship. Jensen won six races, Clark won five. They would spar with each other for the rest of their racing careers — and still do, both men exuding bonhomie and putting their stamp on proceedings with their dominating personalities.

After leaving the air force Ross worked in various government services on technical development and as a mechanical engineer. This was useful while he was building his racing Ford V8s, but bureaucracy eventually defeated him and late in 1951 he set up his own motor business in Newmarket, Auckland, specialising in high-performance and high-dollar motorcars, including Rolls-Royce, Bentley and Healey. At this point he was competing in one of the sleek new Jaguar XK120s entered by a Miss Christie. Things were looking up.

Motor racing in New Zealand was emerging from being a wild hobby into something that would become a professional sport. Ross's speed had been noted, and with the first international New Zealand Grand Prix scheduled for January 1954 on the Ardmore airfield circuit, Ross was approached by Austin importers Seabrook Fowlds about heading up a team of three Austin-Healey 100/4s. The Austin agents for Auckland, Wellington and Christchurch had been given one car each for a top local driver plus limited factory support, including larger carburettors, Alfin brake drums and metal tonneau covers.

Ross had been on the committee formed in 1953 to establish the New Zealand Grand Prix Association. It was a group that included parliamentary, local-government, local-business and motor-racing representatives.

That first New Zealand Grand Prix was a wild affair, with a field ranging from Ken Wharton in a V16 BRM to V8 Specials and prewar

P3 Alfa Romeos and 500 cc Coopers. It was Jack Brabham's first race outside Australia, and his conversations with the UK drivers prompted him to try racing overseas. He finished sixth in his Cooper-Bristol, while Ross was seventh in the Austin-Healey — the second New Zealander to finish, in the first sports car. Ron Roycroft was fifth in his P3 Alfa Romeo. Brabham and Ross met for the first time over the race weekend and formed a bond that lasts to this day.

> Jack and I have had a close relationship ever since. I remember Jack saying that the thing that really fired his enthusiasm for motor racing was the sensational noise of the BRM. They wheeled out the V16, and when the car started, the noise was spectacular. But the amazing thing was that the reaction of the crowd drowned it out. Jack mentioned this again the other day, and I was glad to hear him say it because I was beginning to think it was just in my imagination.

An hour before the Grand Prix, Ross scored his first win in the Healey. He and Ray Archibald's XK120 Jaguar started from scratch in the sports-car handicap race, and Ross won.

New Zealand's first Grand Prix was won by Stan Jones (father of Alan, who would win the world championship for Williams in 1980) in his Maybach Special.

The Healey exercise was a successful one, considering the competition was primarily single-seaters, and a few weeks later Ross was approached by the New Zealand importer of Standard Cars, who offered him a newly imported Triumph TR2 for the 1955 Grand Prix at Ardmore. Ross spent three months modifying the car, fitting an oil cooler and bigger brakes and carrying out a variety of other alterations. He drove it in circuit races and hill climbs, and in the Grand Prix his was once again the first sports car to finish, this time in ninth place.

The winner, in his 250F Maserati, was the diminutive Prince Birabongse Bhanuban of Siam (now Thailand), or Prince Bira for short. (The prince always raced as 'B. Bira', although he came to be nicknamed 'The Drainlayer' after local legend had it that he had disappeared before the start of the Grand Prix only to be discovered pleasuring a local lass in a ditch behind the paddock area.) It was the Siamese prince's last major victory in a long career, and, by a twist of fate, this particular 250F would reappear in Ross's career.

The Austin-Healey Ross had raced in 1954 had been sold to Les McLaren, who worked with his young son, Bruce, to improve its performance. 'We didn't know that the reason the Healey was being put on the market was that Ross was waiting for the special competition "100S" version of the Healey,' Bruce recalled in *From the Cockpit*.

> Pop entered our Healey for the 1956 Grand Prix and we set about modifying it. Everything that moved was polished and balanced. Chrysler pistons were fitted, along with Buick cam covers and pushrod gear, and Chrysler exhaust valves. The ports were opened out and highly polished and a special twin-pipe exhaust system was made up and fitted. A full-length undertray was made and the cast-iron brake drums were re-fitted with plenty of cooling holes and big scoops on the back plates.

The McLaren Healey dropped out of the Grand Prix with gearbox trouble. The Jensen Healey 100S also retired when the flywheel came adrift, but not before Ross had taken it up to eighth place in the single-seater field in a race that was won by Stirling Moss in his 250F Maserati — another 250F that would reappear in the Jensen racing future.

Ross had an eye for a fine car. The Austin-Healey 100S was a customer version of the special competition model Donald Healey had built for the Sebring 12-hour race. The Austin-Healey 100/4 looked comfortable and fun; the 100S was sleeked down and looked as though it meant business.

There was a full series of races in New Zealand (which would eventually become the Tasman Series), and Ross raced at Levin, at Wigram airfield, round the houses in Dunedin, and finally in the Ryal Bush road race outside Invercargill, on the Queenstown road. At Levin there were six races for the 100S, and Ross won them all. At Wigram he finished ninth, and first sports car again, in the Lady

Wigram Trophy race, Peter Whitehead and Tony Gaze finishing first and second in their Ferraris.

Ross had a battle royal in the sports-car race that preceded the trophy main event with Tony Gaze in the HWM-Jaguar, the Aston Martins of David McKay and Tom Sulman, and Ray Archibald in his XK120. Gaze was leading with Ross in second place, getting the better of the two Aston Martins, until two laps from home, when a Buckler, being lapped, ducked the wrong way, forcing Ross into 'the spin of all spins' and into the hay bales. Ross went on to finish fourth. He won in Dunedin, and was racing hard with Sulman's Aston on the fast road circuit when the 100S threw a rear tread a mile from the pits and he retired.

'The 100S was a fine car, and while it was not a pure thoroughbred single-seater it did have disc brakes and the great versatility of being able to be driven between races. I grew quite attached to it by the end of the season, with the racing and the travel. Results were fairly spectacular primarily due to the braking power supplanting track speed.'

At the end of the 1956 season, Ross bought the 100S from Seabrook Fowlds, set about modifying it with twin-choke Webers, and kept on winning in Auckland hill climbs and Levin races.

Ross Jensen and Tom Clark were the top New Zealand drivers, and both were invited to Melbourne's Albert Park, home of the modern Australian Grand Prix, for the Olympic Grand Prix and its companion Tourist Trophy race for sports cars. Clark took his Ferrari single-seater and Jensen the Healey 100S. Stirling Moss and Jean Behra were entered in factory Maseratis in the Grand Prix and the sports-car race, and Moss won both with consummate ease. Ross finished eighth in the Tourist Trophy race and won his class, finishing just behind Bib Stillwell's D-Type Jaguar. Peter Whitehead knew talent when he saw it and offered Ross a lease deal to drive his Monza 750 Ferrari sports-racer in the 1957 international series in New Zealand.

Ross's motor-racing career stepped up a gear. Whitehead's Ferrari Monza was said to have been raced by Eugenio Castellotti in the 1955 Mille Miglia. Ross reckons the Italian had also crashed it, and its capricious handling was eventually traced to a bent chassis. 'It was a difficult car to drive,' Ross says on reflection, 40 years down the line. 'It tested one's mettle.' Nevertheless, in 1957, for the first time, a Gold Star was to be awarded to the champion New Zealand driver, and Ross felt himself suitably equipped with the Monza.

The 750 Monza was a Ferrari 'customer sports-racer', built in a limited run for special customer teams and drivers. Until 1951 Ferrari had championed Colombo's V12 engine design, but when Aurelio Lampredi took over as Ferrari designer in the winter of 1951 he switched to 4 cylinders, reckoning the superior low-speed torque would be best on short, twisting circuits. Enzo Ferrari had been intrigued that Norton could get 100 bhp per litre from its single-cylinder racing-motorcycle engine, and this was to be Lampredi's target. It took him 100 days from drawing board to dynamometer, and in the 750 Monza the 3-litre engine gave 260 bhp at 6400 rpm.

The 1957 New Zealand Grand Prix at Ardmore was an occasion to remember for a variety of reasons. A New Zealand driver started from pole and dominated the opening laps; Ken Wharton was killed in the sports-car race, in his Monza Ferrari, and his death was announced to the crowd as the Grand Prix grid was forming up; Reg Parnell won his last Grand Prix, in his Ferrari; and Ross Jensen won the Leonard Lord trophy as first Kiwi to finish — in his Monza Ferrari.

Ross had a game plan based around the fact that the Grand Prix had been increased from two-and-a-half hours to three hours, which meant that he would need to stop for fuel. 'I calculated that if I increased the Monza's capacity by 10 gallons I could run nonstop to the finish, and the night before the race I installed the extra tankage behind the passenger compartment.'

Ron Roycroft had qualified his 4.5-litre Ferrari Tipo 375 Grand Prix car — the very car that Froilan Gonzales had driven to win the first Grand Prix for Ferrari, at Silverstone in 1951 — in pole position, faster than all the overseas stars and cars, and, to the delight of the crowd, he led his home Grand Prix for 10 laps. Ross found he could stay with Peter Whitehead and Reg Parnell in the 2.5-litre Super Squalos, having qualified quite close to them with his sports car.

'I was staying with them on the opening lap, but as we entered the Cloverleaf at the end of the back straight, the Monza didn't respond as required and it went straight on. I gathered it up but it took the rest of the race to overcome the deficit and I finished fourth behind Parnell, Whitehead and Stan Jones in his 250F Maserati. It's easy to outsmart oneself at times.'

The last-minute installation of the extra fuel tank, with its extra weight, had upset the already fragile balance of the Monza, and Ross had had no chance to track test the modification.

It had been a traumatic day for Ross. He had entered his Healey 100S in the sports-car race, saving the Monza for the Grand Prix, but the engine had refused to fire at the Le Mans start, and in trying to make up lost ground Ross had spun on the eleventh lap when the brakes had locked. Seven laps later and race leader Ken Wharton had suffered his fatal crash. Ross had finished fourth, but the crowd had been hushed as it had waited for the start of the Grand Prix. The fact that Wharton had been killed in his Monza, a sister car to the one Ross was leasing, must have been a worry, even though the crash was proved to be a result of driver error. The accident had also happened in front of the pits and the main grandstand. Wharton's death had been the first in a race at Ardmore.

Ross's fourth place in the Grand Prix earned him the Leonard Lord trophy and £150 for first New Zealander home, as well as valuable points in the inaugural race for the Gold Star.

At Levin the following weekend Ross made no mistake and won the sports-car race in the 100S, but he dropped out of the main race with a gearbox problem in the Monza.

There was another win in the sports-car race with the 100S on the fast, open Wigram airfield circuit in Christchurch, and then the field lined up for the Lady Wigram Trophy in sweltering 33-degree heat. Ron Roycroft was on pole again with the big blue Ferrari, faster than the Super Squalos of Whitehead and Parnell and the cheeky little rear-engined green Cooper of Jack Brabham, which joined him in the front row. Ross had qualified the Monza in the second row between Bob Gibbons in his D-Type Jaguar and Horace Gould in his 250F Maserati.

The baking heat had a profound effect on the race. Roycroft had retired from the Grand Prix a fortnight earlier with heatstroke and had installed improved cockpit cooling for the Wigram race. He led in the opening laps, but the heat again told and he was reduced to racing with his head out in the airstream, desperately trying just to finish after a hectic battle with Whitehead and another with Brabham. Ross had a long tussle with his namesake, Syd Jensen (no relation), in a 1500 cc Cooper, and eventually finished fourth behind Whitehead, Brabham and Roycroft.

On the rough road course round the Dunedin wharves, Ross drove the 100S to a close second-place finish behind Jack Brabham's 1500 cc bobtailed Cooper sports car, which would be bought for Bruce McLaren at the end of the season.

For the first time in that international season Brabham was on pole in his Cooper for the main event, ahead of Roycroft's Ferrari and with Whitehead's Ferrari on the outside of the front row. Gould, Parnell and Ross's Monza were in the second row. Roycroft led in the early stages, but then his brakes and finally his gearbox gave him trouble and he drifted down the field. The two Jensens resumed the battle they had started in Wigram, Syd capitulating only when he clipped a drum. Reg Parnell won from Brabham and Whitehead, with Ross in fourth place. Ross was again the first Kiwi to finish and was still adding to his Gold Star points.

The New Zealand Championship Road Race was on the fast Ryal Bush circuit over closed public roads, and the sports-car race was to be run on handicap. Ross might have been flattered that the handicappers felt the Healey 100S should concede 60 seconds to Brabham's little Cooper. His race became more of a challenge when he was hit with severe cramp down his left side, but he managed to get within just three seconds of Brabham by the flag.

English privateer Horace Gould was a surprise pole sitter in the main race in his 250F Maserati, having recorded the first 100-plus mph lap on any circuit in New Zealand at 100.3 mph — on a track made up of normal Kiwi country roads. Peter Whitehead's Super Squalo was alongside the 250F on the narrow 2-2-2 grid demanded by the modest width of the country road. Ross, fourth fastest in the

Monza, was in the second row beside Reg Parnell in the other Super Squalo. Roycroft's big V12 Grand Prix Ferrari was in the row behind.

The start was hectic. Gould, pumped up to make a good start from his first pole position, made a botch of it, and it was Whitehead who took the lead, with the rest of the field squabbling over the narrow road behind him. Ross lost time in a spin on the third corner caused by the Monza's grabbing brakes, which gave him problems throughout the race, but he came through in fifth place behind Whitehead, Parnell, Gould and Roycroft.

It had been a swansong season for Whitehead and Parnell. Ryal Bush was Whitehead's last major race win, and, with a best lap of 99.53 mph, the British driver came within a whisker of Gould's new record. He was killed the following September in a rally crash. Ryal Bush was also Parnell's last race, in a season that had brought him suitable success. From now on Parnell would concentrate on team management and play a major part in New Zealand racing, bringing teams out for the international series, helping Ross Jensen to a drive in Europe and putting a very young Chris Amon on the road to international success some years later.

Ryal Bush '57 was also the last race at Ryal Bush. The Southland Sports Car Club was pressing on with what would be the first purpose-built permanent motor-racing circuit on a green-field site in New Zealand. The new Teretonga track would play an important part in Ross Jensen's future career.

The international series had finished, but the Jensen team had a final race for both the Healey 100S and the Monza Ferrari a week later, in the Mairehau street race on the northern outskirts of Christchurch. It would be the last meeting held on the Mairehau circuit, and the last race for Ross in the Ferrari. Whitehead, meanwhile, had sold his Super Squalo Grand Prix Ferrari to John McMillan, while Parnell's sister vehicle had been bought by Tom Clark.

This 20-lap national event was run on handicap with Ron Roycroft's 4.5-litre Grand Prix Ferrari on scratch, giving 60 seconds to McMillan and Clark in their new purchases and to Christchurch driver Frank Shuter in one of the wondrous straight-8 supercharged 8CLT Maseratis that had been built for the Indianapolis 500 but never raced there — never raced anywhere, in fact, before Freddy Zambucka had brought them to New Zealand.

Having suffered at the hands of the handicapper at Ryal Bush, Ross was mollified at Mairehau, being given a midfield 3 minute 20 second start over scratch-man Roycroft. Tom Clark took the race by the scruff its neck, adapting instantly to the Super Squalo and storming away with the race once the handicapping had shaken itself out. McMillan couldn't get to grips with his Squalo, and at one stage Ross was in second place with the Monza, but Syd Jensen came through in his Cooper. The race ended with Clark 20 seconds ahead of Syd Jensen, followed by McMillan third, Shuter fourth and Ross fifth.

The season had been a successful venture for the Auckland garage owner. In the Monza Ferrari and Healey 100S Ross had garnered points at most races and, with a total of 35, had clinched the Gold Star. Ron Roycroft was runner-up on 30 points (Grand Prix 375 Ferrari and Bugatti-Jaguar), with Tom Clark close behind on 28 points (Ferrari Super Squalo and HWM-Alta).

Ross Jensen was New Zealand's champion racing driver and facing a career decision. 'If I had not been able to get a suitable machine, I would have given racing away.'

But there was a very suitable machine on the Jensen horizon.

The 250F Maserati is regarded by all red-blooded motor-racing enthusiasts as one of the most gorgeous looking Grand Prix cars of all time. And it was the 250F in which Stirling Moss had won the 1956 New Zealand Grand Prix, still with the distinctive horseshoe on the scuttle, that Ross Jensen set out to buy at the end of the 1957 season.

> It was negotiation by remote control. I was trying to put it all together with Stirling's manager, Ken Gregory, and it was not an exercise I would care to do a second time. This is no reflection on Stirling, but the negotiations were a nightmare. Buzz Perkins, promoter/manager of the New Zealand International Grand Prix Association, and Don Blows, at the Auckland Customs Agency, were a huge help, and the 250F arrived in Auckland just 10 days prior to the 1958 race. It was

quite a hard call considering I had never so much as sat in such a car, having raced only in sports cars.'

Moss had used his Maserati to demonstrate his ability to Alfred Neubauer, the team boss at Mercedes in 1954, and this had resulted directly in his Mercedes works Grand Prix drive with Fangio in 1955. Stirling had insisted that the Maserati factory change the centre-mounted accelerator to the more usual position on the right-hand side of the brake pedal.

The 250F was a 2.5-litre straight-6 twin-cam that developed around 240 bhp at 7500 rpm in works trim (Fangio used 8000 and beyond!), but Stirling decided to keep it down to 7200 rpm to hold maintenance costs to a minimum. Legendary mechanic Alf Francis fitted SU fuel injection and Dunlop disc brakes and disc wheels, but Stirling found that with the new fuel injection, the car's torque characteristics became very peaky. 'It upset what had been its exemplary handling.' When Moss was driving for Mercedes, the 250F was raced on occasion by Lance Macklin, Mike Hawthorn, Bob Gerard or John Fitch.

Stirling lapped the field in the 1956 New Zealand Grand Prix at Ardmore. A leaking fuel line brought him to the pits for more fuel, losing him half a minute, but he still won comfortably. The 250F (chassis 2508) was shipped back to Britain, and Stirling raced it at Aintree in April 1956.

'By that time its disc brakes had been removed and replaced by drums ready for sale and its engine was very tired, so it was a real bonus when I won after Connaught and BRM had driven each other into the ground.'

Moss's last race with the 250F was at Crystal Palace in May, where he won both heats of the London Trophy. 'We then sold the old car. It had played a crucial role in my career, and in three seasons' service had won seven Formula One races in my hands and, most significantly, had helped me into the Mercedes-Benz drive in 1955.'

If the 250F had been a career-maker for Moss, it carried on in that role when Ross Jensen took delivery just before the 1958 New Zealand Grand Prix at Ardmore. Ross quickly settled into his new car, his first single-seater. At Ardmore Brabham was on pole in the Cooper, Salvadori was beside him in Bernie Ecclestone's B-Type Connaught, and Ross was third, with the young Bruce McLaren's Cooper on the outside of the front row. At that stage Ross was the more famous of the two.

Unfortunately for Bruce his gearbox seized up just before the race, and, despite the start being delayed, he was half a lap behind when he finally got away. Archie Scott-Brown had burst through from the second row to lead in the works Lister-Jaguar sports car. Brabham took the lead on lap 4, and by lap 8 the order was Brabham, Les Davison's ex-Ascari Ferrari 500, Salvadori, and then Ross, with Scott-Brown at his heels.

Salvadori's engine went sour, Davison had a huge spin, and Ross found himself in second place behind Brabham. Stuart Lewis-Evans came through in Ecclestone's other Connaught and swapped places back and forth with Ross until the Connaught's Alta engine lost oil pressure and he was out. In the closing laps Ross put himself within six seconds of Brabham, but the driver of a slower car didn't notice the Maserati coming through to lap him so close behind the leader, and Jensen found himself pushed into the oil drums and hay bales marking the hairpin. Damage was minimal, and Ross got back into second place to finish a mere four seconds behind Brabham. He was delighted, hugely satisfied with his first race in the gallant old Maserati, and would say later that this second place meant more to him than his wins later in the series.

The Levin race was run as two heats and a final, and Ross was third behind Brabham's Cooper and Scott-Brown's Lister-Jaguar on the tight course. In the final, Ross was fourth behind Brabham, Scott-Brown and the Cooper of Bruce McLaren, who had been awarded the first Driver to Europe scholarship after the Grand Prix the previous weekend.

Archie Scott-Brown upset the form book at Wigram, hurling the Lister-Jaguar through lock-to-lock power slides and revelling in the power of the Jaguar engine in a race of attrition. Brabham had started from the back of the grid but made it up to fourth by the end of the first lap and then passed Ross's 250F into second place after 20 laps, only to drop out with a broken gearbox. Ross led at one point, when the exuberant Scott-Brown spun, but the Lister-Jaguar battled back into a lead it never lost, and when the flag came out Ross was second, pacing to the finish, comfortably ahead of Lewis-Evans in the Connaught in third place.

The Dunedin Road Race was a Jensen benefit. Ross was fastest in practice with the 250F, even though a timing screw-up had the Englishman Dick Gibson fastest in his 1.5-litre Formula Two Cooper. Ron Roycroft was third in his 4.5-litre Grand Prix 375 Ferrari. Roycroft grabbed the lead from the start but Ross slipped ahead before the end of the opening lap and enjoyed total domination of the race. He won comfortably, 13 seconds ahead of Bruce McLaren's Cooper.

McLaren had a high regard for Ross that season, conceding his compatriot and the 250F were the dominant combination, worthy of the Gold Star for the second year running. Ross would say years later: 'Bruce and I had some great races together, and after a race we'd swap notes with one another. We'd criticise one another if it had got a bit hair-raising, but it would be constructive discussion and part of the learning curve.'

Jack Brabham had missed the Dunedin race. He returned for Teretonga but made no impression at all on the flying Jensen in 'The Grey Lady' Maserati, who led the Brabham and McLaren Coopers from start to finish.

The final race of the 1958 season in New Zealand was a handicap event at Ardmore. Ross conceded five seconds to McLaren, and the result was yet another Jensen win after another battle between the two drivers. McLaren pitted his Cooper when a plug lead came off, and went on to finish ninth.

Ross's crowning achievement that season was his fastest lap in 'The Grey Lady' — a second quicker than Moss's best in 1956 in the same car. 'I broke Stirling's record twice, which was quite something considering he had disc brakes when he set the time.'

Ross's polished drives in 'The Grey Lady' won him the New Zealand Gold Star for the second year running, with a total of 37 points. McLaren was second in his Cooper with 25 points.

Ross's performances that year earned favourable comment when Archie Scott-Brown talked to his team chief, Brian Lister. Ross was offered a works drive in the Lister-Jaguar team, taking over the team leadership after Scott-Brown was killed at Spa.

'I understand that my invitation to drive for the Lister team came as a result of complimentary comments from overseas drivers after that season in New Zealand. I enjoyed the experience greatly, and despite reliability problems I ended up with a good string of results.'

But he worried about those reliability problems. He obviously had the talent but he was not totally happy at Lister. It was decision time for Ross Jensen.

Brian Lister remembers Ross's season, and in a letter to me in April 2001, he wrote:

> When Archie came back from New Zealand in 1958 he said he was most impressed with Bruce McLaren and Ross Jensen. Archie died on May 19th after the crash at Spa and I was approached by BP, who sponsored us and also sponsored Ross, suggesting that we get together.
>
> It was a good relationship and Ross scored a third at Snetterton in July, a second place at Brands Hatch in August and he won at Snetterton in September that season.
>
> Our team got on very well with Ross. He was reliable, with no temperament, a good sense of humour — that was essential in our team! — and in general he was a very happy man. In contrast to racing the way it is today, there *were* happy drivers in motor sport then.
>
> The only reason for me to feel uncomfortable employing him as a driver, looking back over 43 years, was that he was married and I always found that difficult to rationalise with any racing driver I employed. It was obvious that Ross and Hazel were a devoted couple, which only made the dilemma worse.

In 1958 there was genuine concern over the risks drivers took, and Scott-Brown's recent death would have weighed on Ross as well as Lister when they decided not to continue.

Reg Parnell was well aware of the talent Ross possessed as the top New Zealand driver of the day, and he was eager to put together a deal whereby Ross would drive for BRM in Formula One. As Ross recalls:

> After some days of deliberating, I chose to decline in favour of my commercial interests in New Zealand as well as family responsibilities. My wife, Hazel, was always a huge support in my racing but there were other considerations. I had a young family then. Bruce was at the beginning of his career where I was well into mine, and I made the decision that I would pull away. Motor racing had given me a credible and recognisable image for which I have always been grateful.

Jensen had turned down the racing offers in Britain to concentrate on his garage and dealership in Auckland, but this did not mean that he was stepping down from racing at home.

Before he had gone to Britain that season he had sold his 250F to Johnny Mansel and put together a deal to buy Bruce Halford's well-used 250F (chassis 2504), which was the car Prince Bira had driven to win the New Zealand Grand Prix in 1955. Later that year the prince had sold his Maserati to Horace Gould, who in turn had sold it to Halford, who had crashed it almost immediately at Aintree, and the car had gone back to Modena for a rebuild that included a new frame under the old chassis plate.

Ross wanted the gallant old charger to be restyled along the lines of the latest Piccolo models that were being prepared for Harry Schell and Carroll Shelby to drive with the backing of American millionaire Temple Buell in the 1959 New Zealand Grand Prix. Buell had bought a slice of the Maserati racing department when the company had withdrawn from European racing, and his cars were tended at Ardmore by the company's top engineer, Bertocchi.

As part of the promotion for that race, 'Buzz' Perkins, a colonial P.T. Barnum who excelled in putting on a show, decided that the Jensen Piccolo copy-car should be entered from El Salvador, although Ross still isn't sure where El Salvador really is!

The car appeared in New Zealand with a special long-nosed body that had been built by Fantuzzi, one of the legendary artists in aluminium who worked by rule of thumb and later built the bodies on the distinctive 'nostril-nose' Ferraris that dominated the 1961 world championship. The first nostril-nose styling was used on Ross's Maserati. The engine was also uprated, but the 250F retained the 4-speed gearbox and drum brakes, while the genuine Piccolos had 5-speed gearboxes and discs.

Ross was obviously aware that the chassis plate on his car had the same number as Bira's 250F.

> My Piccolo really was the ex-Bira car, but it certainly wasn't to Bira's specification because it wouldn't have been nearly as competitive as it was and it was certainly a better 250F than the Moss car I'd raced. Oddly enough, it could have been the original 1954 chassis, although upgraded considerably, because it was an old-looking space frame with a fair measure of welding evidence where the chassis had been mended in the past.

The new look for 2504 was light blue with a central yellow stripe, but the handsome lines flattered to deceive Ross in the 1959 New Zealand series, most of his retirements stemming from the transmission.

Although the 250F is traditionally regarded as one of the most handsome Grand Prix cars in racing history, it is interesting to hear modern Formula One designer Patrick Head highlighting the shortcomings of its design. This isn't a case of a tomorrow designer simply slagging off yesterday's outmoded favourite, for Patrick's father, Michael, raced C- and D-Type Jaguars in the early 1950s, and Patrick grew up in this historic background.

> If you look at a 250F Maserati now, if you take away its beautiful body, it is disgusting. Not just in the way that it's made, but the load paths wander everywhere, and it still had no real torsional stiffness, there was no real diagonal tubing to add stiffness. It had got as far as adding two longitudinal tubes at the top of the chassis as well as the bottom, but there were just too few vertical chassis bars and a few bulkheads, so it was a pretty low design standard. Nothing like, for

example, the bonded and riveted Jaguar D-Type, which was winning sports-car races at the same time. The D-Type was way in advance of Formula One in terms of application of technology that was available at the time.

Ross remembers his second 250F: 'It was a splendid car but mechanically it proved very brittle, and the 1959 season had exciting prospects and qualifying times but race distances didn't lend enchantment.'

In the 1959 New Zealand Grand Prix, Ron Flockhart was driving his elegant 2.5-litre front-engined P25 BRM against the Coopers of Moss, Brabham and McLaren and a raft of 250F Maseratis. The front row of the grid had Flockhart on pole from Brabham, McLaren and the Maserati of Jo Bonnier. The second row was an all-Maserati affair: Harry Schell, Carroll Shelby, Ross Jensen and Bib Stillwell. Moss, in Rob Walker's Lotus, was at the back of the grid having broken a half shaft in the qualifying heat. Jack Brabham had loaned him a new half shaft — and Stirling would respond by beating him.

Flockhart stalled at the start, and Schell made the most of the mayhem, grabbing an early lead. Ross battled with McLaren until the Cooper spun and dropped back. Ross led McLaren until his clutch pressure plate broke and he had to change gear without it, and he eventually lost another place with a spark plug problem that cost top end revs. He finished fifth and won the Leonard Lord Trophy as first New Zealander home. McLaren was third, a lap down on Moss and Brabham.

Levin had Jensen written all over it when namesake Syd won the main event in his Cooper and Ross was second in his 250F. The other Maseratis had gone home after Ardmore, engineer Bertocchi shipping them back to Italy in disgust because they had proved uncompetitive.

At Wigram Flockhart was on pole again in the BRM, with the Coopers of McLaren and Brabham and Jensen's 250F completing the front row. The race was a long battle between the front-engined BRM and Brabham's rear-engined Cooper, with Flockhart winning from Brabham and McLaren. Ross ran strongly until his gearbox exploded on the back straight.

The front row at Teretonga was the same as at Wigram, but this time it was McLaren who dominated, winning from Flockhart, Brabham and Ross.

In the first race round the streets of Waimate, Ross, the 250F unhappy on the tight course, started in the second row. But torrential rain at flag fall changed the face of the race, and Ross led the field. McLaren spun his Cooper but was working his way back through the field when, just after half distance, the rain stopped and Ross spun. McLaren took a lead he never lost and Ross was second.

McLaren recalled the race in *From the Cockpit*:

A hailstorm didn't improve matters but it drew the teeth of the thunderstorm, the rain stopped as suddenly as it had started and the sun was shining again. A new hazard came with the sun, as we found ourselves groping through clouds of steam from the rapidly drying road. Bedraggled pit signals appeared for the first time and showed the bigger cars were rapidly losing their advantage as the track dried.

I was closing the gap to Jensen in the leading Maserati at five seconds a lap and really enjoying the controllability of the leaf-spring Cooper. Ross had his work cut out holding the big Maserati on the road as the gap decreased and a few laps from the end I arrived at a right-angle right-hander to find the blue Maserati parked backwards on the pavement, with Ross trying frantically to get it back on the street, as I carried on to win.

It had not been a season Ross cared to remember. He had won the Gold Star in 1957 and 1958, but McLaren won the 1959 championship with 50 points, from Syd Jensen with 39 and Ross, in third place, with 28.

To round the season out, Ross shipped the 250F to Australia for the Bathurst race over the Easter weekend. A local race report began, 'When tall, jut-jawed New Zealander Ross Jensen landed in Sydney for the Bathurst 100 he must have been a worried man,' and went on to list the problems Ross had suffered in the New Zealand races. The problems continued when the Maserati broke a cam follower in practice.

250Fs were entered for Ross, Stan Jones (father of the lad who would win the 1980 world championship) and Arnold Glass. Before the race, the local reporter noted the red line on the Maseratis that showed Ross had reached 7900 rpm in practice, Glass 7800 rpm and Jones a modest 7350 rpm. Ross was on the latest Dunlop R5s, Jones had earlier Dunlops and Glass had Pirellis. Ross was in the middle of the front row with Jones to his left and Alec Mildren's 2-litre Cooper on his right.

Jones led from the start, with the Coopers of Mildren and Len Lukey chasing, followed by Doug Whiteford, in his 300S Maserati sports-racer, and Ross, who had made a poor start. After his lacklustre season in New Zealand Ross must have been resigning himself to midfield. Mildren took the lead from Jones with some hectic motoring, and Ross slipped past Whiteford. Things looked even better when he passed Jones: he was now second to the hard-charging Mildren. By lap five both Ross and Jones had passed Mildren, and Ross was surprised to find himself in the lead.

On the seventh lap Jones coasted into the pits with a dead engine, leaving Ross comfortably in the lead, over half a minute clear of Lukey and Whiteford. Mildren was fourth, making a comeback run that would take him up to second place before he spun into obscurity. Brake problems slowed Lukey, and Whiteford went into second place before his transmission failed. Ross was in total control, and he won by a clear minute from Lukey's Cooper and came close to lapping Glass in the third-placed 250F.

The local report ran: 'Probably the happiest man on the circuit afterwards was Ross Jensen. At last his Maserati had come good and won him a little honour and glory, not to mention money. There were few who didn't feel heartily glad for him.'

Ross himself was feeling terrible. He had been unwell all weekend and was glad the race was over. The next day he went down with pneumonia and was hospitalised for weeks.

The 250F was sent back to Modena, and because Maserati was now officially out of racing, Ross arranged for the car to be consigned to Hans Tanner, a colourful figure on the Modenaise scene who had accompanied Temple Buell's 250Fs to New Zealand. Tanner was a motor-racing journalist, famous for his road tests of all the latest sports and road cars from Ferrari and Maserati. (It was only years later, having been an avid reader of his reports and books, that I found out he couldn't drive. He always sat alongside the works tester or one of the racing drivers, which must have been the next best thing to doing it himself, I suppose.) That said, Tanner was something of a wheeler-dealer, and, in hindsight, shipping his racing car to him probably wasn't the smartest thing Ross could have done.

At this point Ross began to lose contact with the car, and it was not until late in the year, when he went on a business trip to Europe, that he visited Italy to try to trace it with the aid of Gianfranco Comotti, a prewar Italian driver of some note who had been suggested to Jensen as a worthy aide by Dennis Druitt, then head of the BP international racing programme.

'This fine man, Comotti, came to Modena with me to sort out the situation, and we found what was left of my original chassis having a big American V8 installed in it. It had been decided by Tanner and the gearbox designer, Valerio Colotti, that they would build a Maserati-engined car of their own called a TecMec, and this Corvette-engined version was tending to materialise out of my car.'

Ross still winces when he recalls the sight of his butchered 250F.

A complicated situation became even more tangled when it was realised that there was a government lien hanging over the car through expenses incurred, and it was not until work had been completed on a 'new' 250F replacement, built in the workshops of Stanguellini, and a large wad of lira had changed hands, that Ross again became owner of a 250F.

'I eventually received what was ostensibly my car with all my bits and pieces on it, but it wasn't the same physical chassis because the original chassis now had the V8 installed. I finally had to tell them, "Look — I don't care what chassis it is, I just want my car back!"'

Legendary motor-racing journalist Denis Jenkinson was in Modena at the time, and he was able to check his notebooks and confirm for me that the chassis Ross ended up with was actually 2523, from a 250F that Jo Bonnier had been using as a rent-a-racer that he hired out to local drivers for their 'home' events.

When the Piccolo arrived in New Zealand, Ross sold it to Brian

Prescott, who raced it in the 1961 New Zealand series with a lack of success, hounded by engine blow-ups. I mentioned to him that his engine failures must have been expensive, but he said it wasn't so bad because he was now using Jaguar replacement connecting rods. But these were still breaking? Yes, but Jaguar rods were cheaper to replace than original Maserati rods.

Ross counted himself fortunate to be shot of the Maserati, and he decided to tackle the New Zealand touring-car championship with a 3.8-litre Jaguar. This was a more relaxed series, and Ross was able to apply his smooth style to heading off hard chargers like Ernie Sprague's Zephyr and Harold Heasley's Humber 80. He won the Saloon Gold Star with 44 points from Sprague on 39 and Heasley on 20.

Ross Jensen has always held New Zealand motor sport close to his heart. He was one of the founding fathers of the New Zealand International Grand Prix Association, which funded the first Driver to Europe scholarship, sending a youthful Bruce McLaren to race overseas, and it is fitting that he is now one of the important names behind the Bruce McLaren Trust, dedicated to keeping the McLaren name and its legend alive in modern New Zealand motor sport.

CHAPTER 7

TOM CLARK

Tom Clark was a giant on the stage of whatever sport he chose to venture into, from Grand Prix cars to ocean yachts. The success of his ceramics company had made him a millionaire, so he could afford good equipment, but that's no help unless there is skill at the helm. Tom was one of New Zealand's top racing drivers at a time when success and enjoyment off the track were as important as on-track achievements, and the racing never suffered just because people knew how to socialise. Tom was a legend from our Good Old Days.

The booming laugh is still the same from the burly, ebullient, wealthy Kiwi sportsman, Sir Tom Clark, now in his late eighties, who raced Grand Prix Maseratis and Ferraris in the '50s, switched to ocean yachts, and later backed Graham McRae's racing programme. Sir Tom really is larger than life, a contemporary of Ross Jensen from a racing era when the cars and the drivers were big and colourful and powerful and the after-race parties were almost as important as the on-track participation.

Tom Clark was born in 1916 and his first interest was in flying. He gained his wings from the Auckland Flying Club and celebrated by flying around New Zealand in a single-engine plane. When the Mark 7 Jaguar saloon was announced, Tom bought one as his road car. He was soon swept up with the racing pedigree of the marque and entered it for a 1952 saloon-car race on the Ohakea airfield circuit, which was so wide *nine* cars started across the front row. Tom won his debut race despite starting from scratch, and he subsequently competed as often as he could in races, sprints and hill climbs. Business kept him from competing in 1953, however, and it was 1954 before he was back at Ohakea and winning the 50-mile saloon race. 'I beefed the Jag up a bit and fitted adjustable shock absorbers so that we could screw it up tight and improve the handling.'

In typical Clark fashion, Tom decided that if he could win he needed a proper car, so why not buy the 1936 straight-8 supercharged 2.9-litre black 8CM Maserati that Freddie Zambucka had imported, said to have been raced — as was every Maserati and Alfa Romeo ever built — by Tazio Nuvolari. 'It used to go like hell in a straight line, but it was a real performance to get it round a corner.' With this feisty acquisition, Tom set a record of 13.7 seconds for the standing quarter and 150 mph for the flying quarter, and went on to win the North Island hill climb title.

Tom loved a challenge. He entered the 8CM for the Grand Prix at Ardmore in 1955 with the goal of being the first Kiwi home. With only a few laps left, battling the tricky performance of the old racer and probably tiring in the heat, Tom went into a corner with locked brakes and stormed into the hay bales. The Maserati reared in the air in an accident that looked a good deal worse than it actually was.

The following weekend Tom proved that the tight little one-mile Levin track wasn't really a 'Cooper circuit' as supposed, winning every race he started despite the fact that the track became rutted in the gravelled grooves and the little Coopers swarmed around his big Maserati. He picked up £240 that weekend, and the party on Sunday evening was one to be remembered.

The 8CM was better suited to Wigram, but the engine bearings failed after a couple of laps. Down in Dunedin for the race around the wharf roads — including a 250-yard stretch of loose gravel — Tom finished fifth behind the Ferraris of Tony Gaze, Reg Parnell and Peter Whitehead and Syd Jensen's Cooper. In the national race around the streets of the Christchurch suburb of Mairehau, Tom was two seconds inside the lap record and favourite to win, but the legendary Clark enthusiasm was his undoing. He spun, crashing over a deep gutter, buckling wheels and narrowly missing a power pole. He motored slowly to the pits with the bent wheels all over the place, but his crew cannibalised another car and sent him back out on odd-sized wheels — to come in third! Tom Clark didn't make up tall tales — he *lived* them.

The next race was on the fast Ryal Bush road course near Invercargill, and Tom qualified third fastest behind Peter Whitehead and Reg Parnell in their much younger Ferraris. In the early laps he was second behind Whitehead, but then Parnell came through. Tom spun on the twelfth lap, plunging six feet down a bank, but the car landed on its wheels. He begged the marshals to help get the car back up to the track, but they were unsure whether they were allowed to offer assistance and it was eight long minutes before permission was received and he was back in the race.

He fought back through the field for 20 laps of the five-mile circuit and closed on Gaze's Ferrari, pressuring him into a spin. Caught unawares, Tom spun as well, crashing into a deep ditch. He was stunned, slumped over the wheel with blood pouring from head and chest injuries. He was taken back to the pits, where he collapsed, but he refused to go to hospital for treatment, preferring, as always, to stay for the after-match party. In the early, rowdy hours of the morning he collapsed again, and this time he woke up in hospital, diagnosed with broken ribs, a cracked chest bone and severe abrasions.

The final race of the season was three weeks later, at Ohakea, and the irrepressible Clark was back in the Maserati, living up to the Nuvolari legend with his chest and ribs heavily strapped — and, of course, he won at a canter, from Roycroft in his Bugatti-Jaguar.

It was time for a faster, more modern car, so Tom sold the Maserati to buy the HWM raced by Tony Gaze and, latterly, by John Horton, fitted with a supercharged 2-litre Alta engine that supposedly turned out 240 bhp. In preparation for the 1957 season, he pulled the engine down but couldn't stop it overheating. He eventually solved the problem by hiring the services of Stan Ellsworth, Peter Whitehead's English mechanic, for three months. He ran the car in local hill climbs but had further problems. In his first race with the HWM, on the Olympic Grand Prix circuit at Melbourne's Albert Park, he shunted through the hay bales in practice and didn't last even a lap in a preliminary race, while in the Grand Prix the HWM stuttered and misfired, ending up in eleventh place with a faulty magneto.

The 1957 New Zealand Grand Prix at Ardmore was nonstop action. Tom qualified fourth fastest for a front-row grid spot, but the drivers were stunned when it was announced over the loudspeakers that Ken Wharton had died of injuries suffered when his Monza Ferrari had somersaulted during the morning sports-car race.

Tom was with the leaders in the early laps, but on the fifth, in the Clover Leaf, he missed a change and lost second gear. Then the gear lever itself snapped and he was left with a four-inch stump. Even with these problems he held his place ahead of Stan Jones in his 250F Maserati, but then the HWM's clutch failed.

A contemporary report described the action:

Despite his various problems, the battling New Zealander roared on. When half a hundred laps had been covered, he signalled that he was about to make a pit stop for fuel. Two minutes later the HWM had 44 gallons aboard and Clark was pushed back on to the track. But almost immediately he noticed that the temperature level of the cockpit was rising. Smoke began to obscure his vision. A lap later, Clark was sitting in what felt like an inferno. There was no sign of flames and so he drove on. During lap 87 the oil pressure began to go haywire and Clark pulled into the pits. Ellsworth soon found the problem — the oil hose into the blower had broken. While he taped the break, the car was refuelled and Clark prepared to re-enter the fray but the car refused to start until Ellsworth fitted a fresh set of plugs.

Ross Jensen was the only New Zealand driver ahead of Tom, and the pair battled it out until one of the HWM's Alta exhaust pipes came loose and scorching fumes filled the cockpit, almost blinding Tom. Then there was a roaring flash of flame and Tom was on the brakes, swerving off the track and clambering out of the car before it had stopped, dowsing the fire with an extinguisher.

By this time Tom must have been thinking that motor racing was a good deal more dangerous, complicated and costly than it really needed to be. He cabled the Alta factory in England, had a new engine block flown out and was on the grid at Wigram, tended by a very weary Ellsworth. He was running fifth at half distance when the clutch let go.

In Dunedin for the road race the following weekend, Tom was well on the pace in practice, with a new lap record, when a rear wheel came off on the very last lap of the session and the HWM spun out of control, ending up between a power pole and the heavy mesh fence of a railway shunting yard. A half shaft had fractured, but as the HWM was put together mostly from proprietary parts, Ellsworth found a spectator's sports car with the necessary axle and did a deal to borrow it for the race. He completed the job a quarter of an hour after the race had started, but Clark stormed out of the paddock and into the fray. 'Needless to say I never caught the others, but I had *fun*.' That comment sums up the difference between racing then and now, between the Good Old Days and Modern Show Business. Do you suppose Michael Schumacher ever *has fun* when he's not winning?

At Ryal Bush, the HWM was short on pace on the long straights and the best Tom could do was fifth. When I spoke to him about his time with the HWM a few years ago, he sat back in his chair, laughed at the memory and said, 'That HWM was the most expensive way I ever found to boil water.'

The overseas drivers used the colonies as a selling plate for the cars they brought out to race, and when Peter Whitehead said he was disposing of his Super Squalo Ferrari, Tom was ready with the funds. He wasn't sailing completely into the unknown, because Ross Jensen was working with him and had arranged for genius special-builder Hec Green to work on the Clark cars, and in his first race with the big Ferrari, around the streets of Mairehau, Tom came to grips with it and pulverised the lap record. He went under the record to take pole, then took a full *seven seconds* off in the race itself, and won every race he entered that day with ease, scratch and handicap. The occasion was celebrated with another megaparty, Clark style.

Tom ran the Super Squalo in North Island hill climbs in 1957 but it really wasn't the horse for the courses. He proved once again that he could outdrive the nimble Coopers on the one-mile Levin course, today only a grown-over outline visible on the infield from high in the horse-racing grandstands. He won the feature race on the programme and two other races that day.

It was time to take the big Grand Prix Ferrari over to Bathurst, long before the mountain circuit became famous for its V8 touring-car epic events. Tom was slated as the main competition for Aussie hero Stan Jones in his 250F Maserati. In the first race he led away, but after 50 yards Jones was out with a broken axle, having been overloaded on the start. In the Bathurst 100, the main event, a piston failed on the Ferrari and Tom was sidelined. 'Lex Davison had been leading the early stages but then he dropped out and I was going like a rocket. Everything was brand new, having just been bought, but it blew going up the mountain.'

An Australian journalist, Pedr Davis, wrote after that race:

Away from racing, Tom Clark is a genial man with an aptitude for entertaining each and every one around him. One of his delights is to fill his ample frame with good food and drink, and his staying power at the most hectic of parties is a constant source of amazement. The burly New Zealander tips the scales at 15 stone, yet he carries no excess weight. At home he is a typical family man, with five children. Mrs Clark is also very keen on motor sport.

Fortunately.

In the Australian Grand Prix with the Super Squalo later that season, Bathurst again proved Tom's undoing.

> I was lapping a guy in a 4CLT Maserati for the second time, and at the end of Conrod Straight I was doing about 160 mph. I was airborne over the hump and hard on the brakes down to the left-hander. The guy in the 4CLT was probably going half my pace. I'd just landed and he came right across in front of me. He didn't know I was there, obviously. I was skating down beside big steel railway irons with eight-by-two planks on them and I was just skimming them. Then I hit his back wheel, tossing the Ferrari into the air, and it came down on top of me. It bloody near did me in. I had a fractured skull, internal injuries that were bleeding and a smashed arm. The hospital facilities at Bathurst weren't up to much and I was flown to Auckland, where I spent two months in hospital battling to survive. It was a further six months before I was fully recovered. Hec Green rebuilt the Ferrari for me and we tried it once before I took it to Levin for the November meeting in 1958, and I think I broke the lap record, but I knew I'd had enough. I said, 'Right. I'm selling it.' And I walked away and looked around for something that was less likely to kill me — like yachts.

Tom was 42, but it must have seemed he had spent a lifetime in motor racing.

> Most of my races were memorable because bits would fall off and I'd have to start again. I remember the race at Albert Park when I'd qualified second to Jack Brabham, and Alex Mildren came down the inside like a rocket. I was halfway round the bend and he took me out. I gathered it all up and drove that whole race with an out-of-balance front wheel, but the engine was going great. It was one of those races when I was holding my breath. There was a line of trees down the straight and I was wondering which one I was going to hit if

something broke after that first-lap crash. I finished fairly well back but it was one of the few times that the car ran absolutely perfectly.

Sir Tom enjoys his senior racing status these days whenever old cars and old drivers get together, and he relives the racing past with his old sparring partner and mentor Ross Jensen, both of them pillars of New Zealand motor-racing history.

CHAPTER 8

JOHNNY MANSEL

New Zealand lost a champion when Johnny Mansel was killed on the Dunedin street circuit in 1962. This account of the dashing driver's career was written for New Zealand Classic Car *in 2001.*

He looked like Hollywood's idea of an Italian racing driver: handsome, tall, powerfully built, flamboyant and fast. Johnny Mansel was only briefly on the New Zealand racing stage but he certainly left his mark. He drove the usual variety of old sports cars and V8 specials in his early days as a mechanic in the 1950s, growing up in Ron Roycroft's hometown of Glen Murray and learning from the master. He bought Roycroft's garage and used that as his racing base.

Johnny came to notice with the famous old P3 Alfa Romeo that Tazio Nuvolari drove to win the 1935 German Grand Prix against the might of Mercedes-Benz and Auto Union. He would have raced well in the Nuvolari era. It was his sort of style. He looked more like an Italian racing driver than most Italian racing drivers. His next car was the 250F Maserati formerly raced by Stirling Moss and Ross Jensen. Then there was a brief flirtation with a 2-litre Cooper, and finally the ill-fated Cooper-Maserati that killed him in a race he should never have been allowed to enter, on the streets of Dunedin in 1962. He was 33.

Johnny's need for speed started when he was a teenager on a racing bicycle and he won an Auckland championship riding for the Lynndale Club. He built his own motorcycle special, fitting a Rudge engine into an old Rex-Acme frame, and competed in local scrambles. He was 19 and working for Ron Roycroft when he bought his first fast car, a Riley 9 with which he started hill-climbing and racing at Seagrove. He had plans to fit a Gipsy Major aero engine in the Riley, similar to the power unit in the Stanton Special, and in fact entered the 'Gipsy Riley' in the 1955 New Zealand Grand Prix, but the project never happened and instead he fitted the little Riley with a Ford V8 after experimenting with an aged 2.2-litre 6-cylinder Continental engine. He drove Ron Roycroft's Bugatti in some events in 1955.

Johnny's next racer was the Marlborough-Thomas that had been built at Brooklands by Parry Thomas in 1923. Thomas, a Brooklands specialist with workshops inside the track, was killed while making an attempt on the land speed record on Pendine Sands four years later, but his Marlborough-Thomas was already racing in New Zealand. When Johnny bought the car from Roycroft it was fitted with a 1937 6-cylinder Chev engine. In 1952 he sold it on, although he would buy it back, fit a Mercury V8 with Ardun heads and christen it the Ardun Special before moving into the major league with the P3 Alfa Romeo. That famous old car had something of a Glen Murray pedigree, having been owned and raced by three residents of the little mining township. Dave Caldwell bought the P3 from Ron Roycroft but had difficulty keeping the Grand Prix Alfa engine running and sold it on to Johnny.

Ray Stone remembers meeting Johnny by way of the Alfa engine.

I was an apprenticed mechanic, and I spotted some interesting valves in an engine-reconditioning company owned by Harold Wallace. I always called him 'Mr Wallace'. He was a special person, an exceptional engineer, and would become my mentor. I asked him if he would put in a word for me with Johnny, as an enthusiastic 16-year-old, and I eventually ended up in the Mansel pits for the 1958 New Zealand Grand Prix at Ardmore.

The valves I had spotted belonged to the P3 Alfa, and a series of long weeks and late nights followed, building one engine from a collection of several old Alfa engines, all in bits. John had purchased the P3 from David Caldwell, a gentleman farmer with tweed jacket, appropriate English BBC accent and lots of style but no great feel for things automotive. Caldwell had bought the car from Ron Roycroft, but lost interest in racing after a major engine blow-up.

Building up the engine was an interesting exercise. It was an in-line 8 made up of two 4-cylinder units bolted together in the centre with a two-piece crankshaft, also centrally bolted, with two Roots-type superchargers centrally mounted and taking their drive from a central gear train.

The one-piece block and head made the fitting of the block-head-camshaft-valve assembly on to the crankcase a somewhat challenging job. Being eight cylinders long with eight pistons and rods all hanging out of the crankcase at different lengths and angles, timing the valve train and blower rotor positions while lowering this great lump of engineering gently down onto the crankcase was definitely a four-person job.

Stone said he used to go down to help Johnny working on the Alfa and then drive home at about 5.00 a.m. in time for work the next day.

It wasn't unusual to fall asleep under the car.

The 'spares' were a motley collection of half-blocks, cranks, blowers, pistons, valves, etc. from the two previous owners' mechanical misfortunes. My first job was to sort through that lot and put aside the 'definitely stuffed' bits, like crankcases with large holes, pistons in two bits, bent valves and stuff like that. Then we looked at the remains and decided what could be restored, repaired and reused. We actually ended up with one good engine.

In those days the old P3 Alfa (or Tipo B Monoposto, to be strictly correct) was regarded as little more than a means to an end, a way to go racing on the cheap, providing you could keep the thing running. It had been designed by Vittorio Jano in 1932 as the frontline Grand Prix car for Alfa Romeo. It won nine races in 1932 and six in 1933. In his book, *Classic Grand Prix Cars*, Karl Ludvigsen wrote:

> Jano's design overcame one of the major disadvantages of the in-line eight: the length of both the camshafts and the crankshaft, which introduced torsional vibrations that harmed both valve timing and reliability. Instead, this was composed of two four-cylinder engines back to back — each with short cams and cranks. With an eye on cost and practicality, Jano made the major parts symmetrical so that one four-cylinder block casting, for example, would serve both ends of the engine. Simplicity also characterised the bottom end, which used plain bearings instead of rollers. Instead of detachable cylinder heads, each of the four-cylinder heads and blocks were unified in a single 'monobloc' aluminium casting with dry cylinder liners. Here were two valves per cylinder, symmetrically inclined at the broad included angle of 102 deg.

This was the pedigree engine on which Ray Stone cut his motor-racing teeth as a young apprentice. It was in at the deep end in anyone's terms. The P3 engine was initially a 2.6-litre and gave 215 bhp, but in 1934 this was increased to 2.9 litres, giving 255 bhp. A novelty of the P3 design was the split propeller-shaft transmission in the form of a V, with the differential at the base attached to the back of the gearbox so that it was sprung weight, and consequently a very light back axle incorporating a crown wheel and pinion for each shaft, the half-shafts being mere stubs.

Between its 1932 debut and mid-1934 the Tipo B took part in 26 races, of which it won 22. In seven of those the Tipo B filled the first three places. It achieved a 92 per cent finishing record from 62 race starts in this period!

By 1958 the famous Nuvolari Alfa was 26 years old and a well-known winner on New Zealand circuits in Roycroft's hands. 'We had a fun season with the Alfa,' Stone recalls. 'It was a magnificent piece of engineering, which pleased me, and we were happy enough with the results.' Johnny was ninth in the Grand Prix.

Stone laughs as he remembers Johnny's performance at Wigram that year.

> John had qualified well, but there was some sort of engine drama so we had to improvise. In those days you collected money for getting on to the grid — and John was broke so he needed to be there, despite his engine problem. We had taken the engine apart to determine what had happened and hung a sack over it to stop dust getting into the valve gear. We put the engine covers back on and wheeled the car on to the grid for the start. As the flag fell, John raised his arms and sat on the grid. When the dust cleared, I rallied the marshals and we pushed the car off the grid, feigning dejection at the sudden demise of the clutch.

Johnny had been in the police force in the early 1950s before going into the motor trade, and had been involved in the watersiders' strike in the Auckland docks. 'John was a striking figure,' says Stone.

> He was over 6 foot, with broad shoulders, large biceps and slim hips. He walked with a natural swagger of confidence and nearly always wore tight black short-sleeved T-shirts. He was an easy-going guy,

and although he had a burning ambition to succeed at whatever he did, this didn't come through in normal day-to-day contact. He had a boyish sense of humour and was always out for fun. I never knew anyone who didn't like him. He probably wanted to be more than a garage owner/operator, and he was also getting involved with Auckland car dealers. I think he saw buying and selling as a way to make sufficient money for his racing and family, while having sufficient time for his racing. He was married to Joan and they had two daughters.

The P3 was sold to ex-speedway driver Brian Tracy, and Stone remembers the old car parked for months at the side of an Auckland street. 'It was nose down on a flat deck trailer. The sight of that big old exhaust pipe facing to the sky and openly inviting rain to run straight down to the engine still makes me shudder.'

Christchurch collector Bill Clark eventually bought the old Alfa and its spare engines, and when it was completely restored it sold at auction in Monaco for close to £1 million!

The Alfa Romeo was replaced for the 1960 season by the Maserati 250F that Stirling Moss had driven to win the 1956 New Zealand Grand Prix at Ardmore. Starting from pole, Moss had set the lap record and won despite stopping for fuel late in the race. Ross Jensen had then bought the Maserati and raced it successfully in New Zealand in 1958, when it became known affectionately as 'The Grey Lady'.

The 250F was a simple design clothed in an outstanding body shape, certainly the best-looking Grand Prix car of its era. It had a space frame with coil-spring/wishbone front suspension and de Dion rear suspension. The 5-speed gearbox was in unit with the final drive. The engine was a 2.5-litre straight-6 that gave around 250 bhp. Altogether, 32 250Fs were built for the works team and for private owners.

Johnny preferred his cars to be black and he always wore black when he raced, so the 250F was painted black with a white nose flash, still with Moss's good-luck horseshoe on the flank, with its seven nail holes. Seven was Moss's lucky number, his mother having been born on the seventh day of the seventh month.

Stone remembers that the 250F was not as easy to test on the gravel roads around Glen Murray as the old Alfa had been. They had rebuilt the engine at 'Mr Wallace's', and in the week before the Grand Prix, Johnny was anxious to practice starts with his new car.

> We both agreed that practising standing starts on loose metal would be a waste of time, but there was a concrete bridge nearby and it was ideal as a practice pad. It was quite something to watch John in the Maser coming off the concrete at full cry with tyres smoking — and then buttoning off before the full-blooded slide onto the loose stuff became uncontrollable. Unfortunately the concrete surface must have had too much grip and we ended up splitting the transmission housing. Imagine the scenario. It's Thursday, and practice is tomorrow, Friday. No time to dismantle, weld, machine and reassemble, and no such thing as spares. However, it was a good opportunity to try new-fangled 'metal-in-a-tube' stuff, and that, with a bit of bracing and drilling and tapping, held it together for practice and the race. It only leaked a bit.

Johnny qualified in the third row of the grid, alongside Ross Jensen in his later 250F, and finished a stylish fifth, winning the Leonard Lord Trophy as first New Zealander home. Bruce McLaren finished second to Jack Brabham but by now was considered as an 'overseas driver'.

At Wigram Johnny was in the second row but his race lasted only half a lap, after which he rolled to a halt with the bolts in the universals sheared.

I became a member of the Mansel team for a short time after that Wigram race in 1960, travelling in the famous big Mark 7 Jaguar, which was painted black to match the Maserati on the trailer behind. The crew included Ray Stone, Bob Wallace (a hot-rodder friend of Ray's) and a young Rod Coppins. After his work on the Mansel Maserati, Wallace would go to Italy and work for Maserati there, before joining the new Lamborghini operation as chief engineer and test driver, the equivalent of Guerrino Bertocchi at Maserati.

The big Jag was quite a tool. Ray remembers Mansel at the wheel.

John would try different lines and explain to me what was happening. He would drop the inside front wheel off in the loose stuff and it allowed the car to slide just a bit and allow a tighter line. Mind you, you needed a bit of speed on for the difference to be noticeable. That was fine without the trailer, but with the trailer on you have to induce a bit of a slide under brakes as you go into the corner. That way the trailer hangs out a bit and doesn't follow the front wheels through the rough stuff. I learned a lot about driving with John. In those days, towing at 80 mph or more wasn't unusual.

Down in Dunedin Johnny qualified in the second row and came through to finish third behind Syd Jensen's Cooper and Pat Hoare's Ferrari. At Teretonga he was in the front row with David Piper's front-engined Lotus 16 and Jensen's Cooper, but engine problems caused him to retire.

The following weekend, at Waimate, was all Johnny's. The circuit was laid out on streets around the little country town, and it was a very popular event. Prerace money was on Syd Jensen's nimble little Cooper, but Pat Hoare surprised by pipping it to pole in his 3-litre Ferrari. Johnny was third fastest. The race was 50 laps, and Jensen jumped into an immediate lead from Hoare and Johnny. For six laps he held his place, then made a rare error at the hairpin, almost spinning, and Hoare was through. Three laps later and Johnny was past Jensen into second place and storming up behind the Ferrari. He took the lead on the thirteenth lap and led comfortably, setting the fastest lap, and when Hoare made an attack late in the race he was made to realise that catching up was one thing but getting past was something else again.

It was Johnny's first big win and the celebrations went on long into the evening. It was late when we piled into the Jaguar and went looking for food. We arrived at the Waimate pie cart as the owner was putting up the shutters, and he refused to reopen for us even though we pointed out that 'our' driver had won the race that afternoon. For reasons that probably had much to do with the length of our postrace celebrations, I took it upon myself to distribute the contents of the cutlery box up the street, and when discretion and immediate flight seemed the best option, the Jaguar had gone. Mild panic, until I realised that Johnny had moved the car round to the front of the pie cart and was endeavouring to hook it up so that he could tow the whole thing away!

Johnny finished third in the 1960 Gold Star championship, but not without drama. The final race was on the wide Ohakea airfield circuit, but the top drivers announced a boycott of the event, the final race in the championship, because the organisers refused to increase the £10 starting money to £30. Wealthy Ferrari driver Pat Hoare was the only confirmed entry because he was second in the points table, one point behind Cooper driver Syd Jensen. The boycotters included Syd Jensen, Johnny, Len Gilbert, Malcolm Gill, Bill Thomasen, Johnny Windleburn, Brian Prescott and Jimmy Palmer. Johnny discovered on the Wednesday before the race that Syd Jensen had reconsidered, probably realising that his stand could cost him the Gold Star for the sake of £20, but when Johnny tried to reinstate his entry in the 250F, the organisers refused to accept it. He appealed to the stewards of the Association of New Zealand Car Clubs for permission to start, and the stewards confirmed to the Manawatu Car Club that he should do so. The Maserati was scrutineered and taken to the starting grid, but as Johnny was about to climb in, police arrived and threatened to arrest him if he tried to take part in the event. The Maserati was pushed away, and the race — and the Gold Star — was won by Syd Jensen by just 0.6 of a second from Hoare's Ferrari.

Stone remembers the passing of the Mark 7. 'One day, in Christchurch, the Jag was turned into two 1948 Ford coupés. John drove one and I drove the other until they were eventually sold in Auckland.'

The black 250F was sold to Bob Eade at the end of the season, and Johnny ordered what must have seemed the ultimate Maserati — a 250F fitted with a V8 racing engine from one of Lance Reventlow's Scarabs. The TecMec appealed to Johnny's need for more power, pace and sheer excitement. The car had been built by gearbox designer Valerio Colotti's Studio Tecnica Meccanica when the Maserati team had closed down. Journalist and entrepreneur Hans Tanner also had an involvement in the project.

What actually arrived in New Zealand was what seemed to be one of the unhappy-looking bodies made for the V12 last-gasp 250Fs fitted with a Chevrolet V8 that had never been near the Scarab workshops. 'It looked the part when it arrived, and we fondly believed it had this super race V8 with a magnificent cast-alloy towerlike Rochester fuel-injection inlet manifold,' says Stone. 'But it soon became apparent that what we had was a pretty standard Corvette motor with standard injection and hydraulic tappets. It was disappointing, but I suppose it was something to race.'

The TecMec was late arriving, and Eade loaned the 250F back to Johnny for the 1961 New Zealand Grand Prix, but Johnny retired after 45 of the 75 laps on the Ardmore airfield circuit.

The TecMec was in Christchurch in time for the Wigram race. Practice was in pouring rain. The big car looked evil, and on the fast open sweeps of the airfield circuit it was a complete handful. Johnny lost it on the fast left-hander on to the back straight, spinning for what seemed like miles on the wet grass before tumbling into a big storm drain part filled with water. The car overturned as it went in, and Mansel was lucky to avoid being drowned as he struggled to get clear. He was just emerging from the ditch when he heard the ominous swish-swish-swish of another car spinning towards him. It was Bob Smith in his Super Squalo Ferrari, which actually struck Johnny as it went in over the top of the TecMec. Johnny had the Ferrari's tyre marks and heavy bruising on his back.

As though this mayhem wasn't enough, a few laps later Brian Blackburn lost control at the same place in his 4CLT Maserati and slammed over the upturned TecMec, driving it further into the ditch, and bounced beyond the Ferrari. I remember taking a photograph of the three Italian *monoposto*s in the ditch but it has vanished in the mists of time.

Stone recalls the incredible scene:

> It was really pissing down, and I ran from the pits across the soaking infield to hear the electric fuel pump still running on the TecMec. Everybody was scared the whole thing would go up. Fortunately I knew where the fuel pump switch was. Here were all these cars in and

Tom Clark at speed in a 8C Maserati in 1956.

*Tom Clark in his Ferrari Super Squalo at Ardmore in 1958.
Engineer Hec Green is in attendance.*

Tom Clark in the Ferrari Super Squalo at Ardmore in the 1957 Grand Prix.

Tom Clark on pole in the Mark Seven Jaguar at Ohakea, 1952.

*Scuderia Centro Sud: Lorenzo Bandini, Guilio Borsari,
Johnny Mansel and Mimo Dei, in 1962.*

Johnny Mansel in the TecMec chasing a Cooper 500 at Levin, 1961.

Ernie Sprague at Wigram in his 4CLT Maserati in 1958.

Ron Roycroft in the 4.5-litre Ferrari GP car at Ardmore.

Eoin Young and Warner Mauger, owner of the aero-engined Stanton Special.

Maurie Stanton racing the Stanton Special. B. Snowden

Bill Hamilton in the 1914 TT Sunbeam at Muriwai Beach.

Bill Hamilton with his Bentley at Brooklands.

Len Southward and Eoin Young with the engine from the Indianapolis Stutz.

The Indianapolis Stutz, 'as found'.

Norman Smith (inset) and the stretch of sand on which he set a new 10-mile speed record.

Stan Jones winning the 1954 New Zealand Grand Prix in the Maybach Special. B. Snowden

out of the ditch. Really spectacular. The TecMec was completely upside down with the floor pan level with the surrounding field. John was running about, probably a bit confused, but making sure that the other drivers were OK.

Fate stalked the TecMec down to Dunedin. The fuel tank drain plug was accidentally torn out as the car was unloaded from the trailer and 36 gallons of alcohol-mix fuel sluiced down the gutter.

The engine wouldn't fire properly on the grid — I don't think we even knew the correct firing order at that stage. John took off after the field and had just passed Tony Shelly's 1500 cc Cooper when the exhaust came adrift on the TecMec. John screamed to a stop, tore the pipe from the car, and rejoined the race for a few more laps before withdrawing.

Johnny sold the TecMec to Rod Coppins, who fitted the centre-seat sports-car body that Louis Rosier had used on the 4.5-litre V12 Grand Prix Ferrari. Ron Roycroft imported the car in this form, had a single-seater body fitted along the lines of the car Ferrari built for Indianapolis, and kept the sports-car body in the rafters of his workshop.

By now Johnny had figured that if he couldn't beat the Coopers with his front-engined cars, he should join them. He bought the Cooper that Denis Hulme had leased from Yeoman Credit for the 1961 season. The 2.5-litre Climax engine had been removed, and Johnny fitted a 2-litre engine and, in a burst of patriotism, created The Silver Fern Team. Stone still has a few team letterheads to remind him of his trip to Australia on the good ship *Wanganella* with the Cooper as his passenger baggage. They had entered for a national race at Warwick Farm.

There was drama at Sydney docks when customs demanded to know why Stone had valued the Cooper at such a minimal amount — only a few hundred pounds — which he'd done in line with common practice. They took his explanation that it was a very old racing car and these things weren't worth much with a very large grain of sea salt. One of them produced newspaper clippings of an interview with

Stirling Moss, who had arrived the week before. 'You do know Stirling Moss, don't you, Mr Stone? Mr Moss says here that his Cooper is worth many thousands of pounds.'

The shortfall in the value of the car was eventually sorted out and Johnny took the grid at Warwick Farm, but he didn't finish. 'The car stopped unexpectedly with some sort of vapour lock in the fuel line,' recalled Stone. 'We weren't prepared for the Aussie temperatures. I don't have any recollection of racing that car in New Zealand or whether John owned it, leased it or was simply taking it out of the country to escape duty.'

Then there was a Cooper-Bristol, which Johnny drove briefly in several North Island hill climbs.

The 250F and the TecMec had given Johnny an affinity with Italian racing, and a deal was cut whereby he would lease or buy — nobody seems sure which — a Cooper-Maserati from Mimo Dei's Centro Sud team for the 1962 season in New Zealand. The team brought out two cars, one for a young pre-Ferrari Lorenzo Bandini, the other, an older vehicle, for Mansel. The New Zealand Grand Prix that year was the last on the old Ardmore circuit — it moved to Pukekohe after that — and is well remembered as the race where it teemed with rain and Stirling Moss was quite simply in a class of his own, winning with consummate ease in his Rob Walker Lotus.

Johnny was not best pleased with his 'new' Cooper-Maserati, struggling home in ninth place. Bandini was fifth in the other Centro Sud car, crossing the line with a flattened nose after a shunt and the water temperature off the clock.

Howden Ganley remembers competing at the same events as Johnny in the 1962 series in his Lotus 11. 'Johnny was a pretty tough character, immensely strong but always very pleasant. He took the trouble to weld up the broken gearbox on my '35 Chevy tow car the previous year in Dunedin because he was the only one who could weld cast iron.'

At Wigram Johnny was eighth and last, finishing with bent valves, probably caused by overrevving because the axle ratio was too low. 'There were bugger-all spares and Centro Sud were not very interested in our old car anyway,' says Stone.

Teretonga was next, and there were clutch problems. Johnny was eighth again, and Stone found that all the valve clearances had closed up.

> John returned to Auckland while I stripped the car in Dunedin and generally got the engine ready for the new valves, which we had made at J. & A.P. Scott in Dunedin, and alternative springs. John arrived back in Dunedin at the end of the week, and by working all night and into race-day morning we managed to get the thing back up and running. We were working in Sid Cottle's workshop at the north end of George Street, and we could hear that the race had started, in pouring rain, by the time we'd run the engine up in the workshop and tried the car up the street. The engine was running better than it ever had in New Zealand when we tested it that fateful morning.
>
> John hadn't practised, but for John problems were just things to overcome. Undeterred, he drove down a back street to come on to the circuit at a road-block access point. The marshals must have figured that he'd just spun off, so they lifted the tape and he set off into the race, long after it had started.

The officials should never have let the driver on to the track, but that is to pass judgement on wet, puzzled, men 40 years on. It is easy to be wise so long after the event. Johnny Mansel was a racer, and he just wanted to race that day. It was his last.

The circuit was like glass, the city streets diesel-greasy in the rain, and cars were going off everywhere. Chris Amon crashed out of the lead in his 250F, Rod Coppins crashed the TecMec sports car, and a young Howden Ganley went off in his Lotus 11. Johnny pressed on for about 10 laps in the middle of the race before losing control on the aptly named Cemetery Hill.

Stone takes up the story of the final minutes of a great man's life and career:

> It was raining and John hadn't practised or even attended the driver's briefing, so he was unaware of just how slippery the circuit was where it climbed up past the cemetery on the bus route, greased with diesel.

On the easy right-hander up the hill, he slid wide and hit a power pole, cutting the car in half. John stayed with the seat and the front half of the car, while the back half, still reasonably intact with wheels, engine and transaxle, disappeared off down into the park below.

Stone didn't see the crash; in fact he didn't see Johnny again until he reached the hospital. Deeply saddened, he took the wreckage of the Cooper-Maserati back to Auckland, but what happened to it then is something of a mystery. According to one version of events, the remains were taken offshore and dumped to satisfy import regulations, as the car had been imported under bond. According to another, the Colotti gearbox, the only salvageable part of the wreck, was removed before the rest was shipped out and is still in New Zealand.

Johnny Mansel left the stage as he had made his entrance — with flair and a flourish, and exuding the sense that racing was about sheer excitement and speed — and as a New Zealand motor-racing hero deserving of a place in our national Hall of Fame.

CHAPTER 9

THE BLUE FERRARI

It was a dream come true, the chance to drive the actual Ferrari that Gonzales had driven into history at Silverstone in 1951. Looking back from fifty years on, with Ferrari and Michael Schumacher so dominant, it is hard to believe that Gonzales' win was the first victory for the Prancing Horse.

It was one of those rare days in motoring when everything exceeded expectation. The first Ferrari to win a world championship Grand Prix, 40 years since that summer of 1951, would be mine for a Sunday-morning drive.

The plan was to start early before the local church-going traffic had stirred. Dawn was cloudless, heralding a clear April morning high up at Euan Sarginson's hillside home in Governor's Bay, at the end of the long inlet of Lyttelton harbour, over the Port Hills from Christchurch.

Sarginson was the top racing photographer in New Zealand when the Grand Prix drivers wintered in the colonies. The sea was like a millpond, and we heard the Ferrari before we saw it as Gavin Bain threaded the historic blue single-seater along the winding road around the bays.

The 12-cylinder exhaust was morning music made legal by New Zealand laws that insist all imported cars have to be taxed for road use and therefore covered for third-party insurance. The laws were an annoyance to the visiting drivers in the '50s, but they provide an interesting loophole that allows old Grand Prix cars to be driven on public roads today.

A *blue* Ferrari? French blue. Froilan Gonzalez drove this car, chassis no. 2, to score the first Grand Prix win for Ferrari, at Silverstone in 1951. Weeks later Alberto Ascari drove it to win the German Grand Prix at the Nürburgring. Chassis numbers were not the religion they are today, and only in relation to these two races is reference made to chassis no. 2.

The car was one of six 4.5-litre V12 Type 375 Grand Prix single-seaters built. Three exist today, but Gavin's has the best pedigree. It was sold to French privateer Louis Rosier in 1952. Almost as soon as Rosier had painted it blue, the formula changed, rendering the car obsolete, so the Frenchman converted it to a sports-racer, keeping the central seat and adding outriggers to carry an all-enveloping body and a tiny 'passenger seat', 10 years ahead of Penske's similar switch with the Zerex Special Cooper.

Pedigrees were not realised in the 1950s, when old Grand Prix cars were simply old racing cars — uncompetitive, obsolete, taking up space. Hindsight is a valuable asset. Ron Roycroft was presumably delighted to sell the 4.5-litre V12 engine to Australian powerboat racer Ernie Nunn, who installed it in his 'Squalo' hull and ran it to a record speed of 134 mph. The Ferrari chassis was bought by local special-builder Ferris de Joux for the basis of a back-yard GT.

Gavin is an avid old-car man with an impressive collection, and he persuaded de Joux to sell him the famous Ferrari chassis in 1968. It was another 12 years before he managed to buy the original engine in Australia and Auto Restorations, in Christchurch, expertly remarried the mechanicals.

We wondered at the wisdom of Gavin driving his pedigree Grand Prix charger up the steep rutted gravel track to Sarge's house, so I phoned him to suggest we meet at road level.

'Do you think this is some modern ground-effect Grand Prix car?' he asked with a measure of mild outrage. 'Just watch me.' It was like discussing ground effect with the owner of a Land Rover. We waited and watched, and the old Ferrari coped superbly, even if it looked absurdly out of place coming up the track and through the farm gate.

The Ferrari had grown in my mind since the day I watched it in action for the first time in the New Zealand Grand Prix on the Ardmore airfield circuit in 1957. Roycroft had bought it from Rosier, raced it a few times with the sports body and then fitted it out as a single-seater with the square nose it has today, closely modelled on the front fashioned for the longer-wheelbase version which was built for the Indy 500 in 1952.

Roycroft seemed an older driver to me in those days, having raced a Bugatti and a P3 Alfa Romeo before graduating to the Ferrari. He was a spare figure in the cockpit so recently filled by 'The Pampas Bull', wearing a T-shirt popular before fireproof uniforms and leading the Grand Prix for eight incredible laps.

This has to be placed in perspective. Roycroft, new to the car, had set the fastest practice lap — 1 minute 29.2 seconds — before Ken Wharton pipped him by 0.7 of a second in a Schumacher-style closing lap at the end of the session in his 250F Maserati. Wharton had also brought a Monza Ferrari to New Zealand for the main sports-car race. Sadly, he somersaulted this and died later of his injuries.

The heat was wilting. It was the fourth New Zealand Grand Prix and the first that had been led by a local, but the big Ferrari was more than the small man's measure and Roycroft gave way to the 3.5-litre Ferraris of Peter Whitehead and Reg Parnell.

Parnell eventually won from Whitehead and the 250F Maserati of Stan Jones, but it was Roycroft's heroic opening laps that added to the legend of the first Ferrari to win a Grand Prix and prompted the present owner to buck tradition and keep the car Rosier blue rather than paint it Ferrari red.

Now the car looked somehow smaller, while the challenge of driving it grew enormously as Gavin ran through the instructions. If I stalled, I was on my own. He wasn't planning on following. What was I like with a crash box? Did I know that the Ferrari transmission was easy to break and *very* expensive to repair? I didn't, but it was now engraved on my mind.

Gavin drove the car back down the track and climbed out, leaving it ticking over on the verge. It didn't seem right. There should have been an excited jostle of Italian mechanics in Pirelli-blue cotton overalls. What had happened to the Scuderia's mystique if Gavin could start the thing on his own and leave it bumbling, ready for me to climb aboard?

The Jaeger rev counter dominates the instrument panel. The gear lever is a silvery wand on the left-hand side. 'Remember the accelerator is in the middle and the brake is on the right.' The horrors of the central throttle have receded somewhat since I have been driving the 1928 Bramwell supercharged Stutz, which has the same footwork arrangement.

A more immediate problem was that the car had thrown a wheel-balance weight on the way over, which may not sound major in today's terms, but was as bad as a horse losing a shoe. 'It's better if you can drive through it,' said Gavin with the casual assurance of an owner-driver.

He also mentioned Roycroft's advice about the brakes: none at all when the car was cold, great for three laps, and then nothing for the rest of the race. The big finned drums looked reassuring. The twin round side mirrors looked tiny. If I had to hit the brakes, it would

THE BLUE FERRARI

throw the car left or right until they were warm. It did.

Let's face it, this was no normal test of a thoroughbred, more an unashamed loiter down memory lane wondering at the drivers and the dreams sighted through the aero screen down the length of the bonnet. Ascari, Gonzalez, Rosier, Roycroft — the latter pair as heroic as the former for accepting the challenge of what was then a state-of-the-art Grand Prix car. Think about borrowing a McLaren-Mercedes from an elderly Ron Dennis, 60 years from now.

Getting in: I am trying not to stand on the seat and Gavin is saying don't worry. Mind the gear lever. No suggestion of seat adjustment. What was good enough for Froilan, Alberto, Louis and Ron is going to be good enough for me. Short-armed. If you can't find low gear, play the clutch in and out. I'm haunted by Gavin's warnings about the cost of ham-fisting the transmission. It turns out to be simple. Well, fairly simple. The wheel shimmy is worse than Gavin suggested it might be, but easy to drive through and then it is bliss.

There can be nothing more satisfying than a well-crafted shift through a crash box, or should I say a shift that doesn't crash. We are not talking lap times or technical expertise here, more an unreal hands-on opportunity to enjoy a dream. The low-speed wheel shimmy is actually a flailing of racing Dunlops that threatens to rip the slim wood-rimmed wheel from your grasp, and then you are into a performance area that exceeds any preconceptions of what the car might be like.

The weather was what you always imagine it might be if someone was foolish enough to let you loose in a car reckoned to be worth £2–3 million if the market settled. The blue of the sky was almost an exact match for the blue of the bodywork. There are those who say that a car with the pedigree of this Ferrari should be repainted red and have the egg-crate grille restored, as when Gonzales created legend with it at Silverstone in 1951. Gavin believes that it should be in the shape and livery it was when Ron Roycroft was creating his local legends at Ardmore and leading the New Zealand Grand Prix that baking January day in 1957. As a Kiwi who watched history being made that day, I agree with him.

Gavin has seen the volcanic top of the collectors' market grow cool, but he wonders whether he might prefer offering his Ferrari in a deal that would include a D-type Jaguar or a 4.5 Blower Bentley — more usable on the road — plus cash to top up a £3-million package.

The few early-morning travellers around the bayside roads must have wondered at the sight of the big blue single-seater and the blast of the exhaust, but it was as much a thrill for me as for them, and one that was over too soon. Sunday mornings will never be the same again . . .

CHAPTER 10

ERNIE SPRAGUE

Ernie Sprague was my home-town hero in Timaru when I was fanning my first enthusiasms for motor racing while working in the ANZ bank, fostering an interst that would take me round the world for forty years as part of the professional Grand Prix 'circus'. This article was written for New Zealand Classic Car *in 2001.*

If Barry Crump had ever written a book on New Zealand motor racing in the 1950s, Ernie Sprague would have been the main character. No question. He characterised the period, the people and the cars. A hard case, certainly, but a racer and a winner. Rough and ready but a made-in-New Zealand legend. A Good Keen Kiwi Racing Bloke. He is probably best remembered for his wins in a variety of heavily modified Fords from the 1940s to the 1960s, but he also raced a 1930s P3 Alfa Romeo Grand Prix car and a 1940s 4CLT Maserati, putting these pedigree chargers onto circuits marked out in farmers' paddocks and up shingle hill climbs with twin rear wheels.

My mother bought Ernie Sprague's house in Kiwi Drive when we moved to Timaru in the early 1950s, but as a teenager yet to catch the racing bug, I had never heard of him. We had a large double garage and only one car, and there was a big, mysterious hole in the garage floor with heavy planks over it. This was Ernie's inspection pit, where he probably worked on a variety of Zephyrs before a race. By further coincidence, when the house was sold after my mother died, it was bought by Leo Leonard.

'I started racing in Timaru after going to Wigram in 1949, when Morrie Proctor won in the Riley,' says Ernie.

> I must have been about 20 and we used to go to motorcycle-club meetings in Timaru because they catered for some car events and they invited cars to a hill climb at Taiko. I remember Hec Green had a single-seater Wolseley Special he had made up out of an old police car. It had a Model T Ford back axle and he'd made up a tube front axle, and he got fastest time. Matthew Wills had his 500K supercharged Mercedes with twin side-mounted spares, and another local driver, Don Marra, raced an old Willys.
>
> We decided to form our own car club for racing, and in 1950 Les Collett and I went up to Christchurch to ask Pat Hoare how we should go about setting it up. Our first races were at Cantwells, south of Timaru, and we used to pay the farmer for the use of his paddock.

Ernie put an ad in the paper for a car he could use for racing and bought a 1930s Riley 1.5-litre, but it had a preselector gearbox and was really too heavy. 'I suppose I raced every car I owned. I had a late '20s Chrysler 77 roadster and then moved on to 1932 Ford V8s. I had three of those altogether. My favourite was the roadster. We built our own engines, fitted big pistons, twin carbs, stuff like that. We also fitted Chrysler hydraulic brakes.'

Gerald McKissock grew up in South Canterbury motor racing and became well known for his work as a clerk of the course at Timaru, Waimate and Dunedin events. He helped Sprague with car preparation, and at one flying-quarter sprint in the V8 roadster the two of them took turns to drive and McKissock pipped Ernie to break the 100 mph barrier, the first time this had been done in South Canterbury.

Ernie raced the V8 at Wigram but then moved on to a Mark 1 Zephyr and a brief dabble in 1956 with a single-seater V8 Special bought from Jack Tucker in Nelson. 'It had a supercharger, but we took that off and used twin carbs. Hec Green built the camshaft. We were pretty well up on Ford V8s by then.'

Ernie raced the Mark 1 Zephyr at Ryal Bush and decided he needed something faster, so in 1957 he paid £500 for the P3 Alfa Romeo that John MacMillan had raced at Ohakea and Wigram, buying the car between the Ryal Bush and Mairehau races. The P3 was one of the true classic designs in Grand Prix history, but in New Zealand in the '50s it was just an old racing car with no intrinsic value other than that it was an exciting car for local events. Today the car is worth millions.

The P3 was a 1934 works Grand Prix car (chassis no. C50006) raced by French ace Louis Chiron in his wins at Casablanca, Montlhery and Reims that summer and in the Lorraine Grand Prix in 1935. It was sold to English specialist Frank Ashby, who modified the engine and supercharger and fitted distinctive twin exhaust pipes that have helped to identify it ever since. It was brought to New Zealand by John MacMillan, who raced it extensively but unsuccessfully for four seasons, apart from a fourth place at Wigram in 1954. It was always the uncertainty of the pedigree power unit that let him down, scarcely surprising in a car still being raced hard 20 years on and far from specialist factory attention.

Ernie wasn't in the history business. He wanted something that was quick and cheap and that he could win with. The Alfa Romeo was *not* a car that he liked. 'It was all right,' he says in a dismissive way that leads you to believe there wasn't much right about it at all. 'It eventually dropped a valve. It had valves like a bloody Wolseley with screw-in tappets and they used to break off at the threads and the valve would drop down.' He had the P3 for one season and raced it in local hill climbs and at the Christchurch Mairehau circuit, and in 1957 he did a deal with Pat Hoare to buy his 4CLT Maserati. The deal included a Renault Dauphine and £500.

The P3 was sold to Bill Harris, who removed the broken Alfa motor and installed a Jaguar engine for beach and circuit racing in 1960, but he was killed in an air crash in the Kaikoura ranges. The Alfa *monoposto* was eventually bought by Leon Witte, who found another P3 engine to complete it. It passed through several owners internationally and is now in the collection of Bruce McCaw, who runs Kiwi Scott Dixon in his PacWest CART team. [Dixon now drives for Chip Ganassi's Team Target.]

The historic 4CLT did not rate much higher than the P3 in Ernie's estimation of how a racing car should work. The 1.5-litre 4-cylinder twin-overhead-camshaft engine had two-stage supercharging and was raced successfully by Reg Parnell in Britain and Europe between 1948 and 1951, when he blew the engine and sold the car to Johnny Lurani, who had it rebuilt and continued to race it. In 1955 it was brought to New Zealand by Pat Hoare.

'It gave continual supercharger problems,' says Ernie, wincing as he remembers his second stint with a European Grand Prix car. 'In 1958 we did Ardmore, Wigram, round the houses at Dunedin and Teretonga.' His best run was at Teretonga in 1957.

> I was actually lapping Pat [Hoare] in his Ferrari. One of our problems was that we didn't have the special Maserati tools that we needed, and we had special tools for the supercharger made up locally by Annett & Darling to stop the rotors from touching the supercharger casing, and it was going good. I was actually lapping Pat's Ferrari at Teretonga when I lost it and put it over the bloody bank.

Tyres were the big problem with the Alfa and the Maser. We couldn't get proper tyres and had to run ordinary Michelin steel radials. We were running on a shoestring all the time. In those days I was only a one-man band at the North Street [Timaru] garage — only myself and a couple of boys.

I swapped the Maser for a wood-over-ply speedboat and a Mark 7 Jag, and the Alfa I swapped for a '46 V8 coupé and a '42 V8 flat-bed truck, and we tossed for the transporter — 50 quid or nothing — and I won.

The old Grand Prix cars were replaced by a succession of Ford Zephyrs — Marks 1, 2 and 3 — all modified to the limit for the hectic saloon racing of the period. Those saloon-racing seasons were the stuff of legend, with Ernie racing his hot Zephyrs against Ray Archibald in the latest elegant Jaguar and Harold Heasley in his amazingly fast Ford Consul and then the Humber 80. You drove your car to the race, raced and drove home.

Sprague stories abound. I like the one in which Ernie is driving home with a friend on a long Sunday-night run back to Timaru after a race. He's driving fast — around 100 mph — when he sweeps past a parked patrol car. The way I heard the story, Ernie brakes to a halt round the first bend and says to his startled passenger, who's been dozing, 'You've always wanted a drive, haven't you? Have a go now.' His mate has only driven a mile when the patrol car comes up with the siren blaring and signals the Zephyr to stop. 'Wonder where he came from,' says Ernie, as his embarrassed mate waits for the cop to write the speeding ticket.

After the Mk 3 we decided to concentrate on long-distance racing. Between times I raced an Anglia. When we took over the Jaguar dealership, I raced a Jag. I co-drove with Ray Archibald at Pukekohe one year and broke a wheel. When I drove my own Jag in the next year's Benson & Hedges, I ran out of brakes and came second to Ray. We won the next race in the 3-litre Zodiac, and then when Brent Hawes was killed, I went into partnership with Leo Leonard and we co-owned the cars for all the rest of the races. We won the Benson & Hedges in a 3.3 Vauxhall in 1969 and again in 1970 with a Chrysler Valiant.

My final race was with the VJ Charger in 1973. My best race? The Charger win with Leo in 1970, I suppose. That was pretty good. My son, Gary, and I won the last Wills Six-Hour in the Zodiac Mk IV. I reckon it's the only time in the world that anyone won a long-distance race in one of those bloody Mark Fours.

Ernie says he never thinks about what might have been, how the modern value of the P3 Alfa and the 4CLT Maserati could have made him a millionaire. In his day, every driver sold what he had to buy something better. Old unreliable racing cars were just old unreliable racing cars. 'I never worry about what I have or could have had. Today is the day I live for.'

The Sprague racing dynasty continued as Gary carried on winning the Benson & Hedges long-distance races in 1975, 1977 and 1981, teamed with Leo Leonard, and now Peter Sprague, Ernie's *grand*son, races a Ford Telstar in South Island touring-car events.

CHAPTER 11

THE LYCOMING SPECIAL

Ralph Watson was a motor racing engineer ahead of his time, an original thinker and creator who combined his advanced ideas in the Lycoming Special, a New Zealand car that caused men like Lotus designer Colin Chapman and John Cooper to revise their ideas on how racing cars could be built. In 1977 I had the chance to drive the car that was part of our racing history.

Bruce McLaren raced it at Wigram and Jim Clark tried it at Teretonga, while Colin Chapman and John Cooper paid such close attention to the technical detail at the 1960 New Zealand Grand Prix that McLaren said he could see the influence of Ralph Watson's intuitive design for the Lycoming Special in later Lotuses.

The story started in 1954 in New Zealand, when Ralph reasoned that a flat-4 aircraft engine would be a suitable basis for a motor-racing special and then stumbled on a pair of 4.7-litre Lycoming engines being sold at scrap price because they were proving too unreliable for an aerial top-dressing company. With the 0-290 Lycoming aero engine as the nucleus, Ralph now cast about for the ideal car to build around it. As always he was practical.

> It was now time to decide on the most suitable type of car and estimate the performance and gear ratios required. To be able to run the car in competitions all over New Zealand meant shipping it to and from the South Island as economically as possible. This would be best achieved by driving the car everywhere, as a tow car and trailer would have raised the expenses considerably.
>
> I also firmly believed that driving many miles on the road was essential to sort out all the little problems and obtain reliability in competition; in fact, every drive, no matter where, should be regarded as a test. It would be much more fun to drive the car, too, than tow it. As tools, spares and some luggage would have to be carried, a two-seater that would also provide transport for a pit manager was by far the best choice. The width of the engine, at 33-inches, was also a point in favour of a two-seater.
>
> The choice between front or mid engine did not take long, as the front engine offered the best air cooling and when combined with a rear-mounted gearbox — the easiest drive arrangement to make — gave an approximately correct weight distribution. Also I had never driven a rear-engine car and felt it might be more difficult to handle.

You have to remember here that Ralph was formulating his new car on a clean sheet of paper with a very clear mind at a time when all serious racing cars had their engines in the front, and yet the New

Zealand engineer considered a rear engine.

Ralph's boyhood home was close to Nelson airport, at the top of the South Island, and he grew up with aviation as his consuming enthusiasm before his family moved to Auckland, where he bought a 1933 Singer Le Mans and went racing in local events. One special Ralph considered building would have used a pair of Triumph Thunderbird motorcycle engines, each driving one pair of wheels, the throttles being coupled to twin pedals so that the proportion of power front or back could be controlled by rocking the foot. Fortunately he found a 1931 BSA sports car and concentrated his development ideas on that, before beginning the Lycoming project.

The chassis for the Lycoming Special followed established practice, with a space frame based on two large tubes as used by Connaught, Aston-Martin and the prewar Mercedes.

'Because of doubts about the torsional stiffness of a space frame with large cockpit and engine openings, two 2.5-inch tubes were used as a base, these being about half the strength that would be needed without the help of the space frame.'

These big-bore chassis tubes doubled as air-cooling conduits to the inboard rear brakes and revealed an unexpected propensity when one of them ingested a sparrow on one road trip. Bath plugs were fitted thereafter for touring between races.

'The front cockpit bulkhead was made from panel steel and formed part of the structure. The top tubes from this bulkhead to the front suspension had to be placed so as to allow for the removal of cylinders and all other accessories without disturbing the crankcase.'

The gearbox was to be in unit with the differential, and a Ford V8 crown wheel and pinion gave a choice of several easy-to-change ratios, while a 1941 Studebaker gearbox was found, fitted with side controls which adapted handily to a remote gear-change lever. Ralph had worked on Ron Roycroft's 1931 supercharged Brooklands Austin 7, and later his Bugatti, as well as the P3 Alfa Romeo that Nuvolari had driven to defeat the German teams on the Nürburgring in the 1935 German Grand Prix and the 4.5-litre Ferrari that Gonzales had driven to give Enzo Ferrari his first Grand Prix victory, at Silverstone in 1951, so he was aware that there were perils in overcomplication.

'Perhaps a racing-car gearbox should have had an aluminium case, but I had more confidence in steel than cast aluminium, in which I had found many worn bearing housings and seen a few fractures.'

The engine was inverted in the chassis and a dry-sump lubrication system installed. Amal advised that they did not make carburettors large enough to feed the Lycoming thirst, so Ralph considered a modified large single Solex and even checked out a Rolls-Royce Merlin supercharger, but fuel injection seemed most suitable, so Ralph made up his own system.

> Most racing cars with large-bore carburettors or injection systems ran rather roughly at low speeds, with the power coming in suddenly later. To me, this was intolerable on a large motor — it just had to run smoothly all the way from idle to maximum rpm. To achieve this, it was decided that the injection should take place where the air velocity was always high, like the edge of the throttle valve, and that the nozzle should always provide a spray, and not dribble at low rates of flow.

The dual magnetos that sparked the twin-plug head in aero form were replaced by a single distributor.

The uneven beat of the Lycoming was a distinctive feature, a clatter on idle that blended into a roar under power and simply hurled the lightweight polished aluminium two-seater forward. Ralph described the noise well: 'With the motor lightly loaded, the piston slap was always there, increasing on the throttle and sounding like a team of panel beaters working in rhythm.'

Ralph drew up a chart of figures to compare the Lycoming's weight-to-power ratio with that of contemporary competition engines in 1954. The Lycoming engine weighed 1472 pounds, the D-Type Jaguar engine 2200 pounds, the Cooper-Bristol unit 1400 pounds, the 250F Maserati engine 1810 pounds and the 1930s P3 Alfa Romeo straight-8 1980 pounds. For horsepower per ton, the Lycoming, on its most highly tuned form of 210 bhp, scored 313, equal with the Formula Two Cooper and just short of the Maserati's 322. Ralph had read that the weight distribution of the 250F Maserati, then the class of the field, varied between 52 and 61 per cent according to whether the fuel tank was empty or full, so the optimum figure for the Lycoming was reckoned to be 60 per cent. When the special had been completed, weight distribution was found to vary between 56 per cent empty and 59 per cent full.

Ralph adapted Morris Minor steering and used a Borg and Beck clutch assembly from an Austin Princess. Suspension was de Dion type with Pegaso radius arms at the rear. Drum brakes were fitted, outboard front and inboard rear. When Bruce McLaren raced the car at Wigram after the Coventry Climax engine in his Cooper had destroyed itself on race morning, he found that the drum brakes were the old special's major limitation, and he subsequently sent a set of disc brakes as a thank you for the loan of the car.

In December 1956 Ralph clocked 14.4 seconds in a standing quarter-mile sprint and realised that his racing special had the hoped-for performance potential. In the 1957 New Zealand Grand Prix at Ardmore in January, he finished seventh against an international field, and he raced, sprinted and hill-climbed the car for the rest of the season. He was tenth in the 1958 Grand Prix and tenth at Wigram, and then arranged for Bob Gibbons to do the racing while he enjoyed reaching his limits in sprints and hill climbs.

In November 1959 the car was sold to Auckland engineering student Malcolm Gill, a serious, bespectacled young man. Gill reckoned he could cover his costs, and perhaps even make a profit, by racing the car with mudguards in the sports-car races, then stripping the guards to drive it in the main events as an 'open wheeler'.

At Wigram, on the fast open airfield circuit near Christchurch in January 1960, Gill was delighted to offer the Lycoming to his hero, McLaren, when the engine of McLaren's Cooper failed on race morning. At last here was the chance that Ralph had probably never dared dream of: a Grand Prix driver was at the wheel of the very special car he had designed and built.

After a few practice laps on Michelins, McLaren asked to have the racing Dunlops from his Cooper fitted, and he was ready for the race. McLaren had been weaned on rear-engined cars but he soon became accustomed to the front-engined special, despite a broken rev counter, and moved up to fourth behind the overseas drivers. The brake linings had completely gone by the closing laps and McLaren, now confident with the handling, was throwing the car sideways into the corners to scrub off pace. In his book, *From the Cockpit*, he wrote:

> It says a lot for the Lycoming that Brabham, Burgess and Piper were gaining only slightly on each lap. To be sitting bolt upright near the back wheels with the engine in the front was a novel change from the Coopers and an interesting experience. It was necessary to change gear only a couple of times on each lap. The immense torque of the flat-four engine from 1000 to just under 3000 rpm had to be sampled to be believed.

Brabham was in a 2.5-litre T51 Cooper-Climax, Ian Burgess had a similar chassis but with a 2.2-litre Climax engine, and David Piper had a front-engined Lotus 16 with a 2.5-litre Climax.

Gill won the national sports car championship in 1960 and 1961, beating Angus Hyslop in his D-Type Jaguar in both seasons. In 1962 he sold the Lycoming to motorcycle racer Forest Carden, who passed it on to Jim Boyd in 1964, who ran strongly in the national sports-car championship, winning it in 1966 and winning the New Zealand Hill-climb Championship in 1965, 1966 and 1967. It was Boyd who let Jim Clark do a few laps round Teretonga, the world's southernmost race circuit. Clark loved it.

As an aspiring young motor-racing writer in 1960, I had ridden in the passenger seat of the Lycoming around Teretonga with Malcolm Gill and been vastly impressed. I certainly hadn't foreseen that I would drive it myself 17 years later, when new owner Ralph Smith, who had bought the gallant old car in bits and totally restored it, brought it to the Timaru circuit for me to try.

In 1977 I wrote:

> The clatter of the engine startled after the passage of years. I had entertained thoughts of one day buying the Lycoming and preserving it as part of New Zealand's racing heritage, perhaps shipping it to Britain for a season of historic racing with, say, Denny Hulme at the

helm. A few laps of the Timaru track were enough to dampen my ardour. This was a serious car, not to be trifled with by a romancer. The torque of the aero engine in the lightweight silver car made it attain instant speed rather than accelerate in the accepted manner. Low gear was for lift-off, second handled the slower bits and third/top looked after the rest of the circuit. Keep the revs down to 3500, they said. Forty-three mph per 1000 rpm: steam locomotive stuff. Watson used 3800 rpm as his 'owner's limit' and 4100 in short sprints. I was bothered by what seemed to be clutch slip on the straight. Watson wondered whether it might have been wheel-spin. I said I wasn't *that* enthusiastic.

CHAPTER 12

THE STANTON CROP-DUSTER

The Stanton Special wrote its own chapter in our racing history, powered by an aero engine and driven by its intrepid creator, diffident engineer Maurice Stanton, who raced it on open airfield circuits like Wigram, thundered up narrow shingle hill climbs and sped down high-speed sprint record runs on country roads, clinching the New Zealand land speed record at the time. I drove it at Ruapuna and reported the experience later for New Zealand Classic Car.

The four big finned pots stood high in the middle of the chassis, four stub exhausts aiming skywards. The cockpit of the Stanton Special looked like a hatch and was almost between the front wheels. I climbed in, noting the sturdy tubular chassis girders. As my knees settled somewhere under my chin, I appreciated that Morrie Stanton was somewhat shorter than I was. And a good deal braver. But this is to get ahead of the story of one of the most gallant specials built in New Zealand to chase records.

The price dictated the choice of engine when Morrie and Charlie Stanton were planning to build the car that would dominate attempts on the New Zealand land speed record for a couple of generations. Morrie was an aircraft engineer, and he read in 1947 that Tiger Moth engines were being sold as surplus for £25. The brothers hedged their bets and bought a pair of used engines for £12 apiece as well as a new one, with the intention of testing one of the used engines to destruction, fitting the new one for record breaking and racing, and using the third as a spare. They never did manage to destroy the first engine, and it powers the car to this day.

The idea of a chain-driven land-speed-record car certainly hadn't been buried with the wreckage of Parry Thomas's 'Babs' on Pendine Sands back in 1927, and by a twist of coincidence the New Zealand speed record of 173.8 mph set by the aero-engined chain-driven Stanton Special was almost identical to the record of 174.223 mph that Thomas had been chasing across the beach in Wales 31 years previously.

The simplicity of the construction of the Stanton Special was as staggering as the risks Morrie took when he set the record hurtling down an 18-foot-wide country road between barbed-wire fences near Christchurch on a blustery November morning in 1958. His time for the flying kilometre was 173.8 mph. He thought he might have been able to hit 185 mph but for the gusts of wind that shifted the streamlined special across to the shingle verges. Drive down Tram Road today and you can't help but whistle in admiration at Stanton's sheer bravery and lack of imagination.

I drove the Stanton Special at Ruapuna several years ago, but to appreciate my impressions of the drive you must first linger on the colourful history of the car.

The Stanton brothers, Charles (the older of the two) and Maurice — always Charlie and Morrie — started motor racing with a BSA three-wheeler which they had converted to a four-wheeler using Austin 7 parts. The price of the surplus Tiger Moth engine appealed, while the engine itself was an ideal basis for a special. The 4-cylinder air-cooled 6124 cc engine was light at 136 kilograms, it required none of the plumbing needed by a water-cooled engine, and the torque of the big four with its lazy 130 bhp at 2200 rpm approached steam-locomotive standards.

Since the shattering torque was unlikely to need a box full of gears, the Stanton Special was supplied with two cogs which sat out on view either side of a locked differential unit borrowed from a vintage Ansaldo sitting in the yard. The Ansaldo was further cannibalised to provide big finned front brake drums when the tiny seven-inch Morris Minor brakes originally fitted proved totally unsuited to the performance in the 1954 New Zealand Grand Prix. Ford Zephyr brakes were fitted at the rear.

The transmission was simple, operated by a 2-speed dog-clutch arrangement. When the gear lever was pushed forward, the small cog was picked up for low gear. When the lever was pulled backwards, the selector moved across inside the differential housing to take up the drive on the large cog for high gear. The cogs could be changed according to gearing requirements for record runs, hill climbs or circuit racing.

'We rather miscalculated the torque for our first runs,' recalls Charlie. 'It would do 138 mph in low — but the acceleration wasn't very startling!' The engine was eventually geared to give 63.5 mph per 1000 rpm, giving a theoretical maximum of 200 mph.

The engine was turned upside down and back to front, and the propeller pick-up used to attach a clutch from a Ford V8 truck with Commer truck clutch springs. In the engine the base of the cylinder barrels were machined to raise the compression ratio from 5.25:1 to 6:1, and slots were machined in the tappet guides enabling oil mist to rise up the pushrod cover tubes to lubricate the valve gear. Two unions were placed in the bottom of the sump (originally the top cover) and these drained into a tank beneath the engine.

Morris Minor torsion bars were used for the front suspension, and the Freikaiserwagen system, with pivoted quarter-elliptic springs, was used for the rear. Chain-sprocket steering was adopted, as this was found to have no play and the further advantage that the ratio could be varied for different types of event. Ford Prefect disc wheels were used. All-up weight, without the record-run ballast, was 545 kilograms.

The brothers entered the car for the first major international Grand Prix at Ardmore, in 1954, but retired when lying seventh.

On its first record attempts that year, the big 'Crop-duster' covered the flying quarter-mile at 128.57 mph and the standing quarter in 13.96 seconds. But these performances didn't satisfy the Stantons, and they wrote to England to ask the Arnott company if they would build them a special supercharger to give the engine a boost of 12 pounds. With this big bespoke blower chain-driven behind the engine and using four Amal carburettors, power soared by 100 per cent to a still modest 300 bhp. The brothers fitted 145 pounds of lead ballast in the nose and Morrie brought his flying quarter speed up to 154 mph and the standing quarter time down to 12.96 seconds.

The rustic shape of the special, which somewhat resembled its parent Tiger Moth with the flying machine's wings plucked off, didn't exactly lend itself to aerodynamic efficiency for record runs, so a special fibreglass streamlined body was made up from a basic Mistral sports-car shell fabricated by Christchurch Mistral agent Bob Blackburn. The Stanton brothers adapted it by moulding in a tail fin. Big-bore hoses carried cool air from the nose slot to, on one side, a giant vacuum-cleaner nozzle aimed at the cylinder barrels, and, on the other, the blower. In this form the special, again with Morrie at the wheel, flashed down Tram Road to set records that stood until Ray Williams bettered them on 16 March 1996, setting a record speed of 316.929 kph in a Porsche 930 Turbo.

With the streamlined body removed, Morrie campaigned the car successfully in hill climbs, scooping local honours with the big special locked in bottom gear. I remember it spraying shingle as it climbed Clelland's Hill, setting new records, in 1958. This was my local event, near Timaru — a 0.7-mile climb and perilously narrow. The entry list included Ron Roycroft in his famous 4.5-litre V12 Grand Prix Ferrari, the car reckoned to have been driven by Froilan Gonzales when he took the chequer at Silverstone in 1951 to win the first Grand Prix for Ferrari. A young guy called Bruce McLaren was also entered, in a 1750 cc Cooper, with his father, Les, in attendance. McLaren had filled the differential with plumber's lead, but this proved *too* effective and he broke a half-shaft. He clobbered a bank on another run and finished up third on 55.3 seconds.

A measure of the Stanton Special's performance and Morrie's courage and skill was provided by the car's new course record of 53.9 seconds. Dick Campbell was second fastest in a Cooper 500 on 54.9 seconds, and Roycroft tied with Duncan Rutherford's Lycoming Special (not be confused with Ralph Watson's Auckland-based Lycoming) for fourth place on 55.8 seconds. Ernie Sprague was sixth in his 4CLT Maserati on 56.3 seconds, David Young's XK120 Jaguar was seventh on 56.6 seconds and Pat Hoare's 3-litre Ferrari eighth on 59.6 seconds.

On a small matter of historical accuracy, I see that Class G (751–1100 cc) was won by Dunedin driver G. Ashton in an Anzani Special in 62.3 seconds, ahead of a certain E. Young in an Austin A30 on 82.9 seconds. I have it fixed in my mind that Ashton never turned up and that I therefore won my class, which was more than 'B. McLaren' managed to do. History has proved me wrong, but at least I was still second in my class while Bruce was only third in his. (You may have guessed that there were only two entries in Class G . . .)

Nobody seemed to want an ageing aero-engined special, so the Stanton brothers sold their historic creation for a mere £150 to gain garage space. New owner Charlie Bensemann did a few hill climbs and sprints in 1963, and then sold the vehicle for a handsome profit at £300 — still an incredible bargain in modern terms — to Christchurch enthusiast Warner Mauger, who appreciated the qualities and historic pedigree of the old charger.

Ten years and two owners had seen the special shorn of its supercharger, which meant it had nothing like the brute urge with which it had started out. The supercharger had been replaced by a giant jug-shaped appendage of a carburettor made by Arnott. The

Duplex chains and whirring sprockets at the back had been hidden from view by a shapely tail. These things are relative.

The Stanton Special arrived at Ruapuna, as befitted its new-found classic glory, on a trailer behind a magnificent 1924 23/60 Vauxhall. I was to drive this historic car that had totally dominated speed events. Bernd Rosemeyer must have felt something like this when he first climbed into the cockpit of the Grand Prix Auto Union in the 1930s. Both cars had the engines in the back. Both of us sat almost up between the front wheels. Both of us were going into the unknown but Rosemeyer would do it rather more purposefully than I.

To the left of the instrument panel was a vintage oil-pressure gauge and dead ahead a rev counter that read up to a stupefying 3000 rpm. There was no screen. The big wood-rimmed wheel dominated the cockpit. On the left was the spark lever ('Push it forward when the engine starts') and the push-pull gear lever. Two speeds: fast and bloody fast. The two mirrors gazed aimlessly about. I could almost reach out and touch the R3 Dunlops on the front wheels. On the rear were a pair of Dunlop racing covers that had been retreaded. 'All in the valley of Death rode the six hundred . . .'

Warner Mauger started the big engine with the aid of a pair of plug-in 12-volt batteries on a trolley. The chuntering chug could have come from swinging the prop on a First World War fighter. We were in business. Warner said the clutch was a bit heavy. He wasn't kidding. I jammed the gear lever forward, there was a juddering *clunk* and nobody moved. I flicked the switches off, thinking that even if the crankshaft had broken there was a brand-new engine lying about somewhere that had only cost £25. A snake lay on the track behind me. Not a snake but a snapped chain — all 9600 pounds of Duplex breaking strain.

'Never mind, just run it in top,' counselled Warner as he unthreaded what was left of the chain on the small cog. I climbed back in, Warner swung the prop, the big four fired and I was in business again. It didn't so much accelerate as charge down the road with a rumbling chugchugchugchugchug. Warner had said that the hairpin at the end of the straight might be difficult in top gear with the locked rear end. It was. I tried to remember the wording on my insurance policy as I charged the bank in full screaming understeer. I was also trying to remind my right foot that the pedal in the middle it was mashing in an attempt to stop was in fact the accelerator. Young Moss had the same sort of trouble in his first Maserati. Happens to the best of us.

In a magnificent shingle-showering save, I thundered back on to the road, checked to make sure that there was a wheel on each corner, slipped the clutch, and charged on. At the end of the next straight I had cause momentarily to ruminate on whether the vintage Ansaldo drums were really up to the job. The front wheels pattered a bit. That unblown engine somewhere back there might only be giving 130 bhp, but it was a punchy sort of power if you tried booting it through the long loop. There was a fine handling margin between 'Oh boy!' as I brilliantly executed a semi-drifting tail-out run between the Ss, and 'Omigod!' every second lap as I lunged off the road on the hairpin — every second lap because on the one following I would take it carefully and negotiate the turn perfectly, only to apply more pace next time round.

With the rev counter needle hovering around 2500 on the straight, the special was a mighty sight to behold. Like a galleon straining under full sail. The stub exhausts testified to oiling problems somewhere in the internals, puffing up a haze each time I accelerated, providing photographic testimony that I was trying.

With my regular run-off at the hairpin and loss of faith in the Ansaldo brakes at the end of both straights, I was still managing to lap in 61 seconds, which, compared with Warner's best of 56 seconds that morning with the full complement of two gears and more intimate knowledge of his pet's habits, I thought was fairly pleasing. Rosemeyer would probably have been faster than Warner.

I know now what was running through Count Zborowski's mind as he bellowed out on to the concrete bowl at Brooklands with the first of his monster specials fitted with a big First World War aeroplane engine. He'd probably prayed for rain the night before like I had, so that he could excuse himself from the test run, but since it was fine he'd buried his fears and climbed into the cockpit, making a mental note to drown his butterflies in cognac if he managed to complete those first test laps unscathed.

CHAPTER 13

BILL HAMILTON

Bill Hamilton was not only the inventor of the jet-boat propulsion system, but also part of New Zealand's early racing history. He drove Sunbeams in the 1920s and in 1930 raced a Bentley to a record three wins in one day at Brooklands. I interviewed him for this feature that ran in Autocar *in the UK in 1974.*

There are no Irishmen at Irishman Creek, the 23,000-acre sheep station tucked below Mount Cook. The mountain is framed in the homestead's front-room window, and a more blissfully unlikely place for a piece of New Zealand motor-racing history to have its beginnings is hard to imagine. The sheep station took its name from matagouri, or 'wild Irishman', the spiky thorn bush that grows along the rocky riverbeds and over the scrub-covered tussock-land that makes up the McKenzie Country, in the South Island. Now it has a mailbox on the main road. Then it was home to New Zealand's first successful overseas racing driver — C.W.F. (Bill) Hamilton — who would also become the father of the jet-boat.

Charles William Fielden Hamilton was 23 when, in 1923, he took a break from the sheep station and visited England for the first time. In those days such a trip was a change of life more than the 'big OE' that modern young Kiwis regard as their heritage. The journey by ship would have taken two months, and what colonials regarded faithfully as 'Home' was quite unlike their home in New Zealand. It seems odd that Bill should have crossed the world to meet his bride-to-be, Peggy Wills, when she lived on another back-country station as one of his distant neighbours. On that same trip Bill bought one of the 1914 Sunbeam Tourist Trophy factory racing cars. There is still some doubt as to precisely which of the works cars Bill actually bought. In later years, Andy Anderson had the remains of the car to restore and he understood it to be chassis no. IOM 2 (in Sunbeam factory parlance) — Algernon Lee Guinness's car, which broke down late in the long race — but as the restoration went on, he began to have suspicions that, mainly because of the number of past repairs to the crankcase, it could have been IOM 3 — Dario Resta's car, which rattled to a halt when a big-end bolt broke at Ramsey, halfway round the opening lap.

The matter is further confused by a later owner, one John Farnsworth, who, in a letter to *Autocar* in 1942, mentions the car as 'winner of the 1914 TT, Sunbeam no. IOM 4'. In fact, Lee Guinness's winning car is listed in Richard Hough's book, *Tourist Trophy*, as IOM 1, so IOM 4 was presumably a spare training car.

I lunched with Bill and Peggy at Irishman Creek Station back in

1974, and we talked about Brooklands and Muriwai Beach as though they were only a few yesterdays before.

For a back-country farmer, Bill showed a remarkable bent for engineering. He had owned a Darracq in New Zealand, and a four-seater Bugatti that he had bought in England on that first trip, but he regarded the latter as 'a bit of a washout and I got rid of it'. He bought the famous old TT Sunbeam for £500, and it was the first racing car he had driven.

New Zealand's racing history proper began on Muriwai Beach (Bruce McLaren named his home in Surrey 'Muriwai') when Howard Nattrass won the inaugural 25-mile New Zealand Motor Cup race against the clock, with competitors starting at intervals, in a stripped touring Cadillac. The races were run at low tide, when the sand was damp and firmly packed. In 1922 the distance was doubled, and Selwyn Craig won in a Packard. The 1923 cup was won by an Australian, C.F. Sanderson, in a 30/98 Vauxhall. With a grid start for the first time in 1924, Nattrass scored his second win, this time with a 4-cylinder American racing Mercer.

Bill prepared the Sunbeam with assistance from Stan Jones, a garage proprietor in the small South Canterbury village of Fairlie, using a long testing run along a dusty shingle road from Irishman Creek Station.

I grew up in Cave, an even smaller country village, 20 miles towards Timaru from Fairlie, and I find it hard to imagine that these top-line old racing cars were prepared with Stan's legendary expertise in a garage where tractors were still regarded as newfangled. Stan also tended Andy Irving's Brescia Bugatti and the 1922 TT Sunbeam of Peggy Hamilton's brother, Matthew Wills. Those long, rolling ribbons of McKenzie Country tarmac are today simply routes for endless tourist buses or access to the ski fields. Think of Bill driving his Sunbeam down to Fairlie in a cloud of dust for a check-up before driving a further 700 miles over rutted shingle roads to Auckland and beyond, to the beach at Muriwai, for his first race. The car was still in its Isle of Man TT trim, with the large round bolster fuel tank behind the driver.

From the rolling start, the Vauxhall raced by Australian Hope

Bartlett (uncle of Frank Gardner, who would carry on the family racing tradition — and still does, with his facility on the Gold Coast) pulled ahead of the Hamilton Sunbeam, but as the cars streamed down the long beach on the straight six-and-a-quarter-mile there-and-back two-hairpin course, Bill led Bartlett by 100 yards from two Fords, a Brescia Bugatti and a Stutz. Bill held his lead to the end of the 50-mile race, winning by 38 seconds at an average speed of 72.5 mph.

The rising tide forced postponement of an attempt on the Australasian five-mile beach record, but with a clear run the following day Bill and Bartlett brought their cars out again, and it was Bill who took the record at 100.27 mph in the Sunbeam.

Encouraged by his success with the car, Bill and Jones went to work to fit a smaller tank, since the shorter New Zealand races did not require TT tankage, and made up a pointed tail not unlike that of the 1922 Grand Prix Sunbeams.

Back at Muriwai in 1926, Bill ran third with the Sunbeam behind Bob Wilson's 1915 Indianapolis Stutz and Matthew Wills driving a 1922 3-litre 8-cylinder TT Sunbeam. Bill led the first 30 miles, but slowed when a crankshaft bearing collapsed.

Bill led the 1927 cup race in the Sunbeam at half distance, but dropped out with a broken oil pipe. In 1928 he was back to challenge Wilson's Stutz, but took the flag in second place, 34 seconds behind the American car.

Bill also raced on South Island beaches, at Oreti, near Invercargill (taking the national record for the flying mile at 109.09 mph in 1928), and at Waikaouaiti, but he was now spending more time on the station and the Sunbeam was eventually used as a road car. 'It was the only car we had for a long time,' Peggy recalled over lunch. Mind-boggling in the new century? The equivalent of racing a GT40 and then using it as your road car because you don't have anything else about the place.

In 1930 Bill and Peggy went to England again, this time buying a 1929 Vanden Bentley 4.5-litre to take back to New Zealand, but a chance meeting with Malcolm Campbell delayed their return trip and resulted in Bill racing the Bentley into the record books at Brooklands.

C.W.F. Hamilton, OBE, was 74 when he was talking about the long-ago conversation with the crusty fastest man in the world that would see him take the Bentley to Brooklands to prove a personal point. Bill was no respecter of reputations if he chose to disagree with a man's opinion. 'He saw that I had the Bentley and when I suggested that with a bit of tuning I could make it do 100 mph he just laughed and rather belittled the idea. I decided I would have to do something about this bloke, so I went to work on the Bentley and entered for the next meeting at Brooklands.'

The 30-year-old New Zealand farmer checked with Bentley Motors for advice on setting the car up for racing. 'They told me I should use castor oil in the engine. I suggested that perhaps I should dismantle the engine and clean it out completely before filling it with castor oil in place of the regular mineral oil I'd been using, but the Bentley men said it was OK to drain one and top up with the other. The engine blew up on my first practice run.'

Back at Bentley Motors the gentlemanly thing was done and Bill was provided with another engine — not a special racing engine, he stressed, but a 4.5 that had been used in a race before — and facilities in the service department to install and prepare it for the Easter meeting. For Bill to participate, the Hamiltons had to postpone their return home for a month, but there was a matter of honour at stake and Bill was determined to top the ton with his touring car.

Was it a case of a long-odds colonial taking the handicappers by surprise? Bill would like to think there was a little more to it than that. He won the handicap race for Bentleys in racing trim lapping at 103.11 mph, a point he hoped Malcolm Campbell had noted. Getting into his stride, he won the Bedford Long Handicap averaging 100.99 mph with a best lap of 107.8 mph, and in spite of a 20-second 'rehandicap' he also won the next race, the Sussex Long Handicap, with a best lap of 106.42 mph.

Bill Hamilton became the *only* driver to win three races in one day at Brooklands with the same car. I checked with Bill Boddy as I was penning these words in the new millennium, and he confirmed that this was indeed the case. He thought that Parry Thomas may have won three races on the same day before but used three different cars to do it. So Bill Hamilton holds that Brooklands record in perpetuity. He also proved a point to a famous land-speed-record breaker.

Delaying the long trip home had all been worthwhile. Malcolm Campbell's supercharged 2.3-litre Bugatti was third in Hamilton's hat-trick race.

After lunch at Irishman Creek that day in 1974, the Hamiltons brought out the three impressive half-gallon silver tankards Bill had been presented with at Brooklands. Obviously the race organisers had not envisaged *one* driver winning three of those hefty identical trophies.

Bill never raced again after that day of triumph on the Surrey speed bowl, a fact that puzzled the New Zealand press, who expected big things of him when he returned home. When Norman 'Wizard' Smith failed in his attempt at the land speed record on Ninety Mile Beach in 1932, one of the newspapers suggested Bill drive the 'Enterprise', with its 1450 bhp Napier Lion, instead of the Australian. Bill ignored the suggestion. 'I doubt if I could have driven it anyway. You've got to specialise in that sort of thing and it certainly wasn't my speciality.'

Bill had his mind on other, more practical, projects as befitted a farmer with a remote sheep station to run. He had built and installed his own hydroelectricity plant to provide power for his home and workshop. To construct the dam to form the lake he had also designed and made special earth-moving scoops. When the Depression of the 1930s put New Zealand farmers on the breadline, he was saved by his diversification into heavy engineering in the small factory that had grown up around his workshop at Irishman Creek. During the Second World War, he switched production to munitions. In 1943 he designed and built a loader-dozer, which was later manufactured under licence in Britain and Canada.

After the war Bill expanded into a new factory in Christchurch, which mushroomed in size and produced, among other things, the Hamilton marine jet, which the farmer-turned-engineer perfected to sell under licence to a worldwide market. The first Hamilton jet-boat was sold in 1955, and in 1960 a team of Hamilton jet-boats headed by Bill's son, Jon, made a 350-mile run down the Colorado River through the Grand Canyon before turning to make the gruelling nine-day run back up the river. It was the first time the Colorado had been conquered upstream as well as down. Sales soared.

* * *

If the Hamilton Sunbeam's racing days had ended in 1928, the car continued to weave a story around itself. In 1940 it was sold to John Farnsworth, who put it into touring trim with a hood, side curtains, dynamo headlights and other creature comforts. In a letter to *Autocar* in 1942, Farnsworth noted:

> Maximum speed in full touring trim was just about 100 mph, this corresponding to 3100 rpm. Third gear gave 65 and second about 40 mph. Road holding was superb, aided by the marked crab-track, and suspension was harsh in the *pur sang* manner. The standing quarter mile could be covered in a fraction under 20 seconds. The safe rev limit was 3300. This was with h.c. alloy pistons; with the original steel pistons the rev limit was 2800. Running around town I regularly obtained 22 mpg on a 50–50 petrol–benzole mixture.

Farnsworth was a flying instructor, but since flying instructors had other things to do in 1940 he was forced to sell the car. It went to Andy McIntosh, who ran a car-wrecking business in Invercargill and had seen Bill Hamilton competing with the car at Oreti. It was not McIntosh's intention that the famous old Sunbeam should join the wrecks in his yard, for he appreciated the car's character, even if it was heavily disguised by this time, having owned a Brescia Bugatti and a Horstman that had run in the 200 Miles race at Brooklands.

It was during a demonstration of the Sunbeam engine in his garage to a friend that McIntosh revved the motor once too often and with a clattering thud a rod came through the side. At that point the Sunbeam did join the wrecks in the yard outside. The axles were sold as trailer sets and the chassis rails were cut up for fence posts. It was some months before word reached Bill that his old Sunbeam was being broken up, and he despatched his nephew in some haste to buy back what parts of it remained.

The next chapter in the Sunbeam saga took place when a vintage rally stopped overnight at Irishman Creek in 1954 and the after-dinner conversation turned to the old car and its fate. Bill mentioned that its remains lay in one of his sheds, and after further discussion agreed that, if the Vintage Car Club (VCC) would undertake to restore it, they were welcome to the parts. A 40/50 Napier jolted down the narrow track from Irishman Creek to the main road that afternoon, loaded down with Sunbeam parts that included a well-ventilated crankcase, the gearbox and chassis subframe, three connecting rods and Bill Hamilton's blessing.

For four years the committee formed to restore the car discussed restoring it, and in 1958 Andy and Mollie Anderson decided to buy the parts from the VCC before they became relics and rebuild the car themselves. The search for the parts lost for 15 years or more then began, with amazingly successful results. In 1962 the front axle was found under a trailer on a farm near Invercargill. Three years later the rear axle was discovered on a lime spreader near Bluff. The original bonnet sides turned up in Invercargill. The round bolster tank Bill and mechanic Stan Jones had removed when building the pointed tail for the 1926 New Zealand Motor Cup was found at Irishman Creek, where Bill was using it as a fuel tank for a stand-by engine in his workshop. The original carburettor was also discovered. Farnsworth had experimented first with the original Claudel Hobson, then twin Acmes, then a single Zenith and finally a single Smith-Bentley from a 1925 3-litre, which gave the best results for touring.

One problem was that the Andersons were unable to get measurements for the original chassis, but these fell into their lap rather unexpectedly after another vintage rally to Irishman Creek. A club member sleeping off the effects of the night before in one of the farm buildings awoke blearily and studied the rafters in an effort to work out where he was and why. To his amazement he saw what appeared to be body sections of a vintage car. They were the side panels for enclosing the bolster tank that had been removed. The 1926 tail had been replaced by the crude touring body in the 1930s, and the sections for this clearly showed the chassis mounting points. From them the Andersons were able to work out the measurements of the chassis, which was in fact an almost standard 12/16 touring Sunbeam chassis, and one of these was located in Auckland to hasten the TT rebuild.

The 3-litre engine was another problem because the patched crankcase had been ruined by the McIntosh blow-up, so it was decided to invest £1,500 in having a new crankcase cast. A fourth connecting rod was carved from a solid billet, and the lightweight 8-to-1 pistons that Hamilton had fitted (in place of the drilled steel pistons from the factory) were replaced by modern 7-to-1 pistons. Brian Middlemass handled the rebuild of the engine while the Andersons pressed on with the rest of the assembly.

One of the first trips for the famous works Sunbeam will certainly be the run from Fairlie along the road across Ashwick Flat — now tar sealed — to Irishman Creek Station, where the New Zealand part of the TT Sunbeam saga started 50 years ago.

Postscript

The consensus from owners and past owners of the TT cars is that three of the four 1914 vehicles were fitted with 4.5-litre engines for the French Grand Prix at Lyon that year, and subsequently shipped to America to race there in 1915. At least two ran at Indianapolis in 1916 fitted with 4.9-litre 6-cylinder engines and larger, stronger gearboxes and differentials to handle the extra power. The empty and outdated 1914 chassis were then refitted with the original 1914 4-cylinder Peugeot-copy 3.3-litre engines and offered for sale through dealers. This accounts for the heavier differential and longer subframe on the cars owned by Neil Corner and Sir Francis Samuelson, and helps to explain why the 'scrambling' of the cars in 1922 has reduced the chance of historians establishing which was the actual winner of the 1914 TT to nearly zero. We know that the Samuelson car had IOM 1 engraved above the Sunbeam badge on the radiator, but this only proves that Sir Francis owned the winning radiator, not the complete car. Andy Anderson sent me a rubbing to prove that his radiator is IOM 2, and the engine in his car has been rebuilt from the original IOM 2. Neil Corner told me that his engine number is IOM 4, but according to the log book the chassis is IOM 2.

CHAPTER *14*

THE INDY STUTZ

The 1915 Indianapolis Stutz was one of the most important early racing cars to compete in New Zealand. Fortunately for us, Len Southward had the foresight to rescue the famous old car from dereliction, restore it, and now exhibits it in his magnificent motor museum at Paraparaumu.

Harry Stutz went to a lot of trouble building three new cars for the 1915 Indianapolis 500 and didn't win. He was out to beat the Europeans with a 4-cylinder 16-valve engine that owed much to the top-end design of the 1914 Mercedes and the bottom end of a 1913 Peugeot. A Stutz started the race from pole position, but it was ironic that after 500 miles and 5½ hours the finishing order was Mercedes, Peugeot, Stutz.

The Stutz that Gil Anderson drove to third place in 1915 raced in the United States for five years and then took on a new lease of life in New Zealand, racing on beaches and speedways until it was finally pensioned off in 1933 after becoming established as the most successful racing car in the country. Following a series of owners and a period on a farm towing a hay rake at harvest time, the venerable old Stutz was rescued and has been restored to its former glory to take pride of place in the Southward Museum at Paraparaumu, north of Wellington.

The Southward collection includes an 8CLT Maserati built for Indianapolis but never raced there, the 250F Maserati that a teenage Chris Amon raced in shirtsleeves, the Monza Ferrari that somersaulted and threw Ken Wharton to his death at Ardmore in 1957, and the 1929 38/250 SS supercharged Mercedes once raced by Lex Davison in Australia. In all, Southward must have 200 cars in various states of restoration in his fascinating museum.

Jules Goux won the 1913 Indianapolis 500 in a Peugeot, and Rene Thomas won the 1914 race in a Delage. This was definitely not good for the American car-makers, who after all had promoted the race as an exciting shop window for home produce, so in 1915 it was decided to drop the capacity limit from 7.3 litres to 4.9 litres. Harry Stutz started work as soon as the new regulations were posted. He was an innovator but also smart enough to copy successful ideas where they could be incorporated in his own overall design, rather than copying for the sake of copying. Thus his new cars for the 500 featured the Stutz combined differential and gearbox as a refinement of the transaxle he had designed back in 1910. His 16-valve 4-cylinder engine reflected Peugeot thinking in the spur drive from crankshaft to cam, and Mercedes ideas in the rocker mechanism and valve operation. The 4887 cc engine had a three-ball-bearing crankshaft and developed 130 bhp at 2800 rpm. Wheelbase was 108 inches and the car weighed 2200 pounds.

A minimum average speed of 80 mph for the two qualifying laps was more than 18 of the 40 entries could manage. Dario Resta set the pace in his Grand Prix Peugeot at 98.5 mph. Then Ralph de Palma went out in his new Mercedes, one of the cars that had swept the board in the 1914 French Grand Prix (it had been shipped just two weeks before the British had blockaded all German ports), and drove his two laps at an average speed of 98.6 mph. The three Stutz cars had yet to run.

Gil Anderson was the driver the fans were waiting for. A Norwegian by birth, he had raced one of the new Stutz cars four months earlier against the dying 7.3-litre formula cars in the Grand Prize at San Francisco and finished fourth. He had always driven Stutz cars and he was known as a charger. But Harry Stutz had other ideas. He told Anderson and Earl Cooper that he wanted them to qualify at 97 mph, and they dutifully made the field at 96.4 mph and 96.7 mph respectively.

The fans were puzzled. So probably were Anderson and Cooper, who knew the cars would run faster than Harry's target pace. Then Howdy Wilcox came out in the third Stutz with instructions to go for the pole and take it at 99 mph. He duly obliged, with a two-lap average 98.9 mph.

De Palma had the option of a second run in the Mercedes but decided to stick with his spot in the middle of the front row between Wilcox and Resta's Peugeot. Cooper and Anderson started on the second row beside a 1914 Sunbeam driven by Jean Porporato.

The race was scheduled to run on Saturday 29 May, but driving rain for two days kept the 33 starters from the speedway until the Monday. Even as the cars lined up a fine rain mist was blowing across the track, but it was drying in the wind and when the flag finally dropped it was Resta who took the lead. Wilcox had been given 'hare' instructions by Stutz, and going into the second lap he swept past the Peugeot and into the lead. He lasted only two laps before a valve spring broke and the big Stutz clamoured on to three cylinders and dropped back. Anderson, third behind the Peugeot, was then given the 'Go' sign and swept into the lead, where he set a loping pace. With 50 miles gone and 450 to go, he had a 32-second lead over Resta. De Palma and Porporato were two seconds down on Resta, with Wilcox (obviously not suffering too badly minus one pot) and Cooper in line astern.

Tyres were to spook Anderson at Indy and haunt the Stutz team for the rest of that season. After 75 miles Anderson could see his front covers fraying and the canvas starting to show. Four laps more and he pitted for a 60-second tyre change that let Resta into the lead. Tyre failures were to cost Anderson eight pit stops and Cooper four — and cost Harry Stutz the race.

Resta had the race in his pocket but on the 137th lap, with 158 miles to go, he blew a tyre and spun the Peugeot. He limped to the pits for new tyres all round, but now De Palma was leading in the Mercedes. Resta was second but the high-speed spin had upset his steering, and Harry Stutz was out at the pit wall urging Anderson and Cooper to speed up and apply pressure to the leaders, never mind the tyre wear. The Stutz pressure tactics almost paid off. Three laps from the finish the engine note of the Mercedes changed dramatically. A connecting rod had broken, and as De Palma rattled over the last laps, still leading, the flailing rod end punched two holes in the crankcase. De Palma won the 1915 500 in his stricken car, averaging 89.84 mph and collecting $22,600.

The Stutz team finished third (Anderson), fourth (Cooper) and seventh (Wilcox), their only consolation being that they were the first Americans home and the only Americans to challenge the continuing supremacy of the Europeans. Oddly, these efforts earn little more than passing reference in historian Griff Borgeson's tome *The Golden Age of the American Racing Car*.

The three-car Stutz team's appearance at Indianapolis in 1915 was their first (although Anderson had raced the prototype in San Francisco earlier), and during the remainder of the season they ran the board tracks and dusty road courses across the States. Tyres robbed them of results on the two-mile Chicago Maytown board track, but fortunes picked up when Anderson and Cooper scored a pair of one-two victories, trading wins in two 30-mile races on the Elgin (Illinois) road course. Resta wasn't at Elgin with his Peugeot, but on the Fort Snelling concrete speedway he turned up with Bob Burman in a sister car. Both French cars went out with engine failure, leaving Anderson and Cooper to stage a side-by-side grandstand finish after 500 miles of racing.

The 350-mile Astor Cup on the banked board track at Sheepshead Bay (New York) resulted in another Stutz one-two victory, Anderson leading Tom Rooney over the line. Cooper's Stutz had swallowed a valve after 46 miles, and De Palma (in a fourth Stutz, built during the season) was sidelined with a seized piston just after half distance.

Harry Stutz had proved his point. His cars were winners, even if they hadn't managed to win the big one, and he withdrew from racing to concentrate on filling orders for production cars.

The four works cars were sold as a job lot to Earl Cooper, the works driver, for $5,000, and he raced each of them for a year before selling them at the end of the season for $5,000. Each.

According to research by noted American auto historian Charles Lytle, after the 1915 season the Stutz name was really only carried by the car that Cooper happened to be racing at the time. As the cars were sold off, they appeared under different names with different owners until the formula changed in 1920 and the capacity limit dropped to 183 cu. in. (3 litres).

Best known of these Stutz privateers was Cliff Durant, who bought the ex-Anderson car that had won one of the Elgin road races and the Astor Cup at Sheepshead Bay. For some reason it was known as 'Number 7', although according to Lytle it never carried this number when it raced in America. It did race as Number 7 when it reached New Zealand, however, carrying on a tradition that is something of a mystery.

Durant entered the Stutz for the 1919 500 as a Durant Special, and Eddie Hearne drove it to second place behind Howdy Wilcox in a Peugeot. The fact that a four-year-old car could finish the classic 500-mile race in second place was a legacy of the war, but the decision to drop the Indy limit to 3 litres was made because Carl Fisher, the track owner, feared lap speeds were rising too high. The same cry is heard today, with qualifying speeds licking 230 mph and the track scarcely changed!

With the ex-Anderson/Durant Stutz rendered obsolete in America, it was bought by New Zealander Selwyn Craig, son of one of Auckland's founding families. In 1922, Craig had won the New Zealand Motor Cup on Muriwai Beach racing a stripped Packard. His first race with the Stutz was the 1924 Motor Cup at Muriwai, a 50-mile race on an up-and-back course between surf and sand hills. Crowd control was difficult and the cars waited 15 minutes at the start, during which time Craig ruined the clutch on the Stutz and the race went to the Mercer driven by Howard Nattrass, who had won the inaugural Motor Cup race in 1921 with a Cadillac.

Shortly after his beach troubles Craig put a rod through the side of the Stutz's crankcase and sold the car as a nonrunner to A.J. Bell, who ran it at Muriwai in 1925 but didn't feature, C.W.F. Hamilton winning in his 1914 TT Sunbeam. Like Craig, Bell was disillusioned with the Stutz and passed it on to Bob Wilson (later to establish the Wilson & Horton publishing group in Auckland and own the *New Zealand Herald*), who completely rebuilt the 10-year-old car with help from Reg Grierson, who was to feature later in the Stutz saga. The rebuild included a new bronze crankcase built by Mason & Porter in Auckland.

It was the start of a new lease of life for the Stutz when Wilson took it to Muriwai for the 1926 Motor Cup race. He led the first lap from Matthew Wills in an 8-cylinder 1922 Sunbeam and Hamilton in the 1914 4-cylinder Sunbeam, and went on to win comfortably.

Opposition was stronger in 1927. On the first lap Wilson tailed the Sunbeams of Hamilton and Australian star Hope Bartlett, but he was ahead of Bartlett on the second, and when Hamilton dropped out on the third he was leading the Australian by four seconds. On the fourth lap Wilson had a half-mile lead, while Bartlett's Sunbeam was 'running irregularly', according to a contemporary newspaper report. Wilson won by a mile.

Any driver who won the three-foot-tall silver Motor Cup three years in succession kept it. The trophy was valued in the 1920s at £105, and has since been given to the New Zealand International

Grand Prix Association, which awards it to the winner of the New Zealand Grand Prix, held at Pukekohe.

In 1928 the Muriwai course was shortened, bringing the straights down to 4.2 miles each way with a total of 11 turns round the hairpin barrels. On the first lap Wilson and H.K. Cutten in the ex-Zborowski Miller arrived side by side at the home turn after 8.5 miles of racing, but on the second lap the Miller slowed and Wilson stormed on across the sand to win the race by 34 seconds from Hamilton's Sunbeam, and to keep the giant silver trophy.

Once the crowds that had poured down across the beach at the end of the race had been moved back, there was an attempt on the Australasian five-mile speed record. A one-mile course was marked out and the Stutz clocked 108.4 mph, Hamilton's TT Sunbeam 95.1 mph.

Since Wilson kept the Motor Cup, the feature race of the year became a 25-mile event called the Australasian Beach Championship, and after a misfire problem midrace, the Wilson Stutz came through to win by half a mile from A.J. Roycroft's Bugatti.

On 23 March 1929 the 1.5-mile Mangere speedway opened, and promoter George Henning presented a silver helmet to the driver who set the first lap record — George Smith, on 76 seconds. A month later Wilson took the noble Stutz to the speedway and lowered the record to 70.6 seconds.

With its formidable record on the beach the Stutz acquired an unbeatable handicap, and because a man like Wilson preferred wins to lap records, he stood down to let Reg Grierson run the car. At the end of 1929 Grierson lowered the Mangere record to 63.6 seconds, and in March 1930 lowered it again to 59 seconds. In January he had continued the Stutz tradition of winning the feature race at Muriwai — the fifth consecutive victory by the big yellow car.

At the beginning of the 1931 season D.C. Sutherland was racing the Stutz. He extended the tradition still further by winning the Beach Championship that season and again in 1932. It was 1935 before the Stutz finally faded from the race results and was put out to grass. It had won the premier race at Muriwai every year from 1926 to 1932.

Sutherland may have sold the car with another broken con rod, for it seems the engine was removed for repairs and then tried in a speedboat. A Roosevelt straight-8 engine was fitted in its place to make the venerable old racing car into a more tractable vehicle on the shingle roads of the day, but the Indianapolis ratios were so high that the Roosevelt never succeeded in pulling top gear.

The Stutz was eventually acquired by Len Stonnell, a farmer in Taranaki, who used it from time to time to tow a hay rake round his fields during the harvest. Farmers tend to be short on appreciation of classic cars, but Stonnell was later prepared to let Ron Roycroft, son of the Bugatti driver who had finished second behind the Stutz on the beach in 1929, collect the remains of the old car on condition that he restore it. The Stutz joined Roycroft's impressive collection, but the restoration was more than he could contemplate and when Len Southward offered to take over, Roycroft approached Stonnell and received permission to hand it over.

Southward was not surprised Roycroft had baulked at the rebuild. The engine had completely rusted up after lying outside for years, and all the running gear on the chassis was badly pitted and corroded after the years of beach racing.

It was the sort of challenge that a sportsman like Southward relished. He had built up a successful business supplying the growing New Zealand motor industry with tube steel. In 1954 he set the New Zealand water-speed record over a kilometre at 109 mph in his 28-litre Allison-engined boat *Redhead*. He was involved in a quiet way with Chris Amon and Graham McRae when they began their racing careers and has always been interested in old cars.

So the Stutz has found a good home. Despite much of the engine having been lost or ravaged by weather and time, the bronze crankcase made up in Auckland in 1925 is still sound. Southward Engineering has been called on for various new parts to rebuild the engine with a new two-piece crankshaft, and painstaking work has been put in on the gallant old chassis.

Harry Stutz would be pleased if he could look down and see the meticulous care and attention Len Southward has lavished on his 60-year-old charger.

CHAPTER 15

NORMAN 'WIZARD' SMITH

The land speed record was a challenge to the British and American speed kings in the 1920s and 1930s, but it was an Australian who got New Zealand involved in the chase. Norman Smith decided to use Ninety Mile Beach to try to best the record in 1930 and 1932. I wrote about his ill-fated attempt for a 1974 issue of the UK Autocar.

Near the tip of the North Island is a long stretch of golden sand that has been a passage for history since the first Maori arrived. On it, 70-odd years ago, an ill-fated attempt was made on the land speed record, and from it the first airmail to Australia took off. Both events involved men who bore the common name Smith in an uncommon way.

For mile after mile, with the Holden sitting on a comfortable 112 kmh, we drove up the apparently endless beach, rolling surf and 2250 kilometres of sea stretching towards Australia on our left, sand hills on our right, and shimmering mirages ahead. The sand was damp and packed as hard as a motorway surface. Occasionally there was a tug at the wheel as we crossed a soft patch.

'Ninety Mile Beach' is a misnomer. The coastal sand flat is only 103 kilometres long, but it has a colourful history largely forgotten today by the tour buses and holiday-makers that drive its length at low tide.

Seventy years earlier, when Holden was still the name of a saddlery company which had switched to building motor-car bodies and was about to be taken over by its largest customer, General Motors, two Australian racing drivers, Norman 'Wizard' Smith and Don Harkness, were working together on a special project. They were building a car to attack the land speed record, and would make their attempt on Ninety Mile Beach.

At the same time a grizzled flyer named Charles Kingsford Smith, with flights across the Pacific and the Tasman already accomplished, was planning a regular airmail service between New Zealand and Australia. He would use Ninety Mile Beach as the stepping-off point for these pioneer flights.

Wizard Smith specialised in town-to-town records, at a time when such speed events in Australia and New Zealand were run on open roads either with official approval or at least under a 'blind-eye' sanction from police and other authorities. The cars he drove in these record runs were stripped versions of American Essex, Pontiac, Chrysler, Studebaker or Hudson models. His door-to-door times across hundreds of kilometres of rutted roads made ideal advertising for Australian agents.

Harkness was an engineer who also had something of a reputation as a racing driver. His stripped and tuned Overland had won, among other events, the first race held on the murderous Maroubra Speedway, in Sydney. Harkness had also built a special car to compete for a $100 silver cup put up for the first Australian to top 100 mph. The mysterious machine had had 'a powerful aero engine in the heaviest car chassis he could find', and in 1925 Harkness had won the cup at 107.14 mph.

It seems highly probable that the first special record-breaker Wizard Smith took to Ninety Mile Beach, in 1930, was a revised version of the Harkness special. It was built from a Cadillac chassis fitted with a First World War Rolls-Royce V12 Eagle aero engine bought as air force surplus for $80. The 18.7-litre engine developed 360 bhp and drove through a 3-speed gearbox. The standard Cadillac radiator was retained with a sloping cowl as a concession to streamlining, and a small tail fin, which carried the national flag and the words 'Advance Australia'.

The engine fired through a battery of 12 stub exhausts, there was a water-temperature gauge sprouting from the radiator cap in vintage touring fashion, and the bonnet was secured by two straps. The vehicle had an overall length of 20 feet, a wheelbase of 11 feet and a track of 4 feet 8 inches. It was painted gold and christened *Anzac*. Tyres for the record runs were provided by Firestone.

Smith took *Anzac* first to Gerringong Beach, in Australia, where he ran a two-way average of 128.571 mph to take the national speed record. With more room to manoeuvre on Ninety Mile Beach, he announced he was aiming for 175 mph, which wouldn't be enough to take the world land speed record, then held by Sir Henry Segrave at 231.446 mph in the sleek *Golden Arrow*, but would be enough to secure the 10-mile record. Smaller bait was the New Zealand speed record of 109.09 mph, set by C.W.F. Hamilton in his 1914 TT Sunbeam at Oreti Beach, near Invercargill, in 1928.

On 11 January 1930, Smith and Harkness crammed themselves into the two-seater cockpit, and Smith's two-way average for the mile was 150.5 mph. He slowed on the return run in drizzling rain, losing 200 revs. Seagulls straying into the path of *Anzac* were another hazard. Bad weather delayed Smith's run at the 10-mile record until 17 January, when, on a wet beach, he was clocked at 148.637 mph, travelling over the last 0.6 of a mile at more than 160 mph on the rev counter, according to Harkness.

In fact Smith wasn't awarded the 10-mile record because of confusion surrounding regulations and timing procedures. But he and Harkness were quoted in Sydney newspapers as saying Ninety Mile Beach was the best record-breaking venue in the world. 'At low tide the water recedes perhaps a quarter of a mile and leaves a perfectly straight course of hard-packed fine brown sand 25 miles long. Even above high-water mark the sand is hard enough to drive on; below it is like concrete.' One of the drawbacks was the presence of toheroa, molluscs with razor-sharp shells, which spelt danger to the thin tyres of Smith's cars.

The shellfish are still troublesome today, and although we had no problems with the Holden, we saw one holiday-maker in a Hillman flapping along with a punctured rear tyre. My two-year-old daughter, Selina, discovered to her delight that you could still scoop up handfuls of shellfish from just beneath the surface of the sand, although these were pipi rather than the scarcer toheroa, which are a delicacy and strictly protected.

Derric Vincent, local historian and editor of the *Northland Age* in Kaitaia, was eager to assist in combing the files of the little newspaper which covered the speed-record events on nearby Ninety Mile Beach. He told us where we could find the remains of a special sand-proof garage built for Smith's second attempt at world records. All that is left now is the concrete foundations and floor, with shell fragments and sea sand in the concrete mix.

From the garage, tucked in the shelter of the sand hills, it was a 50-yard run down to the sand and, at low tide, another 300 yards to the surf. Kingsford Smith later used the garage to service and fuel his Fokker *Southern Cross* for its trans-Tasman flights. In a photographer's shop in Kaitaia we found old shots of the Southern Cross on the beach preparing for take-off in 1934, but photographs of Wizard Smith's efforts had been moved to the Alexander Turnbull Library in Wellington.

Anzac had obvious limitations as a speedster, being, in the words of Henry Manney III, about as aerodynamically efficient as Anne Hathaway's cottage. *Anzac* phase 2, a special car to take the land speed record, had been planned even before phase 1 had made its first runs. The power unit for the new car was to be a 1900 bhp Rolls-Royce R engine, as used in the Supermarine S.6, which had won the Schneider Trophy air race in 1929.

H.J. Butcher, mainstay of Smith's record runs at Ninety Mile Beach following the confusion in 1930, had gone to Europe to buy the latest photoelectric timing equipment to ensure official recognition of any records Smith might set.

The new car was built in Harkness' workshops in Sydney. Segrave's *Golden Arrow* had used a 925 bhp Napier 'broad arrow' engine with three banks of four cylinders, similar to the power unit that had won the Schneider Trophy in 1927 in a Supermarine S.5, so Segrave's speed and horsepower were regarded as par for the record. The shape of the *Golden Arrow* was also regarded as optimum, and Harkness designed a dart-shaped frontal area almost identical to that of Segrave's car, mainly because the application for the loan of a Rolls-Royce aero engine had been rejected by the British government.

It was only after the Australian prime minister had intervened, and a former cabinet minister, Sir Frederick Stewart (after whom the car was subsequently named), had agreed to stand the $2,000 bond, that Harkness was able to get a 1350 bhp supercharged version of the Napier Lion aero engine that had been prepared for the 1929 Schneider Trophy but rejected in favour of the R-Type Rolls-Royce.

Segrave had been loaned an unsupercharged version of the Napier engine, and Sir Malcolm Campbell was able to 'borrow' a supercharged Napier to install in a revised version of *Bluebird*. John Cobb later used a pair of the engines in his Railton Mobil special.

Harkness estimated his design showed a 17 per cent improvement over *Golden Arrow* in frontal area, but this must have been hard to assess as *Golden Arrow* had run with large surface-type radiators slung on outriggers between the wheels, and even when Smith's car was shipped to New Zealand late in 1930 the cooling system had not been settled.

Harkness wanted to cool the engine by circulating ethylene glycol through the water system with methyl chloride being released or expanded through heat exchanger plates. Initial tests showed this to be extremely expensive, and sponsorship money was starting to dry up as the Depression in Australia tightened.

An alternative arrangement was made to fit a radiator ahead of each front wheel, with streamlined water tanks behind the wheels to take either water or ethylene glycol. Final tests were to be done in New Zealand.

Although the car was a year late in arriving at Ninety Mile Beach, and the record had in the meantime been raised by Campbell to 246.09 mph, Wizard Smith was not daunted. 'The chances of my breaking the land speed record with the *Fred H. Stewart Enterprise* on Ninety Mile Beach are about a million to one in favour, as I consider the car is the best designed and built machine which has attempted to break the record,' Smith was quoted as saying in the *New Zealand Herald* on his arrival from Sydney.

Butcher was back from Europe with the special timing equipment, and this was carefully installed in the captain's cabin of the motor vessel *Motu*, which sailed for Awanui from Auckland with the car lashed in place on deck. The timing recorder was packed in cotton wool and rubber in a mahogany case with a waterproof canvas cover and nestled on the master's bunk.

To finance the record attempt Butcher had formed the Auckland Automobile Racing Club, an offshoot of the Auckland Automobile Association, and while he was very much aware of the responsibilities of policing 15–20 miles of public beach, and also coping with the ferocious undercurrents of bad feeling which grew in the camp as bad weather caused delays, he became very unpopular with the public and the press.

Although the *Enterprise* was popularly supposed to have been designed to touch 100 mph in first gear, 200 in second and 300 in third, Harkness later maintained it was geared to better Campbell's record by a margin of only 5 mph. It had a double clutch: a friction clutch to cope while the car was gathering speed, and a positive dog arrangement for higher speeds. The drive shafts ran either side of the seat with a crown wheel and pinion carrying final drive to each rear wheel.

The special 37-inch wheels carried the latest Dunlop Land Speed Record tyres, and it was said the car was slung so low it could flip upside down and still clear the ground. Where the driver was supposed to be at this point was not explained.

The Post Office had laid telephone cables for the electronic timing equipment, and there was further delay when an underground cable had to be checked to find where enterprising locals had cut it to remove its lead sheathing. Initially the timing equipment gave trouble because the shadows cast by seagulls flying overhead kept triggering the light-sensitive cell. Even clouds had an effect and adjustments had to be made.

First tests on the beach soon revealed a serious rift between Smith and Harkness. Smith, unhappy about the untried cooling system, had secretly asked an aircraft engineer to design an alternative system of ice tanks. It failed, and after Harkness had returned to Sydney in disgust, Smith commissioned an Auckland coppersmith to make a three-core radiator. He had this mounted squarely across the front of the car, completely ruining any aerodynamic advantage the chisel nose may have conferred.

At this point, any hope of Smith breaking Campbell's record had been lost. Bad weather and mechanical problems delayed his attempt, while the tempers of the local public, barred from the beach by police manning the entrance roads, stretched extremely thin. The *New Zealand Observer* was moved to comment: 'Instead of the slim, elegant machine exhibited in Auckland, the car is now a snub-nosed monstrosity with a massive box-like arrangement said to weigh nearly 700 lb extending forward from the front axle.'

The dual-ignition, twin-magneto system on the Napier had an Australian invention, Raysola, wired into it with a control on the instrument panel so Smith could adjust the spark to each cylinder individually. This innovation was the cause of one particular incident that subsequently reached Sydney's libel courts.

A Mr Nudl had been detailed to look after the Raysola system, but he clashed with Smith after asking to check the compression on the

Napier. Smith refused, saying the British Air Ministry, which had supplied the engine, desired the compression details to be kept secret, and if an attempt were made to use it, 'especially by a man with a name like Nudl', the permit to use the engine might be withdrawn.

Smith issued instructions that the ignition expert was not to be allowed near the engine unless accompanied by certain named people. He further suggested that if Nudl approached the engine with a compression tester he would throw it — and Nudl — into the surf.

One gathers that the receding prospect of snatching the land speed record was playing on Smith's nerves, and there must have been an explosive atmosphere over the garage in the sand hills as the weather and high seas continued to make an attempt impossible.

Finally, in desperation, Smith called for the timing crews to man their posts on the morning of Tuesday 26 January 1932. The weather was still far from settled, but it was the last day of the full-moon tides and Smith couldn't afford the expense of keeping his diminishing team waiting any longer. Early in the afternoon he was ready to make his first run southwards down the beach, and his time through the measured 10 miles was 3 minutes 59.945 seconds, giving an average speed of 150 mph. He was troubled by wet sand flying up from the front wheels and plastering his patent revolving screen so he had to take a hand off the wheel to clear it.

The toheroa were close to the surface in the stormy weather, and the Dunlop covers were so badly cut at the rear that Smith changed wheels before setting off on the northward run, which he completed more quickly, in 3 minutes 18.848 seconds, at an average 178 mph. The combined average speed over both runs was 164.084 mph, which comfortably broke Mrs Gwenda Hawkes' 10-mile record of 137.2 mph, set in her Derby-modified front-wheel-drive supercharged 1.5-litre Miller at Montlhery.

So the Wizard had broken a record, but it was scarcely the one he had set out to better when he had embarked on the expensive project. He reported he had reached 228 mph on one of the runs, but that was still short of Campbell's speed. Further runs were abandoned, and Smith returned to Australia, this time to face suggestions that he was afraid to go for the one-mile record.

Harkness had cabled the New Zealand organisers to say he would test and drive the car himself in an immediate record attempt. The affronted Mr Nudl was delighted to join Harkness, and flew up and down Muriwai Beach, on Auckland's west coast, reporting smooth sand and perfect conditions. It was even suggested that C.W.F. Hamilton, the sheep farmer who had set the New Zealand one-mile record, should come out of racing retirement and drive the car. Hamilton refrained from accepting the challenge, and the organisers politely ignored Harkness' offer to take up the challenge.

The car was shipped back to Sydney and eventually dismantled during long and costly legal wrangles over a libel case brought by Smith against a now-defunct newspaper named, curiously enough, *Smith's Weekly*. It had published allegations that Smith was a coward and scared to drive the car.

Smith won his case and collected $2,000 of the $40,000 he had claimed. The engine had been bought from the British Air Ministry and was sold to a speedboat owner. Harkness died in 1973, and much of the background information for this story was made available by his widow in the form of his scrapbooks, kept in a Sydney museum.

The whole of the Northland tip of New Zealand was new territory for us, touring the area in our Holden, and research into the exploits of Wizard Smith soon uncovered the story of the other Smith, who had used the beach more successfully.

Charles Kingsford Smith was famous as a pioneer aviator in the South Pacific, and his tri-motor Fokker, *Southern Cross*, was to become as famous in Australasian history books as Lindbergh's *Spirit of St Louis*. His first flight across the Tasman was in September 1928, and in March 1933, to establish an airmail service, he flew from Ninety Mile Beach to Sydney in 13 hours 42 minutes. He made the same flight again in March 1934, clipping 19 minutes from his flight time.

Flying in those days was still an adventure, and while Smith and his crew used the earlier Smith's garage as a hangar and bedded down early for a dawn start, cars arrived from all over Northland and hundreds of people slept in the sand hills. At 4.45 a.m. the three Wright Whirlwind engines were fired up, and by 5.30 a.m. the big Fokker was thundering down the beach. It struggled into the air after a run of 1000 yards, made all the more imperative by the sudden appearance of a car full of drunks careering across the beach in front of the plane.

'The Old Bus', as the Fokker was affectionately known, was quite an impressive aircraft, with a wingspan of 71 feet 8½ inches, a maximum chord of 12 feet 6 inches and a maximum thickness of 2 feet 9 inches. It held 1298 US gallons of fuel for long hauls, distributed about the plane: a fuselage tank held 807 gallons, there was a 107-gallon tank under the pilot's seat, and there were four 96-gallon tanks in the wings. It cruised at 90 mph and had a range of 3818 miles in still air with a 69-mile margin in case of rough weather en route.

The popular story told in Northland is that Smith and his crew took off on that 1934 flight with a hamper of cold roast godwit, which they tucked into on the way across, washing it down with the contemporary equivalent of ice-cold Fosters. Climbing down from their plane at Sydney Airport, they were greeted by a full-regalia municipal reception followed by a banquet — which none of the intrepid aviators could face!

Ninety Mile Beach still curves up the western coast of the North Island, its mile upon mile of golden beach edged with curling breakers. All that is left of the two famous Smiths is the concrete foundation of their garage, hidden in the tussocky sand hills, along with the memories of the history-makers who worked there 70 years ago.

CHAPTER *16*

REVIVING LOST FERRARIS

New Zealand in the 1950s was regarded as a motor racing version of an elephant's graveyard. Several famous Ferraris, regarded as uncompetitive and therefore unsaleable, were sent here to run in the open formula events. Most of them ended up being converted into local specials.

The early-January sun blazed down on the Ardmore airfield circuit as the cars for the 1957 New Zealand Grand Prix were wheeled into position on the grid. In pole position was a 4.5-litre V12 Ferrari driven by local man Ron Roycroft. Beside him were a pair of 3.5-litre Super Squalo Ferraris driven by Peter Whitehead and Reg Parnell.

It is interesting to trace the tale of those three Ferraris, from their Grand Prix days in Europe, through their brief summer of glory down under in 1957, to their sad dismemberment and, finally, their restoration in the care of car collector and connoisseur Gavin Bain, who lives beside one of the many bays that serrate the edge of Lyttelton Harbour.

The mood of the crowd in the makeshift scaffolding grandstands at Ardmore that afternoon was almost solemn as the colourful field lined up. That morning spectators had been shocked to watch British driver Ken Wharton being hurled to his death in the sports-car race as his Monza Ferrari had skated out of control on the corner into the pit straight and somersaulted end over end.

When the flag dropped, it was the diminutive 40-year-old Roycroft who led the dash to the College Corner right-hander, and for eight glorious laps the New Zealand Grand Prix was led by a New Zealander, but the merciless heat of the sun punished both the driver and the drum brakes of the big Ferrari. When Roycroft pitted close to exhaustion, Parnell moved into the lead ahead of Whitehead, who was also having brake problems. Roycroft swigged at a bottle of cold drink, poured the rest down his back, and raced out of the pits again, but he was finished. On lap 63 he was lifted from the cockpit completely overcome by the heat.

The Grand Prix was won by Parnell from his Scuderia Ambrosiana team-mate Whitehead, to give the Super Squalo its first-ever race victory. The British pair shared the rest of the New Zealand series that summer. Whitehead won on the fast open Wigram airfield circuit, Parnell won the 75-mile race through streets around the Dunedin wharves, and Whitehead set new records on the fast Ryal Bush road circuit near Invercargill, leaving the lap record at 99.53 mph. After this winning run both cars were sold to New Zealand drivers. Tom Clark bought the Whitehead Squalo, winning at

Mairehau, in the outskirts of Christchurch, a week later, as well as at Levin. The other car went to John McMillan.

Roycroft battled back against the overseas contingent with their newer machinery, and although he started from pole position again at Wigram he fell back once more, exhausted this time by engine heat and fumes despite the fact that he had cut an extra cooling vent in the scuttle. He drove the final part of the race with his head out to one side in the airstream.

Roycroft raced the Ferrari until 1960, battling overseas teams and the fickleness of the V12, but both the Super Squalos were shipped to Australia at the end of the 1957 series in New Zealand and both were crashed. Clark took more than a year to recover from his injuries, but he brought his car back to New Zealand and entered it again in the 1959 Grand Prix. McMillan despaired of taming the habits of his car, and after rebuilding it he sold it to wealthy Sydney driver Arnold Glass and stayed with Glass to prepare it for him. The ex-Parnell car, now fitted with a 3-litre engine, is in the Giltrap museum near Surfers Paradise, in Australia.

Grid positions for the 1958 Grand Prix at Ardmore were allotted according to the finishing order in the race heats rather than the practice laps, and Roycroft started on the outside of the front row beside Archie Scott-Brown, in a Lister-Jaguar, and Jack Brabham, who was on pole in a 2-litre Cooper. A young local driver named Bruce McLaren was to have started in the second row directly behind Roycroft but his crew were still bolting the transmission back together on his 1750 cc Cooper, and the field was halfway round the first lap before he set out on a catch-up run that was to earn him the first Driver to Europe scholarship and launch him on the path to fame.

Roycroft ran steadily through to third place behind Brabham and Ross Jensen in a 250F Maserati, but the big Ferrari was still misbehaving. An aluminium shaving had jammed the gearbox selectors, and Roycroft could only get third and top gears for most of the race.

Roycroft was never really happy with the car and confessed some years afterwards that 'the Ferrari wasn't a very good car to drive. It wasn't a very good car, full stop. All the years I had the car I never won a single race with it. The best I ever finished was third in the 1958 Grand Prix but by that time the car was uncompetitive. It really was a most frustrating car.'

Last-minute problems with the Ferrari in 1959 saw Roycroft bring his Jaguar-engined RJR Special out of retirement for the Grand Prix, but he spun and damaged it in practice and was a nonstarter for the race. The 1960 Grand Prix was his swan song but again the Ferrari jilted him. The car popped and banged with a magneto malfunction and he finished twelfth. After announcing his retirement, Roycroft put the Ferrari up for sale.

Although Clark's Super Squalo was ready for the 1958 Grand Prix following its crash in Australia, Clark himself was still recovering from his injuries and didn't race again until the Grand Prix in 1959. He finished tenth, well astern of the Cooper one-two-three wrapped up by Moss, Brabham and McLaren. At Wigram he dropped from fifth place after a pit stop to drag newspaper from his radiator. At Teretonga he held fifth, at Ohakea he was running second until a spin dropped him to third, and after winning the final race of the 1959 season, at Levin, he announced his retirement from racing.

The burly Auckland businessman went on to race ocean yachts and provide sponsorship for Graham McRae through his company, Crown Lynn Potteries. His Super Squalo was sold to Bob Smith, something of a mystery man, who started in the back row of the grid in the 1960 Grand Prix at Ardmore and didn't feature in the results. Smith campaigned the Ferrari with little success until he sold it in 1963, and by 1964 the car was sitting forlornly in an Auckland used-car lot.

Thus it was that the Roycroft V12 and the ex-Whitehead Super Squalo effectively ended their competition days waiting unhappily for buyers, who refused to be tempted.

In their European Grand Prix heyday, both cars had been put out of business by unforeseen events. Louis Rosier had bought the 4.5-litre Ferrari from the factory for the 1952 season and then found that the world championship was to be for Formula Two instead, so he had hedged his bets and bought a Ferrari Formula Two car as well. Alfa Romeo had retired from Grand Prix racing at the end of the 1951 season, and there was little point in continuing to run a formula with only one competitive works team — Ferrari — operating.

When the Type 555 Squalo (the word means 'shark') Ferrari first appeared in 1954, it was essentially a development of the previous Type 625 but strengthened for the 2.5-litre formula. The multi-tubular space frame tapered at the rear, and there was a transverse tubular structure in front to mount the steering box and front suspension. Rear suspension was by de Dion, with unequal-length wishbones at the front and a single leaf spring front and rear. The 2.5-litre 4-cylinder engine had twin overhead camshafts driven by gears from the front of the crankshaft. Power output was initially 250 bhp at 7500 rpm, but by 1955 modifications had raised this to 270 bhp at 7500 rpm. Individual exhaust pipes from each cylinder joined into a single high tailpipe running beside the cockpit, which was a distinctive feature of the car. A new multitubular space frame was built for the 1955 model with two large-diameter tubes and a superstructure of smaller-gauge tubes to carry the rear suspension, body and fuel tanks. The new car was known as the 'Super' Squalo.

The Super Squalos were effectively finished the day Alberto Ascari was killed testing a Ferrari sports car at Monza a few days after his crash into the harbour at Monaco. Lancia withdrew from Grand Prix racing with its team of advanced D50 cars, and its equipment and personnel were handed over to Ferrari, which at that stage was struggling with the Super Squalos against the might of the Mercedes, Maserati and, until then, Lancia teams. Designers Jano and Massimino were put to work to sort out the Super Squalos halfway through the 1955 season, and although they made vast improvements, introducing 5-speed transmission and better handling characteristics, the V8-engined D50 Lancias obviously held greater development potential, and the works effort was soon put into these.

Two of the Super Squalos were bought by Peter Whitehead and Reg Parnell, and the 2.5-litre engines were replaced with 3.5-litre Type 860 Monza sports-car 4-cylinder engines, which gave an extra 40 bhp and were more reliable — an important factor with a series of races so far from the factory.

French champion Rosier was a privateer who had majored with Talbots, winning the Belgian Grand Prix at Spa in 1949 and in 1950 with a two-seater version of the 4.5-litre Talbot Grand Prix car. He won the 24-hour race at Le Mans driving 20 of those hours himself while his son paced the car for the other four. For the 1952 season he bought a 4.5-litre V12 Ferrari and a 2-litre Formula Two Ferrari, winning the Albi Grand Prix in 1952 and 1953 with the 4.5-litre, but with races for this car becoming scarcer he repeated the Talbot recipe and converted it into a sports car.

As Rosier ran a body-building business in Clermont Ferrand the conversion presented no problem, and the finished article resembled the factory sports car of the period, although it was in fact a one-off centre-seat sports car with a tiny seat to one side in token compliance with the regulations of the day.

The 4.5-litre Ferrari was the car that broke the Alfa Romeo dominance in 1951, when Gonzales won the British Grand Prix at Silverstone and Ascari followed up with wins in the German and Italian Grands Prix.

Aurelio Lampredi designed the V12 engine with a single overhead camshaft for each block of six cylinders driven by a chain from the front end of the crank. The valves were operated by two hairpin-type springs, and the crankshaft ran on seven main bearings. The engine had twin Marelli magnetos and two spark plugs per cylinder, a modification introduced during development in 1951, which raised power from 330 bhp at 6500 rpm to 380 bhp at 7500 rpm. It ran on an alcohol/benzole fuel mixture — Rosier detuned it to run on pump petrol — and lubrication was by wet sump with an external oil radiator. The chassis was based on two parallel rectangular tubes with a de Dion rear axle, independent front suspension and a single transverse leaf spring front and rear.

Roycroft had been racing in New Zealand since 1935. He started with a Wolseley Hornet, moved on to a Brooklands Riley, and in the early 1950s was racing the famous P3 Alfa Romeo that Nuvolari had driven to win the German Grand Prix in 1935, along with a Type 35A Bugatti fitted with an XK120 Jaguar engine. When Rosier advertised his Ferrari sports car for sale, it seemed like the answer to Roycroft's prayer for more performance in the Antipodes.

After a series of letters from the other side of the world, Rosier agreed to the sale and had the car driven from Clermont Ferrand down to the docks at Marseilles, but at some point on that exciting road trip the engine was overrevved and some of the valves were bent. The car arrived in Auckland just too late for the 1956 Grand Prix and Roycroft raced his Bugatti-Jaguar in the New Zealand series instead, but the temptation of his new car in Auckland proved too much. For the last race of the season, at Mairehau, he flew back to the city and drove the car some 500 miles down to Christchurch for the race. 'It went pretty well, but I was disappointed that it didn't go better,' recalls Roycroft. He hadn't touched the engine, presuming he had bought it ready to race. After breaking an axle he freighted the car back to Auckland, and when he and his father carried out an engine check, they discovered that it was only running on nine or 10 cylinders. During that winter the sports-car body was removed and a replica of the 1952 Indianapolis Ferrari body was built on the car locally.

With the characters and cars introduced, we can return to the stage where both cars had been pensioned off and were waiting to be sold.

The Super Squalo was in a sad state and getting sadder. The instruments were stolen as it sat in the car yard and soon the big wood-rimmed steering wheel disappeared. Eventually, despairing of a sale for the complete car, the owner removed the engine and offered it as a speedboat motor. At this point Wellington museum owner Len Southward stepped in and bought the engine to keep it in safe hands. The chassis went to a hot-rod builder, who installed a Corvette V8 engine and then shaved the lightweight chassis superstructure down to the main tubes and mounted a Morris Minor body so that the hybrid would qualify vaguely as a saloon car for the special all-comers category that was currently popular. The car looked evil and performed in a very ill-bred manner as befitted its mixed parentage.

It was in this bastardised condition that the Super Squalo was bought by Gavin Bain, a 29-year-old importer of fine china and jewellery to New Zealand. Bain set about the long task of restoration

*Legendary motor racing writer, Denis 'Jenks' Jenkinson and photographer
Euan Sarginson at the Barley Mow in Surrey.*

Roly Levis in his RAL Special.

Chris Amon in the Ensign at the 1976 Swedish Grand Prix. He crashed out with mechanical failure. PETER NYGAARD

A road race in Dunedin, 1956: Tony Gaze, Ferrari (4), Tom Clark, Maserati (5), Arnold Stafford, Cooper 500 (14).

Johnny Mansel had star quality; here he signs his autograph for fans at Ardmore.

*Johnny Mansel in the Cooper-Maserati during the
1962 New Zealand Grand Prix at Ardmore.*

Tom Clark haymaking with his 8CM Maserati at Ardmore in 1956.

Eoin Young and daughter, Selina, taking part in the South Island rally in a Truimph TR2.

The supercharged Stutz Black Hawk.

Eoin Young with the Stutz before the plate was changed (Septic Tank stood for Yank).

Ross Jensen in the Maserati 250F Piccolo at Levin in 1959.

Eoin Young with the ex-Gonzales/Rosier/Roycroft Ferrari GP.

Eoin Young, spoiled for choice, talks to Ferrari owner, Gavin Bain.

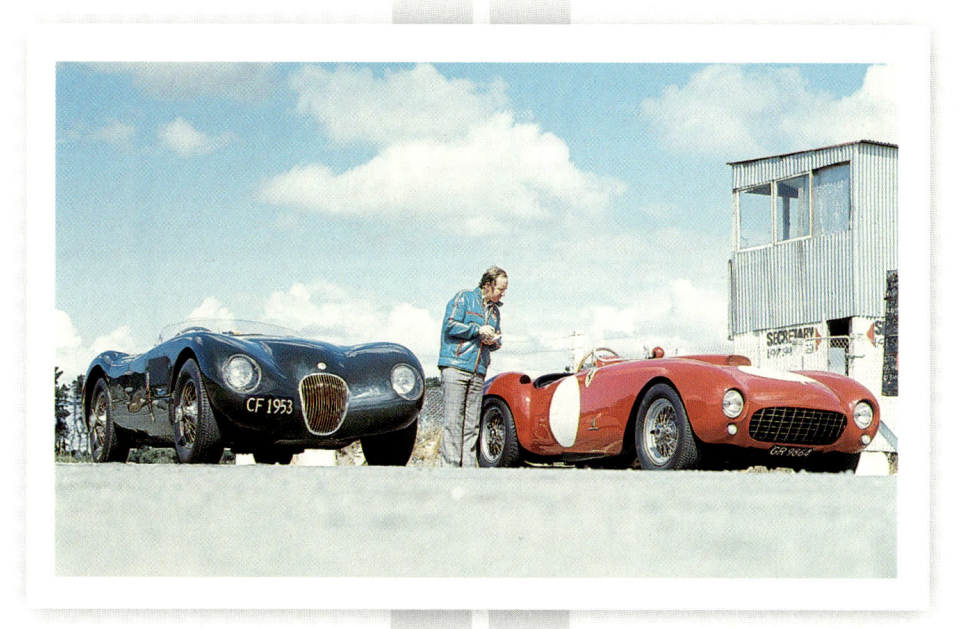

The sleek lines of a Ferrari and a C-type Jaguar complement each other at Ruapuna.

Denny Hulme with Susie and Stirling Moss

The Bruce McLaren memorial at Goodwood. From left: Howden Ganley, David Piper, Innes Ireland, John Surtees, Rob Walker, John Cooper, Peter Gethin, Keith Duckworth of Cosworth, Ken Tyrrell and Stirling Moss.

with a specialist firm of car-builders in Christchurch. When Southward heard what Bain was doing, he made the 4-cylinder sports-car engine available to him, as it was precisely for an opportunity like this that he had rescued the engine from the Auckland car yard. Southward's large collection of cars, soon to be exhibited in a new museum at Paraparaumu, included one of the 8CLT Indianapolis Maseratis as well as the 250F Maserati that was used as a guide when the first front-engined 2.5-litre BRM was being built and, later, was one of the first cars raced by Chris Amon as a teenager.

Fate decreed that Bain would also come to own the 4.5-litre Rosier/Roycroft Ferrari that had shared the front row of the grid in the 1957 Grand Prix at Ardmore with the Whitehead Super Squalo.

The gallant old car had languished for some months in Roycroft's sprawling garages at Glen Murray, 60 miles from Auckland, and prospective buyers showed little interest even at £1,050, which seems absurdly modest by modern standards. Finally Roycroft received a telephone call from Sydney speedboat racer Ernie Nunn, who bought the engine sight-unseen for a powerboat that was to set the Australasian speed record on water at 138 mph. Nunn paid Roycroft £1,200 for the engine. The chassis was then sold to Ferris de Joux, a local car stylist in glass fibre, who fitted a Jaguar engine in the GT frame and clothed it in a remarkably handsome GT body. It was a comedown for the old warhorse but it was better than being dressed in the hand-me-down body of a side-valve Morris Minor.

The de Joux GT went through several changes of ownership before winding up in the hands of the public prosecutor after one would-be buyer had failed to keep pace with his hire-purchase agreement. Then Bain entered the picture again. He bought the car from the government office and started restoring the Ferrari chassis to its former Grand Prix glory. He sold the GT body and then, with enthusiastic support from Roycroft, set about rebuilding the Ferrari. Roycroft supplied the single-seater body panels, the steering wheel and the instruments, as well as the original chassis data he had received from Rosier and the race book his father had compiled during the late 1950s.

It was a long and rocky road from Maranello through the hands of breakers and back to makers in New Zealand, but now the cars have been restored to the sort of condition that would certainly earn Enzo Ferrari's approval.

CHAPTER 17

NUVOLARI'S P3 ALFA ROMEO

Not every writer has the chance to be involved first-hand in motor-racing history. My opportunity came through car collector and restorer Bill Clark, who invited me to drive his immaculately rebuilt P3 Grand Prix Alfa Romeo — the actual car that Tazio Nuvolari had driven to beat the German works teams at the Nürburgring in 1935. This article ran as a cover feature in the American magazine Autoweek.

The first thing that catches your attention is the long, lithe bonnet with its ranks of louvres. It glistens bright, shiny, toffee-apple red, almost rippling in the sunshine like the flanks of a just-groomed stallion. The P3 Alfa Romeo *monoposto* has always been a car that is visually stimulating. It oozes vintage action.

Close to, it is smaller than I had expected. The seat is an overstuffed club armchair. The drainpipe exhaust marches down the side. Up there on the nose is a familiar badge — a black prancing horse on a yellow background: Ferrari. The clues start coming together. A P3 Alfa Romeo with a Ferrari badge. A prewar works car entered by Enzo Ferrari in the days before he built his own cars. In fact, it is the very same car that Tazio Nuvolari drove to glory that July day in 1935 when he won the German Grand Prix on the Nürburgring, defeating the massed might of the Mercedes-Benz and Auto Union teams. The Führer was most definitely not amused. It was one of the feats that feed the Nuvolari legend. A great man in a great car in 1935 — and I am being offered a drive in 1979. These days the most famous of all racing Alfa Romeos is in New Zealand, a prized possession of Bill Clark, who has painstakingly restored it to its former glory.

The mind races to take in the detail past and present, grappling with the tangled history of the car, coping with the awe of sitting where Nuvolari sat all those years before in this Italian terrier that whipped the German pack of Alsatians.

Nuvolari was a lot like that. What he lacked in stature he made up for in cubic courage. There was a magic about the little man which gave him the power to add pace to the cars he drove. He could extract those vital extra fractions of seconds that only a handful of drivers after him could muster — drivers like Fangio, Moss, Clark, Stewart. He was a driver who created legends, and those legends created a driver larger than life.

When he walked to this very Alfa Romeo that morning in July 44 years ago, Nuvolari must have looked almost Chaplinesque in his yellow jersey and red leather helmet. In the Mercedes-Benz and Auto Union pits the German drivers, in their immaculate white uniforms, appeared almost as supermen by comparison, and the huge crowds had been massing since before dawn around the 14.2-mile mountain course expecting nothing less than a Cup Final battle royal between the two top home teams. It was inconceivable that this little man in the ageing Alfa could keep up, let alone set the pace.

The race is history now. Ferrari had endeavoured to update the P3s for that season with a new Dubonnet front suspension, but he knew, and his drivers knew, that this was not enough. The Nürburgring itself turned out to be the leveller, as it was to be in so many races afterwards. Nuvolari made up in skill and agility what he lacked in horsepower. At the end of the first long lap he was in second place, 12 seconds behind Caracciola's Mercedes. Second time around and the Alfa was engulfed in a silver pack as Rosemeyer passed him in the Auto Union and von Brauchitsch and Faglioli in their Mercedes.

In his efforts to catch the leading Mercedes, Rosemeyer slammed a bank and lost places with a pit stop to fit a new wheel. Nuvolari was fighting back now as his fuel load lessened, improving the balance of the P3, and with 10 laps gone he was actually leading. Another lap — half distance — and the leaders pitted for fuel and tyres. The race switched from drivers to mechanics. Von Brauchitsch was first away after a stop of only 47 seconds by the Mercedes pit crew. Caracciola and Rosemeyer rejoined the race in second and third places respectively, but the Alfa Romeo was still in the pits as mechanics struggled with churns of fuel. The handle of a special pump for refuelling had broken off in the excitement, and Nuvolari could only rage as his lead was frittered away. In total his pit stop took 2 minutes 14 seconds, and he would have to make up every second in pure talent.

The rain helped. The more powerful cars on full tanks were tricky to handle. It was a challenge Nuvolari could accept; his rage at the pit-stop chaos merely served as an additional goad. He picked off the midfield runners with ease and then started to climb steadily up the huge illuminated scoreboard in the pits. With seven laps to go he was back into second place and hacking at von Brauchitsch's lead. As the two drivers headed into the very last lap the German was 35 seconds ahead, but the pressure was telling. Von Brauchitsch, never known for nursing his cars, was thrashing the Mercedes with merciless abandon, haunted by the spectre of the little Italian, who he knew to be snatching a second or so on every turn. At the Karussel he could see the flash of red in his mirrors.

Now that his pursuer was visible instead of just a number on the scoreboard, making the race more immediate, von Brauchitsch hammered his tyres and brakes to the limit and beyond. Only seven kilometres from the flag, the left rear tyre on the Mercedes burst, flailing rubber as von Brauchitsch took the only course open to him and stormed on as fast as he dared on the rim. Nuvolari sped past into the lead and almost before the big scoreboard had had time to register the change the red Alfa was in view and flashing across the line to win. The crowd was stunned.

The pundits have said since that if von Brauchitsch had not been so hard on his car, Nuvolari would not have won. On the other hand, if von Brauchitsch had been driving a more sober race, Nuvolari would probably have passed him anyway. Alfa Romeo fans point out that the Mercedes tyre failure merely evened the score for the Alfa pump handle snapping off during the pit stop.

You sit behind the wheel with a broad spread of legs to reach clutch and brake spaced either side of the transmission tunnel. The gear lever is cranked out to the left. Clark explains that the shift pattern is odd in that you move the lever forward for first then across to the right and forward again for second, using the two top legs of the conventional H rather than slicing straight back for second. The P3 was originally fitted with a 4-speed gearbox, but as the engine capacity was increased, so the transmission had to be beefed up, and because there was no room in the standard P3 casing for bigger gears, they chose to drop one of the forward speeds and go for three fatter cogs.

We are making our runs on a deserted country back road near Clark's farm, and louring skies are urging us to hurry.

I have a moment to wonder why the driving seat is so high when the P3 has inherited the split propshaft from its Type A ancestor, which boasted two engines side by side with crankshafts geared together. There are those who say that the car should really be a

Type B if the Alfa Romeo family tree is to be strictly followed, but it was called a P3 in the Italian papers soon after it started winning in the 1930s and it has been a P3 ever since.

The clutch take-up catches the rear wheels and you don't just move forward, you have a feeling of being flung — catapulted up the road. The polished quick-release caps for the reserve fuel tank on the scuttle and the water radiator so far forward along the slim, red, strapped-down bonnet become rifle sights with the narrowing stretch of bitumen as the target.

As the Alfa gathers pace the front wheels start to dart and I ease back. I accelerate again and once more the car takes control. It is really quite frightening knowing you are behind the wheel of a car worth so much that the owner has put it in a family trust rather than leave himself open to the temptation of selling it for one of the growing offers he has been turning away. I try to drive through the speed at which the front wheels begin their dance, but it isn't possible: the shimmy merely increases.

It is then that I recall Roy Salvadori recounting his experiences with this car when he owned it in the late 1940s. He wasn't at all impressed with the P3. At Chimay 'It was a toss-up whether you passed the car in front, hit it, or went through the fence. It was fast, but it was all over the place.' So perhaps I'm not alone in my assessment. Nuvolari must have been a superman to have coped with this on the Nürburgring for four hours. I explain the feeling to Clark but he is reluctant to listen to criticism of a car that has cost him so much care, time and money. Something, it seems, is not as it should be — but who is to know if they aren't all like this? Didn't Salvadori confirm the quirk?

A few weeks later I receive a letter from Murray Jones, an engineer and friend of Clark's, who has thoroughly examined the front suspension of the P3 in the light of the handling symptoms described to him, and discovered that the stepped keys which determine the castor angle have been reversed in the rebuild, giving positive instead of the required negative castor. 'It must have been like driving at high-speed in reverse in a front-wheel-drive car,' he says in his letter. He and Clark have cured the problem, taking a couple of hours one

Sunday afternoon to transform the handling so the car is once more the thoroughbred it must have been when Nuvolari raced it and they knew which way the castor keys were supposed to go. One assumes all this was a mystery to Roy Salvadori in the days when suspension setting-up was called putting a few more pounds in the tyres.

After I have climbed out of the P3 and watched Clark drive away, memories and emotions until then held in check by the excitement of actually driving flood my mind. The smell. The aroma of Castrol R and dope fuel that wafted back into the cockpit — the perfume of what racing used to be like when you could see the driver at work. And the noise. The sound of the supercharged Alfa engine provides yet another dimension to driving. Not so much a noise, more a piece of Italian piano excitement that rises to a crescendo. At a 1500 rpm idle, the beat is slightly uneven, but as the revs build up, so the music gathers force, the supercharger chiming in as accompaniment. It's difficult to capture the sound on paper, but the P3's solo on a straight exhaust is always commented on when people first hear it. It has something in common with the excitement and urgency of Italian music, a likeness more striking than in the case of a Bentley or Bugatti.

The P3 was sold at the end of the 1935 season, and in 1936 it came to race in Britain with Austin Dobson at the wheel. But Dobson was looking for more power and pace and sold it to Kenneth Evans in favour of the Bimotore, or twin-engined, Alfa. Evans campaigned the P3 extensively before the war, and Clark feels that Evans' ninth place in the 1937 German Grand Prix on the Nürburgring as a private entrant was, in its way, as fantastic an achievement as Nuvolari's victory two years earlier.

When racing began again in Britain after the war, Evans wheeled the P3 out once more and raced it several times before selling it to Roy Salvadori, who drove the old charger for a full season. It was advertised for sale but there were few drivers interested in taking on a car which was off the pace and fairly cantankerous. But it was in the late 1940s and early 1950s that New Zealand and Australia became popular as 'dumping grounds' for cars that were no longer fast enough for racing in Europe. The P3 was bought by motorcycle speedway racer Les Moore, father of Ronnie Moore, and taken back to New Zealand in 1950 with the ex-Earl Howe 2.3 long-chassis Alfa Romeo sports car that turned out to be the vehicle that had won at Le Mans in 1931.

The P3 enjoyed a new lease of life in the colonies. Moore won the Wigram race in 1951 and 1952 on the airfield circuit near Christchurch and built a reputation for the car sufficient to find a new buyer in Australia. The car was actually in Auckland en route to Australia when A.J. Roycroft intercepted it and offered £1,500, topping the Australian bid and keeping the machine in New Zealand for his son, Ron, to race.

The P3 kept on winning. In 1953, Roycroft scored victories at Wigram, Mairehau and Dunedin. The car was painted black now, with a silver stripe, and known as 'The Glen Murray Express'. In 1954 Roycroft was fifth, and the first New Zealander, in the Grand Prix at Ardmore, but he broke his winning run at Wigram by retiring on the first lap when he forgot to turn the oil on. In 1955 he scored one win, at Dunedin. After retiring from the 1956 New Zealand Grand Prix he sold the car to David Caldwell, who seems to have done little but put con rods through the sides of two engines. Johnny Mansel, a driver definitely in the Italian mould, colourful and quick, raced the car to ninth place in the 1958 Grand Prix. Then Brian Tracey raced it briefly in 1959 before it changed hands again. The new owner only drove it up the road and back — on neat petrol, which did little for the pedigree engine.

Bill Clark entered the picture when he heard that the famous old P3 could be bought at a reasonable figure, and a deal was done for £350 — including trailer. Ron Roycroft was able to supply further P3 spares, plus two motors in pieces and the 3-speed gearbox, which he and his father had replaced with a 4-speed Wilson preselector box to gain the extra ratio. Clark's rebuild included reinstallment of the 3-speed box.

It took nearly 20 years for Clark to find the time to complete the restoration of the P3, which stood in his motor-house together with eight Cooper single-seaters of various vintages, the ex-George Smith GCS (one of the more famous New Zealand specials), a Speed 25 Alvis, a 1928 4.5-litre Bentley, an MG TD, a one-owner 1923 Chevrolet, a 3.5-litre Jaguar and a GTV Alfa Romeo.

I was always aware that the Alfa Romeo was progressing and was always anxious to drive it, but every year, when I visited Christchurch, it was still 'not quite' finished. It took the thirtieth anniversary event at Wigram to spark the final work, and for the first time Clark was able to drive the car that had such a tremendous history.

Coincidentally, the sister P3 fitted with Dubonnet suspension for the 1935 season was owned by Leon Witte, a farming neighbour of Clark's, and between them the two enthusiasts owned a TecMec chassis. The frame of the Bimotore Alfa that Austin Dobson had bought on quitting the P3 was brought back from Christchurch to be rebuilt for Tom Wheatcroft's collection at Donington.

Wheatcroft has tried on various occasions to secure the Nuvolari P3 for a central feature of his motor-racing tableau at Donington, but Clark has always resisted these offers and insisted that the car will remain in New Zealand as a permanent mechanical reminder of the days when it enjoyed a new lease of life and became a winner again 15 years after Nuvolari's miracle victory at the Nürburgring with a car that was 'too old'.

POSTSCRIPT

In 1989 the famous Nuvolari P3 Alfa Romeo sold at auction in Monaco for £1.8 million.

CHAPTER 18

THE BRAMWELL BLOWER

Allan Bramwell is a legend among real enthusiasts for motorcycles and what he would regard as 'proper' cars. It was Bramwell who rescued the chassis of a famous Stutz Black Hawk and had it rebuilt to emulate the Stutzes that raced at Le Mans in the late 1920s.

Racing history tends to be selective in its consideration of the 1928 Le Mans 24-hour race. In recent years Bentley had been dominant on France's Sarthe circuit, but that year there was a particularly strong challenger from the USA that almost defeated Bentley. 'The Stutz was particularly formidable, with its lower frame and superior cornering to the Bentley, and its 4.8-litre 8-cylinder engine.' Bentley supporters should not denigrate the writer of that passage, for it was the great W.O. Bentley himself, and the words are quoted from his memoirs.

The Stutz Black Hawk was driven in 1928 by the Argentine-born, French-based Edouard Brisson, who would drive Stutz cars at Le Mans every year until 1932. That first year was to be his finest. Birkin's Bentley led the opening lap, with the Brisson Stutz on its tail. 'Brisson was a very good driver and the Stutz was obviously faster than I had thought it was going to be,' wrote Bentley.

Brisson traded the lap record with the 4.5-litre Bentleys of Birkin, Barnato and Clement in the opening stages, but as darkness fell he was leading. Birkin had blown a tyre and lost time, while Clement had been delayed with a broken oil pipe. At dawn the Stutz was still leading but its handling was suffering from a full fuel load. After fuel stops the lead would sometimes change but the Stutz would regain the upper hand as its load lightened. The race was between the Barnato Bentley and the Stutz, with nothing in it, when, with only an hour-and-a-half to go, the Stutz started to jump out of top gear — some say it lost second in the 3-speed box. Barnato also had his problems in the Bentley, which had broken its frame. He limped across the line to win and preserve Bentley's record. The American Stutz, having led for much of the long race, finished second.

History remembers that period of Le Mans racing as being dominated by Bentley. Scant mention is made of the near-terminal Bentley chassis-breakage or the Stutz domination of the 1928 race.

It is interesting to consider this in modern terms. When I mentioned my Stutz experience to Grand Prix designer Harvey Postlethwaite over lunch, he mused: 'Wouldn't it be interesting if the Stutz had won Le Mans then. The impact of an American win in Europe, beating the Bentleys, would have changed motoring history.

There would be a Stutz Division in General Motors and we'd all be driving around in Stutz Cavaliers!'

As it was, Bentley went on to become the most famous of vintage cars, the car you see in your mind's eye whenever the word 'vintage' is mentioned. In fact, both the Bentley and Stutz companies were victims of the 1929 Wall Street crash and the Great Depression, and Le Mans 1928 was as close as Stutz came to international acclaim in racing. The marque was well known on American tracks, and the Bearcat was already a sports-car legend.

The straight-8 Black Hawk series was designed to provide smooth American horsepower allied to a low 'safety chassis' that helped provide European-style handling. This ideal marriage was revived in New Zealand by Allan Bramwell.

It was one of those happy coincidences that sometimes occur in the old-car world. In 1988 a Stutz came on the market in New Zealand, offered without a body. History was repeating itself, for in 1928 the Stutz factory had offered a few very special right-hand-drive Black Hawks in chassis form for export only and to be bodied in Britain. An issue of *Stutz News*, the magazine of the Stutz Club in the USA, notes that these cars had a special 127$\frac{1}{2}$-inch wheelbase, down from the 131 inches that was standard on the home market. 'These Black Hawks had the 8-cyl Stutz engine, a 3.8:1 rear axle ratio, two shock absorbers for each wheel, different lighting equipment, knock-off hub caps, the barest minimum in fenders, hood straps and were right-hand drive. These Black Hawks were the hottest of all Stutz cars.' The idea was that the Stutz dealers in Britain would fit wood-framed, fabric-covered Weyman bodies.

The Bramwell Stutz came with no history other than its documented arrival in New Zealand in 1938 and its capacity of 5.3 litres.

To appreciate this special car you have to appreciate Allan Bramwell, a man who loves old cars but doesn't care for old-car committees. He makes his own rules. He founded the Country Gentlemen's Motor Racing Club in Christchurch simply because he wanted to enjoy racing with his friends without being bound by what he regarded as the pettifogging regulations laid down by motor sport's national controlling bodies. He invited like-minded people to take part in his races. There were no entries. If you weren't asked to come along with your car, you didn't come. Bramwell had the *Sunday Times* airmailed from London to New Zealand each week. He christened his Cooper 500 Jilly and then called on Jilly Cooper during a visit to Britain to ask if she minded. She was delighted.

Bramwell is a free spirit when it comes to his cars. The upholders of vintage authenticity may demand that old vehicles should be as original as the day they left the factory, but Bramwell regards this as something of an infringement of his personal liberties. He likes to adapt whatever he has to his own driving preferences. He bought a Phantom II Rolls-Royce, had Auto Restorations in Christchurch clothe it in a superb touring body — and then fitted a Jaguar XJS gearbox because it made the big tourer more relaxing to drive over New Zealand's long town-to-town distances. And up boulder-strewn riverbeds to remote fishing spots, where the lofty ground clearance was a distinct advantage. He also raced the Rolls-Royce when the fancy took him. No ordinary vintage-car driver, as you may have gathered by now.

At 5.3 litres the Stutz had muscle enough in its standard form, but Bramwell decided to create the ultimate in vintage touring cars, based loosely on the Stutz cars that ran at Le Mans in the late 1920s. Murray Jones was the engineer behind the project to supercharge the big overhead-camshaft straight-8, and he produced pages of notes to establish the use of a cabin blower from a Fokker Friendship passenger plane as a supercharger. It is driven from the front of the crankshaft by a belt to a countershaft running back to the blower, which sucks from a $2^{1}/_{2}$-inch SU carburettor and blows into the engine at a maximum of seven pounds. The blower is geared at 1.6 times engine speed.

Supercharging a Stutz is legitimate in spirit since in 1929 Stutz made an abortive attempt to supercharge their entry at Le Mans, but their efforts did not achieve the success of colonial technology six decades later.

The Stutz had a 4-speed gearbox but Bramwell opted for a 4-speed XJ6 gearbox with overdrive. 'I don't have any problems with a crash box, but I wanted this to be a car that I could let my mates drive.' It was to be a fast car for vintage-style road use, so Bramwell fitted the original large-diameter headlight shells with modern sealed beam units behind metal mesh guards. He kept the original lighting equipment; he simply didn't wish to be inconvenienced by 60-year-old illumination. He also kept the original gearbox. The worm-drive differential he replaced with a 9-bolt American Ford unit grafted into the Stutz axle housings with a final drive ratio of 3.7 to 1. He says the whole car can be converted back to its original state in a couple of days.

Bramwell sketched the lines of the body before putting the work in the care of the local Auto Restorations craftsmen, and the result was a superb high-stepping, two-door, four-seater, close-coupled tourer with cycle guards, Stutz-pattern running boards, a fold-down main screen and twin aeros and a hood that furls and erects with ease and actually enhances the period lines of the car. The slab tank holds 56 gallons with a rear-mounted spare wheel, because Bramwell doesn't care for side-mounts. There is new Connolly Leather hide throughout and a small walnut-lined cocktail cabinet in the right rear armrest with a flask and four shot-glasses.

It amounts to a brand-new vintage car that is probably the fastest Stutz road car in the world. It has been raced by Bramwell and ERA-racer Bill Morris, who rates it enthusiastically.

The primary consideration when driving the Stutz is to discipline your mind to the fact that the accelerator is in the centre. A couple of stamps on the throttle when I needed the brake and the brake when I needed power tended to engrave the pedal layout on my mind. The car demands comparison with the 4.5-litre Bentleys it raced at Le Mans and comes out comfortably faster — as well as a good deal easier to drive with its measure of modernization. The addition of the supercharger simply adds to the vintage mystique, the high-pitched whine under power bringing the hair on the back of your neck to attention and recalling all the stories you've ever read of those comparisons with Caracciola in the SSK Mercedes attacking Birkin in the Blower Bentley at Le Mans.

The Stutz would have been effortlessly powerful without the blower, but its addition provided easy acceleration in top gear, and in its modern overdrive the car lopes along at 90 mph with around 110 mph as a maximum. 'It does 37.6 mph per 1000 rpm in overdrive,' says Bramwell, 'and I've often seen 2800 rpm on trips.'

If the Stutz Club authorities say the original version of this short-chassis model was 'the hottest of all Stutz cars', the Bramwell Blower must be the hottest in Stutz history.

POSTSCRIPT

The glorious Stutz is now in the impressive private collection of vintage racer Bruce McCaw, in Seattle. I have driven it since its relocation and couldn't think why it seemed so much easier to operate. Bruce had moved the accelerator pedal to the 'proper' side of the brake pedal.

CHAPTER 19

BLACK HAWK BLAZING

I was so infatuated with the background history and the performance of the Bramwell Stutz that I bought it and in 1992 took it on a famous South Island rally.

Euan Sarginson, the New Zealand photographer who covered the Tasman Series in its down-under heyday for *Autosport*, has a healthy disregard for vintage motoring, having done his share of it, including in an SS 100 and an Alvis Grey Lady. 'Old cars,' he says, 'are like old movies. They're no bloody good.' I'm beginning to think there may be something in what he says. In February 1992 I tempted him away from his fashion models to cover the Southern Festival of Speed for classic racers, travelling with my 1954 Triumph TR2 and supercharged 1928 Stutz Black Hawk. I am not yet as jaundiced as Sarginson about the old-car scene in that I subscribe to the theory but am technically useless in practice.

The underside of the big straight-8 Stutz might as well have been a map of Mars for all the sense it made to me. I'd never seen it before, and the experience was very much a baptism of fire. Picture the scene: driving away from the motel, heading for the first race in the series at the Levels track near Timaru, top down and aero screens up, at 10 o'clock on a brisk late-summer morning. In an open car you get to smell what is happening around you as well as seeing it, and the lorry ahead of me is definitely having a problem. I can't define the smell, but it seems as if something is getting hot. Burning, even. Then I realise there isn't a lorry in front of me and the burning smell is coming from the Stutz.

Clouds of smoke are starting to issue from the louvres in the bonnet sides. No power. The worst scenarios flit through your mind at a time like this, and getting a couple of tons of American vintage hardware stopped at the side of the road becomes imperative. Opening the bonnet requires a series of Gilbert and Sullivan manoeuvres even in noncrisis times — unscrewing locknuts and wing nuts and hinging back aero screens and the main screen to clear the vast upwards-opening bonnet sides. Smoke comes billowing out of both sides of the hefty 5.2-litre supercharged engine, but there is no real indication of where it is coming from. At this point I slide underneath the car and begin a crash course on Stutz cartography.

The long finned sump gleams like the hull of a small submarine. Further back is the clutch, then the gearbox, the overdrive and — Omigod, whatever's at the back of it all is ablaze! Not just smouldering and smoking but fully alight with flames all round it. I wonder fleetingly how metal can burn, then I'm mentally measuring how far the conflagration is from the 45-gallon petrol tank across the tail, how far I'm parked from the nearest house in case it all goes up, and, more practically, how much the Stutz is insured for.

I slide out from under the massive motorcar to see a new Mazda coupé has just braked hard to a stop in front. Boyd Wilkinson, organizer of the racing series. Improbably, he asks if everything's OK. I assure him it is *not* and that the (expletive deleted) car is on *fire* and would he go and find an extinguisher just as soon as he can manage it. Please. Like *now!*

There's a Mobil service station a few hundred yards away, and Boyd is back with a big extinguisher. I pray he'll know how to operate it since my line of work doesn't really cover situations such as the one I've unwittingly found myself in. He leaps from the Mazda, rushes up with the extinguisher and says, 'D'you know how these things work?' Help! On the assumption that fire extinguishers are designed to be worked in moments of great stress by dummies like Boyd and me, I pull the pin and dive under the Stutz again. By now the fire has spread and the flames are licking along the floor. From my terrified viewpoint it's a horizontal scaled-down version of *Towering Inferno*.

Point the nozzle and hit the lever. The CO_2 blasts out in a frightening, choking white fog. I roll out from under in haste before it extinguishes me as well. Under again, and it's still burning but the worst of the flames are out. Another blast of extinguishant and the fire is defeated. I still don't know what has been burning or why. (In retrospect it's clear it was the grease and oil of ages encrusting the underside, but practical thoughts like this desert you in moments of stress.)

A small crowd of competitors and race-goers on their way to the track has gathered, displaying the sort of curiosity reasonably afforded a pair of legs sticking out from beneath a giant black open vintage car. Ernie Sprague is among them. After seasons handling the mechanical complications and inbuilt perversity of old Grand Prix cars like a P3 Alfa Romeo and a 4CLT Maserati, in which flash fires are almost to be expected, Sprague sums up the situation in a few succinct comments. I explain what happened and describe the inferno below. 'You left the handbrake on, didn't you?' Not a condemnation, just a statement of fact. 'It's got a cardin shaft transmission handbrake, and if you leave it on, it grabs tighter and tighter and catches fire. If the fire's out, it'll be OK. Remember to let it off next time.'

How could I have forgotten? Sprague's diagnosis is correct. I telephone former owner Allan Bramwell a few days later for further instruction since it was he who found the Stutz as a rolling chassis and created the big beauty with the engineering assistance of the late Murray Jones.

We have been over 90 mph but the rev counter has failed since the fire and I have kept to around 65 mph through the alpine grandeur of the Lewis Pass on the way to Queenstown, a lope that the Stutz seems to enjoy. The water temperature flits up to 180 and then dips, but I'm not sure whether 180 is too hot or why it dips for no apparent reason. 'It's called a thermostat,' says Bramwell. 'You don't know about these things, do you, Young? Don't worry about 180 degrees. It can go to 200, 220 even, but don't let it go beyond that.' I tell him the overdrive has been locked in, and the overdrive warning light on, ever since the fire. 'It hasn't got an overdrive warning light,' he says. 'That's the generator warning light and if the battery isn't flat now it soon will be.'

Sarginson is right. Old cars and old movies definitely have something in common. I'll stick to my Ford Sierra Cosworth.

CHAPTER 20

THE MILLE MIGLIA FERRARI AND LE MANS C-TYPE JAGUAR

I was spoiled in my early race-following days in New Zealand, because I generally travelled as David Young's passenger in his C-Type Jaguar, the car that had made history at Le Mans in the early 1950s. In 1975 I was allowed to drive the C-Type at Ruapuna and compare it directly with Gavin Bain's 375 Mille Miglia Ferrari. The following article appeared as a colour feature in an early issue of the UK Classic Car.

It must be difficult for a motor-racing generation that grew up with the 1200-horsepower turbocharged Porsche 917 sports racing car to regard the 375 Mille Miglia 4.5-litre V12 Ferrari as a monster when it developed little more than a quarter of the power and looks almost lithe alongside the brutish lines of the Porsche. Back in 1953, however, the Ferrari was the 917 of its time — a tamer of men, a brute of a car with aggression in its chip-cutter grille, the long nose and the determined cut of the air scoop to feed those 12 angry cylinders. In those days 1200 horsepower would have covered the front row of most sports-car grids.

During a lull in the 1975 Stuyvesant series of F5000 races in New Zealand, I took time out to try the only ex-works 375 MM Ferrari sports car in captivity south of the equator (perhaps in the world?), which is being restored to its former thundering grandeur by Christchurch enthusiast Gavin Bain. Bain prefers to be regarded as an enthusiast than as a collector. 'I don't like the word collector. It sounds as though you wrap cars up in cotton wool and put them away.'

Three days earlier Bain had been racing the Ferrari in a special historic event at Wigram. It had arrived in New Zealand from England only four months before, with the engine in the passenger's seat, the Pinin Farina body battered with straw-bale bruises and dents filled with dollops of fibreglass. Panel craftsmen at Auto Restorations in Christchurch had done a tremendous job and the engine bay was next on the list. 'We pulled the top and bottom off the engine and it looked OK for the moment so we bolted it back together for the Wigram race.' My only instructions before I went out for a track acquaintance with the Ferrari at Ruapuna were not to use too many revs and not to spread it all over the circuit.

Any observations on track performance by me would be superfluous to the record of this famous machine built late in 1953 as a works team car and which won first time out in the Casablanca 12-hour race with Farina and Scotti at the wheel. In January 1954 Farina shared the car with Maglioli for the first long-distance championship sports-car race to be held in Argentina, on a 5.88-mile course that used the outer perimeter of the Buenos Aires Autodromo as well as a stretch of the neighbouring dual carriageway complete with an intersection and a roundabout. The field of 37 included works cars from Aston Martin, Ferrari and Borgward, plus an Ecurie Ecosse C-Type Jaguar. Farina made a leisurely start but soon worked his way up from fifth place into first and set a lap record of 3 minutes 34.6 seconds (at an average speed of 98.79 mph) before handing over to Maglioli with a safe lead.

The DB3S Astons were the best of the rest but no match for the 375 MM, and after 66 laps the second-placed Aston of Parnell and Salvadori went out with electrical problems and Farina and Maglioli won the opening race of the season by a clear three laps from a 3-litre Ferrari driven by Schell and de Portago and the Aston Martin of Collins and Griffiths. It strikes a nostalgic note to observe that the 4.5-litre Ferrari driven by Trintignant and Rosier, which led on the opening lap then held second place to Farina until it slowed with pit problems to an eventual seventh place, is also owned by Gavin Bain. The car has been restored to its original Rosier Grand Prix configuration and awaits a V12 engine in the museum at Queenstown. Carrying historical coincidence almost too far, Collins and Griffiths' DB3S is owned by Bain's near-neighbour, Leon Witte.

The Ferrari works team for 1954 was to be made up of more powerful 4.9-litre cars so the superseded models were sold off, chassis number 0370AM going to colourful American privateer Masten Gregory. True to what was about to become his 'form', Masten almost wrote the Ferrari off against a tree in his first race, and the car went back to Maranello for a rebuild. Masten then campaigned the car throughout Europe during the 1954 season, finishing fourth in the Reims 12-hour race with Biondetti in July, third three weeks later in the Portuguese Grand Prix for sports cars at Monsanto, second in a short sports-car race at Goodwood in September, first at Aintree in October and second at Montlhery, and then shipping the car across the Atlantic to win the Bahamas Automobile Club trophy in Nassau. He kept the Ferrari in the States for national events, claiming it was the best racing car he had ever owned, and at one point it was maintained by the legendary Alfred Momo, who cared for the Cunningham stable. History has an annoying habit of clouding over various periods of the lives of famous cars, but we do know this particular 375 MM rested for some time in the private collection of Carl D. Bross before it was brought to England and eventually acquired by Bain.

Although Bain won't accept the label 'collector', his stable consisted at that time of the 375 MM, the Rosier 4.5-litre V12 Ferrari, a Super Squalo Ferrari in the process of being rebuilt, a 1920 Brescia Bugatti, a 1924 3-litre Bentley, a 37.2 H63 Hispano Suiza, a 1908 Humber, a 1912 Silver Ghost Rolls-Royce, a pair of 1924 Humbers, an XK120 Jaguar, a 1935 Bentley 3.5 litre, the famous Bimotore Alfa Romeo (or, more correctly, the Aitken Alfa and now, sadly, minus engines), a share in a 1935 2-litre Alta and 'a dozen assorted motorcycles'.

It must be the wish of every red-blooded enthusiast to take the wheel of a car like the Ferrari for a few laps of a track, but that day on the little Ruapuna circuit, on the outskirts of Christchurch, I found myself in one of those absurd pinch-me situations that occur perhaps once in a lifetime. I had driven to the track in the ex-Peter Whitehead C-Type Jaguar, burbling through suburban traffic and blasting when the road was clear, parked in the pits and climbed into the Ferrari. Probably nobody — unless Mike Hawthorn had the opportunity in 1953 or 1954 — has ever stepped straight from a C-Type Jaguar into a works Ferrari. It was a chastening thought.

The C-Type drive had been something of a lifetime ego trip for me, although it had done nothing to dilute the thrill of the Ferrari. It was in the same C-Type that I had ridden to New Zealand sports-car races back at the dawn of my interest in motor sport, when I had tagged along with David Young, who was then racing it. The car was subsequently owned, and occasionally raced, by Ray Archibald, the Jaguar dealer in Christchurch who made a formidable reputation in the 1950s and early 1960s with his fluid style at the wheel of various racing Jaguars.

It had been delivered to the Whitehead brothers through Henlys Garage in London in April 1953 and raced by both Peter and Graham, before Peter had taken it to Australia for the Mt Druitt six-hour sports-car race, retired with unspecified problems and sold it to

New Zealander Jack Tutton, who was at the race. Tutton had later set a national Class C speed record of 144 mph in New Zealand before selling the car to Des Wilde, who had sold it on to David Young. In 1961 it went to Garth Forsythe, who began a rebuild he never finished, and the Archibald brothers bought it in 1966 for £1,100. Ian Archibald first raced the C-Type at a local race in 1970, surviving an early-morning spin on black ice on the way to the Levels track in South Canterbury and a second spin during the race. After that the driving was taken over by brother Ray.

But back to the Ferrari. I shoe-horned my head into Bain's crash helmet and adjusted the period goggles, which I discovered were reflected back at me disconcertingly from the five instrument dials, like five images of a ham racer in one of those dreadful motor-racing movies pre-*Grand Prix*. (Or maybe including . . .)

The throttle pedal was stiff, but the surge of the V12 was supersmooth as I drove out on to the track. The engine was based on the 4.5-litre Ferrari Grand Prix engine but was not in fact a Grand Prix unit. It had a compression ratio of 9:1, delivered a maximum 340 bhp at 7000 rpm and had a single cam per bank with three inverted 4-barrel Weber carburettors. The gearbox was 4 speed and the brakes drum. The car had a tube chassis with independent front suspension via upper and lower wishbones with a transverse leaf spring and stabilising rod, and a solid rear axle with four pushrods, longitudinal leaf springs and Houdaille shock absorbers as original equipment.

The Moss gearbox on the C-Type had handled fairly slowly, but the tall lever on the Ferrari was a real butter-slicer. Bain had suggested a rev limit of 6000 rpm but I volunteered 5500 rpm, reckoning caution to be less expensive than lead-foot valour, Ferrari racing parts being what they are these days. Through the big slim-rim wheel were the rev counter, which ran to 8000, the speedometer (disconnected), which read to 300 kph, and, grouped between, dials for Benzina, Olio and Aqua.

First impressions were of sitting very low and looking over an endless bonnet. My second impression was of the heaviness of the steering into the tight hairpin and the howling of rubber as I bansheed through it. There was a medium-speed right and left, which was fun to try and perfect in second, and a climb to third on the short back straight and through the long loop, then it was up into top on the long straight. Probably the wrong slots, but wildly invigorating nevertheless. The hairpin became more and more of a challenge as I came in later on the brakes, and turned later, until the tail started taking over on about the fifteenth lap and with all the available helm wound on I seemed to be cruising with frightening ease (and all sorts of tyre noise) straight into the half-tyre course markers. Fate intervened and the Ferrari stopped before its pristine nose was crinkled. I imagined my own suffering in similar fashion, which seemed like the signal I had been waiting for to stop being a hero in a car I couldn't afford to unbend, let alone buy.

I made one last long attempt at getting the loop right, then peeled off into the pits, leaving Gavin and photographer Harry Ruffell wondering whether I had really parked it permanently this time. My earlier effort at the hairpin had registered with them at the loop as a long, rising howl of rubber, followed by a stunning silence, and then a nervous dab of throttle through the twin tail exhausts.

I swapped for a few laps in the C-Type before our track time expired. First time into the hairpin using Ferrari limits I discovered the Jaguar was altogether a different motorcar. It was more petite, catlike in its advance to a corner, light to the touch and not needing a long strong-arm push to the top of the wheel to hold it in the long turns of the loop and the hairpin. (So that's where Farina got the idea of the arm-stretch driving position. The Ferrari wouldn't take a hairpin any other way.) It was darting from lock to lock before I managed to gather it up and set off for the right and left, which I had sorted out to my personal satisfaction in the Ferrari. Again I was in too deep and too late on the brakes and the rounded tail was dancing out. The Ferrari brakes had been heavy but positive; give the Jaguar anchors a tap and the wheels were locked.

A few laps in the C-Type were enlightening but probably suffered from my longer drive in the Ferrari, so I ended up feeling that if I had been in a position to own either car it would probably have been the Ferrari (if I'd been able to discount my romantic ties with the Jaguar). I had confounded my own plans by driving the Ferrari first.

I'd done something similar a couple of years earlier at Silverstone, when I had driven Tom Wheatcroft's 1969 4-wheel-drive Cosworth 3-litre Grand Prix car and then the ex-Nuvolari 1933 8CM, which had felt like a toy after the tussle with the complexity of the Cosworth. If I had driven the Maserati first I would have been more impressed with both cars instead of treating the 8CM with relative ease after the Cosworth.

But it was a day to remember at Ruapuna. I had driven both cars that had battled together that summer 20-odd years before, when Ferrari and Jaguar had proved equally capable of winning at Le Mans, and been cheered to the echo as they had rolled on to the grid instead of being politely inspected as neo-vintage collector's items, as they are today.

CHAPTER 21

THOSE NEW ZEALAND RACES

On discovering this delightful coverage of the first international New Zealand Grand Prix in the April 1954 issue of Motor Sport *I was intrigued by the chatty style, which was* most *unlike the dry wordage of the magazine in those days. It reads almost like a long letter to the editor, and I am tempted to believe this is what it is. I was also fascinated to learn the identity of A.M. Disclosure comes in the text when the author reveals himself as Arthur Moffat and* gives himself a mention in the report of the saloon race at Wigram. William Boddy, the doughty editor of *Motor Sport*, was always W.B., and the legendary Denis Jenkinson (Jenks) was always D.S.J.

Now, when every race is shown live on television and there is a plethora of motor-racing magazines, it seems unthinkable that we waited six to eight weeks for the latest copy of *Motor Sport*, with its comfortable green covers, and devoured every word of the reports within as though the races had taken place only the day before. Moffat's report of our first Grand Prix makes a wonderful trip down memory lane — just like being there, which is the mark of a good writer — even if Arthur was probably surprised to see it in print.

NEW ZEALAND'S FIRST INTERNATIONAL GRAND PRIX

Our chartered De Havilland, 'Dominie,' took off from Christchurch, in the South Island (the finishing place of the England–New Zealand air race), at 5.30 a.m. on a beautiful clear day and we were soon winging over Cook Strait on the first leg of our journey. We landed at Palmerston North to refuel both the plane and ourselves and before long were over the rugged King Country, in the heart of the North Island. Our English pilot took us some miles off course in order to bank low over the scene of the tragic railway disaster [at Tangiwai] about which you have no doubt heard, in which nearly 150 people lost their lives. Our position gave us an unusually terrifying idea of the magnitude of the smash. Telescoped and splintered carriages were spread over a wide area of the streambed. Some were half submerged in the thousands of tons of silt which had suddenly washed down the river from the burst crater lake, smashing the bridge just as the express approached. However, as your journal deals with things automotive rather than locomotive, I will not dwell on this subject.

At 11.00 a.m. we landed at Mangere, the airfield of the Auckland Aero Club, and took a taxi to the venue of the race — Ardmore, formerly an advanced fighter-training station, about 20 miles south of Auckland. We were amazed at the volume of traffic heading out to the airfield. Later we learned that over 70,000 people saw the race, making it one of the biggest sporting events in the history of the country.

We found we had missed some curtain-raisers in the form of motorcycle events (A.J.S. swept the pool), and a Formula Libre event for cars not in the big race. However, we were in time for an excellent sports-car race. As it was a handicap there is not much point in giving the placings. Suffice it to say that the Austin Healey 100s were most impressive, the team of three making a very pretty sight as they circulated in line ahead. One shouldn't be fooled by their polite exhaust note. They were very fast indeed, and later were to frighten many more expensive cars.

A luncheon break followed, but any interest in food was quickly lost as a shattering scream came suddenly from the pits. No, it wasn't a harassed marshal ejecting the unauthorised persons who always manage to get into the pit area! It was, of course, the BRM. To those of us who have so often read about this really fantastic exhaust note in our *Motor Sport*, it was a particularly thrilling experience to hear it for the first time and for it to be just as we had imagined.

The grid start was a really tremendous spectacle, few of us having seen before the type of acceleration which goes with smoking tyres in the higher ratios. (Personally, I have up to now been quite proud when I could raise even a faint squeak in low cog from the rear wheels of my unfortunate $2\frac{1}{2}$ Riley at a sprint event.)

Wharton led into the first bend, which was rather a surprise as we had been led to believe that the BRM was a slow starter. However, Whitehead's Ferrari was flat out, only to be repassed by Wharton a second or two later. The BRM held this lead for 10 laps. The positions at this stage were BRM (Wharton), Ferrari (Whitehead), Maybach (Jones, Australia), HWM (Gaze), Alfa Romeo P3 (Roycroft, New Zealand). I should have mentioned before that the distance was 200 miles (100 laps).

Wharton entered the corner before the pit straight too enthusiastically and spun out, taking a marker drum with him. But no damage was done and he was going again in a few seconds. However, he lost five or six places. By lap 23 he had managed to repass all but the Maybach and 'Gonzalez'(!) Gould's Cooper-Bristol. With 90 miles gone Wharton came in for rear tyres and fuel. The offside hub nut refused to budge for some seconds but finally yielded to some really heavy blows and then the BRM was away again in the fairly good time of 44 seconds. This gave the Maybach the lead again, but not for long as Wharton repassed in five laps.

Meanwhile, Whitehead was lucky to escape serious injury when his front universal broke at 130 mph and the clutch housing disintegrated, cutting him about the legs and arm with flying fragments. Not being badly hurt he managed to retain full control of the car, but it was particularly unfortunate that the accident should have happened because many had looked upon him as favourite for first place, having regard for the BRM's bad reputation over long-distance races. Apart from that (and perhaps I am stepping on thin ice here) Whitehead struck me as being easily the most polished driver in the field. He really made the job look easy. No fireworks, but he was pushing the BRM hard all the time, and the Ferrari motor was beautiful to listen to. Let us hope the car can be repaired in time for us to see this fine combination in action again.

Of the three Cooper-Bristols Gould's was undoubtedly the fastest, and from half distance Gould really began to live up to his distinguished nickname, 'Gonzales'. [Both Froilan Gonzales and Horace Gould were burly drivers.] He began a really vigorous drive, hurling his car into the corners. It was then that the outstanding handling qualities of these remarkable cars really began to show. Time and again Gould went into his corners at seemingly impossible speed, with a remarkable camber on his front wheels, but the car appeared steady as a rock. The same cannot be said for the BRM. Somehow she seems too 'flat'; anyhow, she appeared to spin far too easily, and even some of the local specials were coming out of corners ahead of her. Of course, this is no reflection of Ken Wharton's driving. It is obvious that he obtains the utmost from a very tricky car (although her handling seems to leave a lot to be desired — a lot of road was taken even during cog swapping), and the acceleration can only be described as staggering. In the earlier stages, Whitehead's Ferrari was the only car able to hold the BRM.

In this respect the Cooper-Bristols were just a little disappointing. One remembers reading of their phenomenal acceleration in, say, the first two-thirds of their speed range, and, in particular, the time when at Charterhall last year Mike Hawthorn in a Cooper-Bristol easily held a BRM to the unbounded delight both of the crowd and of *Motor Sport*! The Cooper-Bristols at Ardmore certainly proved to be quite remarkable all-round performers, Gould's in particular, but none of them held a candle to the BRM in sheer meteoric urge in all gears. But perhaps she was in particularly excellent tune that day! What really fascinated me was the way in which the revs went straight up in any gear. In fact, in the first two or three changes I heard I could have sworn that Wharton had actually missed the cog.

But to return to the race. Wharton came in at 57 laps with smoke and boiling fluid spewing from the front disc brakes and, as the damage seemed to be irreparable, these were disconnected and poor Wharton had to use his gearbox for braking and put up a remarkable show, but had slowed down considerably. The very fast and steady Maybach was now in the lead again with Jones driving an unruffled and masterly race. This car is powered by an ex-Nazi scout-car engine, a 6-cylinder of 4 litres, and its fine performance against world-famous cars entitles its driver and its designer, Mr Charles Dean, to the highest praise.

Tony Gaze was now driving fiercely as the BRM's failure had put a different complexion on the possible outcome of the race. He fought his way into second place, passing Gould and Roycroft, the latter driving his P3 Alfa Romeo with great regularity. His technique was unobtrusive yet he was never below fifth place. His cornering lines were perhaps the most accurate of all. This is saying much for his cool skill and for the grand qualities of a 20-year-old car.

More pit drama was to come as Tuck limped home with a broken fuel feed in his Cooper-Bristol. He had driven a fine race and was hard on the heels of the leaders all the way. Then Gaze came coasting in with an empty tank and a dead engine. He had already reached round and undone the fuel cap as he reached the pits, but, although he lost only a few seconds, the BRM was past him again and into second place. However, in the closing laps, Gould, by dint of desperate driving, managed to head off both Wharton and Gaze, but the Maybach proved too tough a nut to crack. All the while the team of Austin Healeys held their impressive formation, although in the later stages the car driven by Jensen seemed faster and began to pull away, eventually to gain a very creditable seventh.

So after 200 gruelling miles Stan Jones, in his wonderful special, received the flag, with Gould second, Wharton third, Gaze fourth, Roycroft fifth, Brabham (Cooper-Bristol) sixth and Jensen seventh. Of the 24 starters, 16 finished.

The Maybach's win was interesting largely because of the fact that it had thrown a con rod in practice, and it is reported that mechanics worked in shifts all night to fit a truck rod, a proper replacement not being available. The car was only started 'with a prayer' but never missed a beat — a marvellous advertisement for the makers of the truck in question. [It was a GMC.]

There appeared to be some argument over the preliminary placings, Gould being placed fourth. He protested, claiming first place. After some days of examining all the lap-scoring documents the above placings were confirmed and photostat copies were sent to the RAC. The winner's time is the only one confirmed at the time of writing, at 2 hours 45 minutes 20 seconds.

(*The Motor*, in the UK, reported the result thus: 'Five days after the race a third set of results was issued but it is understood that a further protest has been lodged against these. No further investigations will take place in New Zealand and photostat copies of lap-scoring documents are being sent to the RAC in London. In each set of results, the Australian Stan Jones has been placed fourth, though Horace Gould, originally placed fourth, has claimed the race and maintains that his Cooper-Bristol completed 101 laps before the Maybach Special finished its hundredth. As a result of these representations, Gould is now placed second instead of fourth, displacing the BRM, now announced as third, though at one stage given fifth place. Tony Gaze (HWM), originally believed to be third, has been moved down to fourth position, and New Zealander Ron Roycroft

(2.9-litre Alfa Romeo), temporarily promoted to third position, has been put back to fifth place again.' Complicated or what?

The Motor continued: 'The sensation of the race was the Maybach Special driven by Stan Jones. The engine of this car came to Australia in a German scout car captured during the war. The scout car was sold to a junk dealer for £10, and he in turn sold the engine for £40. This was modified and tuned by an Australian engineer, Mr Charles Dean, and the Maybach Special, in the hands of Jones, has proved to be Australia's most formidable racing car.')

So there it is. Now we can begin to look forward to the race at Wigram, Christchurch, the Ferrari, BRM and HWM being definite starters. Peter Whitehead did some phenomenal long-distance telephoning to Italy and England to arrange for spares to be sent!

The flight home was uneventful, except for a rather dicey landing in gusty conditions at Palmerston North.

THE LADY WIGRAM TROPHY

This event was run at Wigram air station on 6 February. The aerodrome is only a few miles from the centre of Christchurch, and in view of this it was a little disappointing that only about 15,000 turned out. Perhaps the reason was that there was a Canterbury Jockey Club meeting on the same day. Also, no temporary stands had been erected, which may have deterred many people. However, I heard that the contract quote for the erection of such stands was in the vicinity of 17s a seat, so the Motor Racing Club could not be blamed for baulking at the idea. It is possible that had stands been erected the extra admission might have caused a smaller crowd still, and perhaps an actual decrease in total gate takings. It must be understood that Wigram is an active airfield and has a full flying programme all the year round. Only the generosity of the Air Department coupled with the interest of certain sporting MPs make this annual event possible. Virtually all temporary buildings, sound equipment, straw bales, etc. must be erected and dismantled on the day of the race, which, you will agree, is a monumental task, and any armchair critics of race organisation would do well to first digest the above fact.

I always think the last-minute tinkering and the scrutineering and briefing on the day before a major race are almost as much fun as the race itself! The unexpected meeting of friends from other clubs, the first sight of exciting new cars, the feeling of satisfaction when the scrutineer's OK is pasted on one's humble saloon-car entry, and the pleasantly unsettling feeling of anticipation all combine to make the day before the race a most enjoyable one for all but the poor officials.

The BRM was flown down from the North Island in a National Airway's Bristol Freighter, and prior to the race was on display in the window of a large Christchurch department store. Other overseas entries were Peter Whitehead (2-litre Ferrari) and Tony Gaze (HWM). The three Cooper-Bristols which raced at Ardmore were very much missed, but, as you shall see, although the race lacked their entries it certainly did not lack drama!

I could not help thinking how lucky we were to have these cars way down here. Despite the fact that the BRM has in some ways gained a certain notoriety, it is nevertheless a most interesting heap of metal, and I venture to suggest that many in England would give their right arm to casually stroll round the car as the public have had many opportunities to do in New Zealand. Ken Wharton no doubt has endeared himself to many local enthusiasts by taking a genuine interest in their specials, be they the usual run of 747 cc Austins and Ford 10s or the more advanced type, of which we have quite a selection. He was to be seen outside the scrutineering garage with the nose cowling of the BRM on the footpath, with a race programme attached thereto, busily photographing. I'd like a peep at his album!

Saturday dawned sunny, but with a strong northerly wind. Rubber dust was blown into people's lunches, tricky gusts caught the cars in the earlier races as they rounded the Hangar and Control Tower turns, and at one time during the sports-car practice period straw bales actually were rolling on to the track! However, the wind dropped considerably before the main race, to the relief of the drivers of lighter cars.

The two-mile course is run in an anticlockwise direction and is composed of five mild left-hand turns, one sharp one, and a mild right-hander. The surface is very abrasive. I say this with some feeling, as I 'did' three tyres on my 2½ Riley in the preliminary races in only 40 miles. The racing cars can all do 100 miles on one set, and Wharton told the press that he thinks the course is a really excellent one and reminds him of Goodwood.

Two curtain-raisers were held: a handicap for sports and racing cars of 25 miles, sponsored by Redex, and a 15-mile saloon-car handicap. Both these proved relatively uneventful, except that in the first race T.A. Shadbolt's Shadbolt Special (Kieft-like) got into a bad slide while entering the pits straight and lost a rear wheel. The car overturned amongst the straw bales on the outside of the circuit, but the driver did not appear to be injured. R.J.N. Archibald's very fast XK120 came through the field from the back mark to take second place. I can safely say that this is the best prepared XK we have seen to date, and it is probable that the suspension has been modified in some way, as there was no indication of the inside-front-wheel lift we have seen on other XKs. The brakes appeared to be doing their job admirably, too. J.L. Holden's Jupiter was surprisingly fast, but couldn't make up his handicap, and Ted Reid's smart little Morgan Plus Four (such likeable cars, these) handled beautifully, but developed that annoying habit most of us have experienced of cutting out just as he pulled out to pass a slower car, thus robbing him of a higher place than fifth. Keith Roper spun his Austin Healey 100 but otherwise went very impressively and managed fourth place. Third place was taken by G.A. Rand, who had a good ride in his handsome little A40 Special. The winner was J.K. Kerr, driving a Singer SM roadster. This car was deceptively fast and handled much like the Morgan, but the handicappers did an excellent job, for when the Singer crossed the line, Archibald's XK was only six seconds behind. Not an exciting race, but an interesting one.

The public like to see more everyday vehicles showing their paces, and on listening to some of the comments from behind the ropes, it is clear this applies even more to saloon-car races. A good cross section comprising 19 cars faced the starter in the 15-mile handicap. Three

Morris Minors and an Austin A30 were first away. In a few hundred yards the twin-carburettor conversions began to pay dividends! Citroens, Zephyrs, etc. moved off, and then the back markers, in the form of three prewar Yanks, three 2.5-litre Rileys and a Mark V Jaguar. There was a race within the race between the two Zephyrs of Womersley and Mauger. These two had a great dice together and heeled alarmingly, but always seemed under control. The former just managed to pip Mauger for fourth place. Third was W. Crosbie in an A40. Although this car was absolutely standard, the driver himself was astonished by its performance, as he was hard on the heels of the Rileys! Of these last-mentioned Rileys, Moffat's proved itself the fastest by taking second place (at the expense of much rubber!) but could not catch Ian Archibald's Citroen, which had been considerably underestimated by the handicappers. Ian, like his brother, is an excellent driver, and really hounded that Citroen round.

Now it was practice time for the Trophy Race cars, and there was the usual excited gasp from the crowd as the banshee scream of the BRM rattled the eardrums. Grid positions were arranged according to lap times and, as was expected, the three English drivers filled the front positions. I was lucky in having a pit job so I could watch the BRM and Ferrari crews, and would not have missed the fun that followed for anything!

At flag fall Whitehead was first away, the beautiful Ferrari engine sounding really happy, but the BRM's tremendous middle-range acceleration pushed it into the lead after a few hundred yards. Wharton was to easily retain this lead for most of the race. Whitehead did not appear to be particularly worried about catching the BRM, but was content to remain about 150 yards behind, with a similar distance to Gaze, whose throaty HWM sounded very healthy.

One got the impression that Wharton was taking things very seriously, that Whitehead was playing a waiting game, with more speed available if it proved necessary, and that Gaze was doing his utmost to catch Whitehead. In the meantime some of the local cars were putting up an extremely good show. On lap two fourth man was Frank Shuter, driving his Ford V8-based Edelbrock Special, in company with Hec Green in his RA Special with locally built rear-mounted 2088 cc engine. Sixth and seventh were, surprisingly, the Austin Healey 100 of R. Jensen and the previously mentioned very fast XK120 of R.J. Archibald. Following these were the P3 Alfas of J. McMillan and Ron Roycroft. The latter popular and successful car had unfortunately been run without oil when warming up and Roycroft, not being sure if any damage had been done, wisely pulled out after a couple of tentative laps rather than cause unnecessary damage. There are still three more major races this season and Alfa spares are hard to get at short notice!

Meanwhile, Shuter pulled out with smoke pouring from the engine and Kennard called in to check the relief valve on the radiator cap of his Fiat 1100-engined car. Fred Zambucka's prewar Maserati was forced in with no oil pressure, and a little later Jensen's Austin Healey had to retire. I have not been able to ascertain the reason for this as yet.

At about three-quarter distance the order of the first three was unchanged, and they had lapped nearly the whole field. Archibald, by sheer good driving, had gained fourth place by lap 31, when he suffered a blowout. Before regaining the pits for a new wheel the XK120 collected a straw bale, which was shunted along the course for some hundreds of yards to the surprised pit crew. This stop cost Archibald four places, two of which he regained before the end.

Before the race both Gaze and Whitehead had decided that a tyre change would be necessary, so in due course Gaze came in and his mechanics really showed us how it should be done when they changed both offside wheels and topped up the fuel in under 30 seconds. The stop would have been even briefer had an official not insisted on Gaze getting out. Gaze appeared to be under the impression that it was not necessary for a driver to be out of the car during refuelling provided the motor was stopped. However, the rules state definitely that it must be so. And then the drama began. Whitehead was called in for his tyre change but, to the chagrin of Gaze's crew and the surprise of his own, Whitehead made a negative sign and settled down to drive even faster! One wonders if Whitehead had an idea of what was to happen a lap later, for the BRM pulled up in a hurry at its pit, leaving a trail of oil along the track. A gallon was hastily poured in but came out of the bottom just as fast. It looked as though the oil filler pipe was fractured where it met the tank. In the meantime the Ferrari and the HWM had moved into first and second places, and McMillan was now in fourth place, with Stafford, whose little half-litre Cooper-Norton was circulating with amazing rapidity, fifth.

After a hurried consultation, Wharton decided to risk the consequences in a desperate attempt to regain his first place. But it was not to be. Two more laps and Whitehead acknowledged the chequered flag, with Gaze crossing the line 40 seconds later. Wharton still held a comfortable lead over his nearest New Zealand opponents, which was just as well for him, for 400 yards from the line the gremlin which had caused the brake trouble at Ardmore, and all the thousand and one other troubles in the unfortunate car's chequered career, dropped its usual spanner in the complicated works, and poor Ken's ride was over. So he got sadly out and began to push — and he pushed, and he pushed, and his mechanics walked beside him making encouraging noises, being powerless to help in a more practical way. It was all very dramatic, and not a little sad. Slowly the heap of dead alloys rolled into the short pit straight, where waited the flag.

About 20 yards short of the line the car stopped rolling, and it was clear that Wharton was nearly fainting from sheer exhaustion. It may have been the kind words of officials; it may have been the sympathetic applause from the crowd; but somehow, slowly, painfully, he managed to get the car rolling again. A great shout of pleasure went up as the car trickled over the line into third place with 40 seconds still between it and the McMillan Alfa. Then Wharton literally collapsed on the ground near his pit, and we lent a bucket of water, which was unceremoniously tipped over his head. A little later a tired and rather forlorn man was to be seen sitting alone in the back of a saloon car. And he said, 'This is not the first time. It's just that trick of fate that has been with us all along!' We are sincerely sorry about it, too, Ken. We think you are a great sport and a great driver, and hope that soon we will see you driving something more reliable.

But all the excitement was not yet over. Hec Green, trying hard for sixth place, was passing the control tower when his car burst into flames. (Something to be said for rear engines on such occasions!) Anyway, he managed to slow down enough to bale out with safety. Halsey Logan, in a single-seat blown 1500 cc HRG, slowed down and threw his fire extinguisher to Green, and a moment later the fire engine arrived and the blaze was put out before the car was badly damaged. Yes, a lot of excitement was piled into the last few minutes!

At a cabaret and prize-giving that evening, all three visiting drivers made pleasant little speeches, Tony Gaze pretending to be very annoyed with Whitehead for not stopping for a tyre change. We're glad you did though, Tony, for now we see how it should be done. The trio also said they hoped to come to New Zealand again next year. We certainly hope so too.

A.M.

CHAPTER 22

YOUNG AND FREE IN A TRIUMPH TR2

The Triumph TR2 is a classic British sports car from the 1950s. Mine was even more famous, being the actual car driven to speed records in New Zealand by Leon Witte. My daughter, Selina, and I took the TR2 on a rally linked with an early running of the now internationally popular Southern Festival of Speed.

New Zealand is the best kept motoring secret in the world, a paradise for old-car people offering time-warp driving conditions where my Triumph TR2 could easily have been whisked back to 1954, the year of its birth. Beyond the town limits not a lot has changed on the roads since then. Geographically, New Zealand is the same size as the British Isles but it has the population of Paris. Motoring is bliss. Cars we regard as classics in Britain are still used as everyday transport: a handsome Mk V Jaguar in the airport car park at Queenstown; a 1935 Morris 8 outside the motel in Alexandra; a bronze Mk II 3.4 Jaguar driven with verve up the serpentine climb of Dyers Pass Road. You don't remark or point at the elegant old Armstrong Siddeley in the Christchurch traffic. Thirties American cars are commonplace.

The Southern Festival of Speed, held in February, was a two-race series at Timaru and Dunedin with what they called a Sub-alpine Rally taking cars and competitors over the Lewis Pass to the resort of Queenstown in the week between.

Sponsorship for this mini-series at the other end of the world came from the *Otago Daily Times*, freight company New Zealand Australia Direct and computer-systems company Cardinal Network. An enthusiastic American contingent of 10 brought cars ranging from Peter Giddings' ex-Whitney straight-8 CM Maserati, with its distinctive heart-shaped radiator, through Triumph TR3s to a Saab Sonnet. The cost of the adventure from the west coast of the USA was reckoned to be around $10,000 for a car and two people and considered well worthwhile. A five-car group came down from Hong Kong, and Bob Harborow brought the original Maybach Special from Australia, the car Stan Jones (Alan's dad) had driven to win the first New Zealand Grand Prix in 1954.

A club race at Ruapuna and the first festival event at the Levels track near Timaru served as warm-ups and shakedowns for the Dunedin classic. Giddings, a British ex-pat in California, battled to get the 1934 Maserati Grand Prix car firing on all eight cylinders, a problem eventually cured when new extra-lean needles and jets were made up by local engineer David Diamond. Bob Sutherland had the 8C Maserati Giuseppe Campari had driven to win the 1933 French Grand Prix at Montlhery a week before his death at Monza, but was plagued by a persistent water leak. Bruce McCaw was finding the long loops at Levels playing hell with the oil pressure on the big V8 Chrysler hemi-head engine in his 1953 J2X Le Mans Allard. This car, with its all-enveloping body, had been supplied new to Masten Gregory, who had raced it at Sebring in 1953 and then switched to Ferraris.

The Lycoming Special, restored and raced by Ralph Smith, is a true Kiwi heritage racer, created by Auckland engineer Ralph Watson and featuring ideas so advanced that when Colin Chapman visited the early Tasman races he 'borrowed' some of Watson's developments. Bruce McLaren borrowed the car itself and raced it at Wigram when he cut the Climax engine of his Cooper in half during practice, and Jim Clark was intrigued enough to try it for a few laps at Teretonga Park, near Invercargill, the world's most southerly race circuit. At 73, Ralph Watson is still fiercely enthusiastic, and drove his much-modified 1931 BSA sports car down from Auckland for the race at Timaru. He had converted the air-cooled twin to rotary valves himself.

The rationale for the two-seater layout of the Lycoming Special is interesting. Watson reasoned that, although a single-seater would be smaller and lighter, a two-seater tractable enough to be driven on the road between meetings would obviate the need for a tow car and trailer, saving on transport and ferry costs.

I was travelling the series with my daughter, Selina, and photographers Euan Sarginson and Don Donovan. We made our way by TR TWO and STUTZ 8. These may sound like a pair of code names out of *Star Wars* but were in fact the number plates of the TR2 and 1928 Stutz rescued, bodyless, by Allan Bramwell, in Christchurch. He had commissioned Auto Restorations to build new coachwork along the lines of the Stutz Le Mans entries that so nearly beat the Bentleys in 1928; the lead Stutz lost a gear in its 3-speed box on the Sunday morning and finished second on the heels of Barnato and Rubin.

The Triumph had been a lucky find on my previous trip to New Zealand, when I had discovered it for sale in Gavin Bain's Fazzazz emporium in Christchurch. It was the white TR2 raced to such effect in hill climbs and sprints in the '50s by Leon Witte. He'd worked on the engine, balancing, polishing and porting the motor that had begun its design life in a Ferguson tractor, and, in 1958, had fitted an undertray and a special streamlined cowling on the nose, and set a national class record for the flying kilometre at 122 mph. In the TR2's announcement year factory tester Norman Richardson ran 124.889 mph on the Jabbeke Highway in Belgium.

Witte had been to Europe in 1955 and was at Le Mans when Pierre Levegh crashed his Mercedes into the crowd. He and his friends were watching at the esses at the time of the crash and were amazed that the crowd pushed back to stand in the charred area of the crash only hours after the dead and injured had been removed. Witte had sold his MG TD to finance his trip, but the TR2 was not top of his shopping list when he came home. In fact, the early TR2s had a poor name locally after a spate of serious roll-over accidents. He was probably able to acquire his near-new original long-door model with low mileage because of its poor reputation. He eventually sold it in 1960 and it went through a succession of owners, eventually being put into storage in pieces.

John Barrett, in Christchurch, recognised the TR's history and set about a thorough, ground-up restoration from which the Triumph emerged probably better than new, crisp and tight and eager for top-down motoring. It came to New Zealand with all the options, including wire wheels, overdrive and leather upholstery, and now has the hardtop and solid screens offered with later TRs. We took the hardtop off and ran the entire trip with the softtop furled, using the tonneau when we left the car during the day or in motel car parks overnight.

TR motoring took me back to the late '50s, when I had borrowed a TR2 and driven it from Timaru to Christchurch and back, a 200-mile round trip during which I had seen my first indicated 100 mph. I had made a private promise to myself then that one day I would own a car that would do 100 mph, but I hadn't imagined I would be repeating the ton on the same road in a TR2 of my own. Top-down sunshine sports-car motoring is all very well, but where do you put the luggage? In fact, we found the boot of the TR, plus the space behind the seats, served surprisingly well for soft bags strategically packed and stowed.

The Sub-alpine Rally served to deliver the competitors from Timaru up past Lakes Tekapo and Pukaki, with distant views of Mount Cook, and over the Lindis Pass to Queenstown. Some enjoyed the versatility of their competition cars, and a pair of C-Type Jaguar replicas were in their element as they growled along the sweeping, deserted back-country roads.

In Queenstown, motoring visitors were offered a bewildering choice of excitement, from bungy-jumping 300 feet off a bridge and looping-the-loop in a Tiger Moth to jet-boating down roaring river canyons, white-water rafting and parachuting. American Peter Talbot came to grief when he tripped at the edge of a cliff as he was about to launch his parachute and broke an arm and three ribs. The 76-year-old Saab Sonnet driver told his wife in hospital that it only hurt when he breathed.

We visited Rav Larsen's workshops in Queenstown and saw the one-off Abbott-bodied four-seater XK120 Jaguar awaiting restoration between a production XK120, allowing us to see the differences aft of the windscreen, and a Mk II 3.4 saloon with the nose of a Lotus 15 sports-racer perched on top. Larsen and others are building six replica HWM Jaguar single-seaters based on an original Formula Two car. I felt they might have done better to recreate the original two-seater HWM racer, which at least could be used in the type of event we were enjoying. Larsen has also built D-Type and Lister Jaguar replicas.

I'd inadvertently left the Stutz handbrake on in Timaru, and the Cardan shaft transmission brake had set itself alight. I'd managed to get the fire out but nearby wiring had been burned, which meant that the rev counter no longer worked when top gear was engaged, at which point the generator warning light came on. Mark Neroj, at Middlemass Automotive in Queenstown, cleaned extinguishant off the big battery and rewired the burned-out bits, which immediately restored the rev counter and put out the worrying warning light.

The drive from Queenstown to Dunedin included 21 miles over a rough mountain track in 34°C heat. It was like driving over the mountains of the moon as we passed rock formations seemingly sculpted by the wind. Sarginson thought this impromptu route hilarious.

The Dunedin road races were held on the Cemetery Hill circuit, part of which had been used as a track in the early '60s. The course was bumpy and Bruce McCaw was the first casualty, his J2X Allard sustaining a broken differential. Steele Thurkleson had changed Bob Sutherland's 8C Maserati from alcohol to petrol for the Sub-alpine Rally (it was a Mille Miglia car, after all) but the supercharged straight-8 refused to run cleanly after a change back to racing fuel, and continued to falter when returned to petrol as a last resort. Peter Giddings, on the other hand, was delighted with the performance of his later-model 8CM, which was running perfectly for the first time since he had bought it. The Giddings stable in California includes real rarities: a Monza Alfa Romeo, a 250F Maserati and a Talbot Lago Grand Prix car.

New Zealander Gavin Bain, who owns and races the Gonzales British Grand Prix-winning 375 V12 Formula One Ferrari and a 375 MM sports-racer, was invited by Australian Kerry Manolas to race his Ferrari 196S, the beautiful 2-litre, scaled-down version of the Testa Rossa. The Rodriguez brothers had raced this car in the 1960 Targa Florio, leaving the road several times, damaging both ends of the car and finally rolling it on the way to seventh place. Later owners included Jo Siffert and Rob Walker.

There were more than 200 entries, the relatively moderns merged with the older classics — an uneasy mix since there were too few cars like the Maseratis to make a race, and they inevitably paled in comparison with the performance of later cars. Handicaps and reversed grids made for exciting racing, though. Maintaining the fun recipe of the series there were no published winners, but at the after-race function in Dunedin, Jonathan Harris, from Hong Kong, received the award as best driver of the day for his spirited conducting of his 1964 S1 Lotus Elan. Peter Talbot's wife, Judy, received Peter's award for Worst Paraglider of the series.

As with all old-car races, much of the pleasure was in looking at the cars, talking about the event beforehand and discussing it long into the night afterwards. The series was adjudged so successful that there are plans afoot to add more events to the Festival of Speed in 1993, making the trip more viable for overseas competitors.

CHAPTER 23

CANAM TESTING WITH BRUCE MCLAREN

They say those who can, do; those who can't, write about it. Bruce McLaren underlined the truth of that when he took me for several sensational laps of Goodwood in his McLaren CanAm car in 1967. I've written about that experience endlessly. It has become part of my history!

I'm rather short in the wheelbase and wide in the rear track, if you know what I mean, and the FIA hadn't taken into account that chubby chaps like me would be squirming down into the token passenger seat of things like Group Seven McLaren sports-racers when people like Bruce McLaren were testing. The mechanics had thoughtfully removed the fire extinguisher from its mounts where my bottom was about to be and rehoused it with sticky tape on top of the side tank by my left shoulder. There were a couple of large-bore water pipes alongside my left hip going back and forth to the radiator. Under my left knee the arm of a front wishbone poked through the monocoque to a mounting point rather hazardously situated from my point of view.

The green screen was sloped so gently it wasn't hard to see over it. McLaren hopped over the side screen and slid straight down behind the wheel while I was trying to figure out which cheek I would roast on the water pipes. He flicked his safety straps over his shoulders and thoughtfully asked if the fact that he was securely strapping himself in made me nervous. I forced a confident if rather weak laugh. Since racing cars like this weren't meant for passengers, I had no safety straps.

McLaren switched on and pressed the button, and the big 5.8-litre 500-horse Chevy V8 thundered into life behind our heads. He graunched the stumpy gear lever up on the right into first, and I sat there, smugly glad I hadn't made such a racket in Mr Hewland's gearbox. Then we were off with a rumble and a rush, and Madgwick loomed as a never-ending right-hander. McLaren was peering at his wristwatch, and I'm thinking, 'For God's sake, watch the road, man!'

Those giant front wings in bright-orange fibreglass give me the impression I'm peering down the cleavage of some sort of automotive pin-up girl. The road starts rushing by and we're on top of St Mary's. Then it drops away to the left and I hope that he's better on left-handers than I am. The engine waffles away behind our heads. There's a little window in the front guard and I can see the fat, flat Goodyear riding up and down, but then my mind is jarred back to the job in hand as I realise we're never going to make Woodcote at the end of the straight at this speed. Yet somehow we do.

KERISTE! Someone's built a wall across the road. Take your partners for a fatal road accident. But it's just the chicane. A broad arrow on the wall points to the right, where there seems to be no visible means of exit. As we thunder straight at the uncompromising wall some earnest lamp-rubbing on my part works the genie trick and a narrow gap opens at the end. We snick through and we're accelerating past the pits with such a burst that my borrowed helmet slams back against the chromed roll-over bar, completely destroying the composed 'I do this every day' picture I was endeavouring to convey to the pit watchers. But the lap hasn't been so bad from where I'm sitting, alongside the master. I'm thinking that this big-banger racing can't be so hectic after all. I haven't seen him do anything yet that I couldn't do. P'raps these fellers really do get paid too much.

I'm a bit uncomfortable sitting sideways, and those two big central-heating pipes don't make things any better. My thigh feels as though it's alight. The water temperature gauge says 70, but it's obviously wrong. The bit going past my leg is easily 100. A couple more laps and I'm seriously thinking of tapping the shoulder of the masked racer on my right and asking if I can have a go. Then he changes down, going into Madgwick at the end of the pit straight, and I think, 'Funny, he hasn't done that before.' At which point it all starts happening and the scenery blurs. I think his brain has snapped — or perhaps the throttle has jammed — but he looks pretty composed about the whole thing. It's really a bit hard to work out what's happening in the McLaren mind even if the man is just crammed a shoulder's width away. He might be chuckling hysterically to himself behind that Protex mask and taking a bead on the bank that ended Stirling Moss's career at St Mary's five years ago ... But we thunder at the right-hand sweep into St Mary's, drop a gear, and, then, defying all the laws of gravity and road holding, we're skating down through the left-hander.

There's starting to be a hot smell now — a mixture of hot engine, brakes, rubber and just *speed*. Then the sharp right at Lavant looms like the end of the road and from what feels like 200 we're braking ridiculously hard and my knee feels as though it's slicing into the riveted dash panel. I'll have to tell Ralph Nader about that. My crash helmet slams the roll-over bar again and we're charging away from Lavant, scrubbing through the funny kink after it and blasting out on to the straight as though we're on a drag strip.

The road is flashing past underneath us like one of those drummed-up sequences in Cinerama, only this is real and I'm in it. I've forgotten about the tyre riding up and down in the little window, and become acutely aware that someone has loaded Woodcote corner into a cannon and fired it at us head-on. I'm watching the rev needle climbing absurdly steadily to 5700. I convert that quickly into some impossible speed and then transfer my thoughts instantly back to personal self-preservation and Woodcote, which suddenly looks like a cul de sac. Those new brake pads he's trying out — what happens if he dives in deep and they don't work? I scan the bank for a soft spot and try to imagine what Masten Gregory would have done in my fraught situation. Masten specialised in jumping out just before several of his celebrated sports-car crashes. I'm Graham Hill at the Nürburgring in practice for the German Grand Prix and the Lotus isn't going to slow enough for the corner and Colin Chapman's going to be real annoyed . . . Then I'm back to me again and after forever McLaren is on the brakes and the car is arrested in flight. Woodcote is lined up and he's booting it through and out the other side.

He's easing off now, and for the first time I realise that I'm suffering. My thigh is on fire from those damn water pipes, and the left-hander at St Mary's is suddenly the best corner on the track as it eases me off those twin branding irons. I want McLaren to do another quick one, but then I weigh my enthusiasm against my burning leg and tap him on the shoulder, pointing to the pits. He slows and pulls in. I'm trying to slide out of the cramped seat as professionally as McLaren slid into his, but I make a complete hash of it and collapse back into the narrow space and onto the hot pipes. I clamber back to my feet and perform an impossibly agile leap over the curved-in perspex screen.

I put some of my pent-up queries to the still-masked McLaren. How fast on the straight? 160 mph. Hmmm. How fast through St Mary's? Umm, about 110 mph. Ulp . . . I remember the Guild of Motoring Writers motor-show test days at Goodwood, when there were five or six more corners than there were today — damn tricky ones, too — I wonder what happened to them. What was our lap time on the horrendous quick one? Team manager Teddy Mayer says 1 minute 22 seconds. That's an average of 105.37 mph. That was the lap record that Stirling was chasing the day he parked his racer in the bank. The BARC used to award the Goodwood Ton trophy to everyone who could lap the circuit at over 100 mph. Wonder if they'd give me one as a sort of associate member?

POSTSCRIPT

Three years later Bruce McLaren lost his life at Goodwood in a test session with his new CanAm car for the 1970 season. It was a freak accident: the rear body section came adrift and lifted, slewing the car off the track at high speed and slamming into a track-side concrete marshal's post, long unused since the track had closed for racing.

CHAPTER 24

GOODBYE DENNY

This is the text of my eulogy to Denny Hulme at his memorial service in Chelsea Old Church in London on 11 November 1992. Other addresses were by Innes Ireland and Rob Walker, both of whom, sadly, have since passed on.

History was made in silence at this very moment 74 years ago. The eleventh hour of the eleventh day of the eleventh month — the day the guns stopped firing and the Great War ended in 1918.

But we are not here to listen to silence on the day we remember Denis Clive Hulme. Denny. The Bear. Our mate.

And to all of us he was our mate, which is why we're here today to remember him, but he was a different sort of mate to each of us, if we think about it. Each of us remembers Denny in a different, personal way, because he had that effect on people.

That great motor-racing journalist Denis Jenkinson once said that he thought it should be compulsory for everyone to be able to read their obituaries before they died so that they would appreciate what everyone thought of them. Denny would have been delighted, I think, because journalists around the world regarded him as a friend — for all his reputation as a grouchy bear.

And his friends around the world all had their memories of the man, and none of them seemed to equate with a racing driver who went out of his way to be difficult.

Denny had as many facets as a diamond. A rough diamond, maybe, but a gem of a man nevertheless.

To all of us he was the Denny we knew, but to the rest of the world he was an international sporting star — with a reputation beyond the imagination of his homeland, which ignored his achievements when they set up a Hall of Fame and left him out. He was a world champion in Grand Prix racing and king of the CanAm series. When he won the world title in 1967, he plucked the two most difficult races to win — Monaco and the Nürburgring. The two races Stirling Moss won with the little Lotus against the Ferraris in 1961.

In racing and human terms, Denny was a giant compared with the intellectual pygmies who become champions these days.

I had lunch with Frank Gardner over the Grand Prix weekend in Adelaide, and he had his memories of Denny as a racer and as a friend. They were of an age and shared a common knock-about bond as colonials who had been there and done most of it, and they had a mutual respect for each other's ability. It was Frank's BMW that Denny was racing at Bathurst when he suffered his fatal heart attack.

Frank said, 'Denny had won more races in more cars on more tracks for more years than anyone I know and yet he seldom had an accident. He had that mix of ability and reliability that the young blokes these days just don't understand. And yet he could understand the young blokes. He was ideal to have in the team because he was almost like a father figure, and I've seen him sit down with one of our young guys and talk him through whatever problem he was having with the car or the track. That doesn't happen very often these days, but Denny was good at communicating in a way that those young guys never forgot.

'I mean, at the end of the day it all boils down to less brake and more throttle, but Denny had a way of talking his way through the problems some of these eager young guys were stuck with.'

I count myself very fortunate to have spent a week with Denny over the Monaco Grand Prix in May this year. In an odd sort of way he bridged a Grand Prix gap for me, because I had decided for the first time in 30 years to give the race a miss and watch it on television at home in England, selfishly jaded with the way Grand Prix racing has been going.

But Denny was adamant that he wanted to be there, and I was trying to tell him that it wasn't at all as he remembered it — overcrowded, overpriced, awful people. But he insisted. Why? Because it was 25 years since he had won the race. And 25 years since he had won the world championship.

So I changed my mind and went with him for a week that took us both back to that summer of 1961, when we gypsied around Europe with his Cooper Formula Junior on a trailer behind his Mark One Ford Zodiac, often running in convoy with fellow Kiwi Angus Hyslop and his crew.

I was dreading sharing a room for that length of time with *anyone*, but it was one of those time-warp situations that spanned those 30 years as though it had been the day before. The sort of 'quality time' when you meet up with someone after all that time and you can pick up the conversation as though you had just popped into the kitchen to get a drink. We were neither of us particularly tidy, and at one point he said, 'God, Eoin, I'm glad this room isn't any bigger because

I'd never be able to find *anything*!'

Denny had the sort of presence that is so difficult to define, and if you could define it you probably wouldn't automatically assume that someone like Denny would have it. And yet he could charm the birds from the trees, despite his reputation as a gruff, tough Kiwi.

He was delighted with his reputation as 'The Bear', but I think it was really his way of covering a basic shyness, a shell he could retreat behind. When he won the world championship in 1967 he said he would rather have let someone else have the title if it had meant he wouldn't have to make the speeches and do the socialising . . .

In the late '60s and the early '70s I travelled back and forth between CanAm and Indycar races in North America one weekend and a Grand Prix in Europe the next. We did that all summer long for years, and it seemed like a job. Looking back now it was a time when Denny was making racing history.

It was the time of 'The Bruce and Denny Show', when the McLarens were unstoppable in the CanAm sports-car series. Most of the team were Kiwis, but they worked more like a family than a team and some of those mechanics are here today, remembering their mate.

Other teams had drivers and mechanics, but on 'The Bruce and Denny Show' they were all mates sharing the good times and the bad. The bad times came in 1970, when Denny suffered appalling burns to his hands in a fuel fire at Indianapolis and then Bruce was killed at Goodwood.

Denny was inconsolable. Ken Tyrrell remembers those awful days: 'Denny was in tears all day long, saying that if it hadn't been for his burns he should have been driving the car at Goodwood instead of Bruce. He was a hard man and yet he could be so gentle, but if there had been a war I know who I'd have wanted in the trench beside me — Denny Hulme.'

Denny's dad, Clive, would have liked that remark — he was awarded the Victoria Cross for his bravery in Crete. But for all his pain and misery that June it was Denny who rallied the team and kept it together when it could so easily have fallen apart, Denny who gave the guys the will to carry on and keep winning.

This is not something I wanted to do, not somewhere I wanted to be standing today, but I'm honoured to have been able to remember the mate I knew and I'd like to think perhaps I have reminded you all of the different sides of the Denny you knew too.